Why I Don't Like Sex

(and other conundrums)

D. Alan Petersen

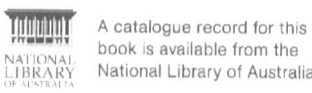 A catalogue record for this book is available from the National Library of Australia

Contact D. Alan Petersen:

petersenalan59@gmail.com

Copyright © 2023 D. Alan Petersen
All rights reserved.
ISBN-13: 978-1-922727-94-7

Linellen Press
265 Boomerang Road
Oldbury, Western Australia
www.linellenpress.com.au

About the Author

How many times have we been to a presentation, watched a panel show such as Q&A, or picked up a book, especially the non-fiction kind, and had the qualifications and claims to fame of the speaker, panelist or author espoused gushingly by the host, or proudly proclaimed in the first few pages the book? And if the person's credentials are not declared, we Google them on our smartphones to check them out.

Why do we – myself included – feel the need?

Why don't we simply listen to, or read, what they have to say without interference from the "framing" [1]? A framing designed to misinform as much as inform. Those spiels are like resumés, all the good bits exaggerated and all the weaknesses quietly forgotten. And yet we rarely seriously question their biases and hence listen and read less critically. Is it really a good default strategy?

Though I lack a string of credentials from prestigious universities to dazzle you, I am not totally uninformed, have a tertiary qualification and, more importantly, in my sixty-plus years, have read widely and done a lot of critical and honest thinking.

This collection of essays and anecdotes, writing between September 2015 and January 2023, is a distillation of my quest to better understand the world. There won't be tales of heroism or inspiring rags-to-riches stories but it will provide something in short supply: the facing of awkward questions on real-life issues that few are prepared to answer thoughtfully and honestly.

All these essays and anecdotes were sparked by events in my life, as well as those reported in the news media – newsworthy events that may have impacted upon your world and hence are worthy of mutual consideration.

I entreat you to be brave and read an essay, or better still, a handful, and then make your own unguided judgements, whilst bearing in mind the inaccuracies inherent in small sample sizes.

One can read this collection from first to last, which is the order they were written, or treat it as a smorgasbord of topics to be tasted according to flavour.

Please note that some of the essays presented will be variations on a theme – themes that benefit from being viewed from a variety of viewpoints and timeframes. It should also be noted that *repetition* is a large part of the process by which any novel concept is comprehended and remembered.

I hope you will read on and see to what *degree* I am right or wrong on the various aspects of life I have chosen to mull over. In doing so you may find yourself entertained, possibly enlightened in some modest way, and will have learned, without Google's assistance, something about this author, *David Alan Petersen*.

[1] *Framing* is one of many biases that interact with our innate mental architecture, fully discussed in *Thinking, Fast and Slow* by the behavioural economist Daniel Kahneman.

Contents

About the Author...iii
Contents..vii
1. The Art of Giving..1
2. Just Do It...8
3. How Depressing..16
4. Big Hands..19
5. Thinking to the Shops...27
6. Mika*..38
7. Tea and Chocolate..43
8. Inside the Ride..55
9. The Man on the Beach..63
10. Aimlessness..69
11. Ennui...71
12. The Reluctant "Robot"..74
13. Insignificance..76
14. A Life in Three Acts...84
15. Friends, Strangers, Enemies...95
16. Knowing When...121
17. The other side of Sunday..125
18. The Wife...135

19. Forgive and Forget	143
20. Intimacy	148
21. Snobbery	154
22. Enslavement	160
23. Understand	174
24. How Few	179
25. Responsibility	182
26. Cogitations on Entertainment	185
27. The Wedding Photo	196
28. The Red Hibiscus	201
29. Für Elise	206
30. Taking the Offensive	210
31. Asperger's Syndrome?	218
32. Like the Sun	227
33. That's Just the Way It Is	232
34. Messiness	243
35. S'wonderful	254
36. COVID-19	257
37. Social Evolution	260
38. In Our Image	265
39. Statues of Stalin	271
40. Living on Scraps	274
41. War and Eden	280
42. Why I Don't Like Sex	290
43. Water Under the Bridge	296
44. Celebrations	302

45. Opinions 310
46. Doing It for Money 319
47. Silence 326
48. Enlightenment 334
49. A Chat with Solon the Wise 344
50. The Truth Issue 356
51. Like Me! 368
52. Warrior Culture: Part One 372
53. Warrior Culture: Part Two 379
54. Type Two Happiness 386
55. Happily Ever After 388
56. The Law 400
57. Believe in God 404
58. J.P. Uncensored 414
59. Unreasonable People 423
60. Philosophising 431

1. The Art of Giving

The health food shop in Kalgoorlie is a lean affair sandwiched between a shoe shop and a cut-price clothing store. It was a Tuesday, late afternoon, and there were only two customers, the dear wife and I – more so the wife. She browsed, slowly and systematically, with her silent progress watched intently by the only other person, the mature gent behind the counter – who looked suspiciously like the owner. After a while, the silence grew thick and uncomfortable. Too uncomfortable for me. Seeking relief, I lobbed a few desultory remarks for him to respond to.

He made noncommittal replies then surprised me with a question: 'So, what do think of Kalgoorlie?', said with a poker face but a voice full of expectancy.

An easy enough question. But not for me. It froze me solid. My philosopher's mind instantly converted his words into a swarm of inadequate replies that required all my mental capacities to frantically assess.

My first choice was to mention the super-pit, that astounding feat of mining engineering within spitting distance of our location in the main street. I moved on quickly to consider remarking upon the amazingly wide roads – designed to enable a camel-train to turn with ease. But dumped both, for not being sophisticated enough, and then thought about mentioning the impressive architectural legacy of the goldrush era, such as the courthouse with its gold-plated dome, and of course, the countless two-storey federation-style hotels, one on every corner it seemed.

I continued to stand mute, torn between a desire to be

diplomatic and a stubborn determination to be accurate. My mind an outclassed tennis player, dashing furiously from one idea to the next and back again, in a desperate attempt to find the winning response.

But it takes time to distil the essence of a town with any real meaning, and this was only my third visit.

The first was a weekender, when I was barely passed thirty, and, being with my bride-to-be, I was too much in love to remember anything *of the town*.

The second time was twenty-five years later, a year before this current visit, but that five-day encounter was mostly spent babysitting my wife's American visitors. They had ruined that visitation by their constant complaints about the flies, and the lack of the civilised trappings to be found in US cities.

Towards the end of that stay the assault on their middle-class sensibilities reached a climax with their visit to a hotel for dinner. As they dined, they had to suffer the hideous sights, and sounds, of a bunch of inebriated Aussie girls having a hen's night in the adjoining room. I think they may have suffered a new form of post-traumatic stress induced by the squealing, screeching laughter of the young women as they repeatedly attacked each other with enormous inflatable penises.

The upside of that episode was that it almost blotted out their memories of the Aboriginals, who accosted them for donations whenever they went to stretch their legs with a stroll around the main street.

This time around, it was just the wife and I, and my main motivation for visiting was not the town itself but the surrounding countryside. I'd fallen in love with its red soils, vast skies and the slender beauty of the trees of the surrounding open woodlands.

But time was slipping by at an unforgiving rate, and the pressure to utter some sort of remark had me about to explode.

A nanosecond before my brain shattered, I blurted out: 'Every place has its good and bad side.'

Then as control strengthened, I stammered on, 'I love the wide streets,' before finally confessing weakly, 'but most of all, I love the desert trees.'

He seemed happy with that, didn't ask any more of me, and then thankfully turned his attention to my wife who had arrived at the counter with her selections.

Seeking relief, I stood back and watched the interplay whilst continuing to mull over my reply. What else could I have said?

Out of respect, I couldn't mention the air of neglect endemic to mining towns, where the ethos of making a fast buck and a hasty exit pervades. The evidence was there in the unkempt gardens and the dilapidated state of many of the houses.

And I definitely couldn't admit to my impotent sadness at having to witness the loitering groups of Aboriginals, who, like tumbleweeds, drifted aimlessly along the main street, or were found lodged, dejected, on benches, or on the ground against walls. They seemed, for the most part, drained of vitality, though occasionally a group would burst into life with loud, animated shouting matches, using words mostly starting with f or c.

But for me, the most unsettling aspect of my indigenous brothers was their begging. We had only been back in Kal for two days, and most of that had been spent driving around sightseeing, and yet twice, in strolling past one of them I had been asked, casually, for a two-dollar donation. So far, I had resisted the temptation.

The Buddhists reckon that each person we meet is a Buddha reincarnated to teach us lessons in life, lessons that will be repeated until we master them.

The next day, Wednesday, I was given another chance to learn how to respond to begging.

The wife and I had gone to the Coles supermarket at the back of the main street, and were queuing at the checkout. We were behind a short, overweight, middle-aged white lady, in front of whom stood a tall, very black, youngish African lady, probably from Sudan, wearing a simple long blue dress. She was delightfully rounded and had marvellous smooth satiny skin.

Whilst we waited a tall, slim, well-presented young African man appeared at the window, stopped, put his face to the glass and stared in at us. He seemed to recognise someone, the Sudanese lady I presumed, and then rushed for the entrance and strode inside.

He ignored his compatriot and instead came up to me, looked me in the eye and boldly asked: "Uncle, can you spare me two dollars for a drink?"

If he'd sandbagged me, it would have had the same effect. Dazed, I stood silent for a long moment until the heat of the collective disapproval from the people around me, including the Sudanese lady, forced from me a muttered rejection. The man walked off unperturbed.

The queue moved. Somehow, I returned to outward normality, paid the lady at the checkout and wandered off in search of our car which we'd left in the undercover car park. We almost made it unscathed.

But my African *nephew* hadn't given up. He'd caught sight of us and dashed over to again press his claim for filial largesse on my behalf. This time I couldn't resist. I dug out my wallet, and after a long and futile effort to find some small change settled upon my smallest denomination, a ten-dollar bill, which I slipped into his outstretched hand. He accepted with a white, toothy smile, turned and departed with a spring in his step. But I felt like an anti-drugs campaigner caught paying a pusher for a hit. In numbed silence, I opened the boot, chucked in our plastic bags of groceries and then cautiously drove back to our rented apartment.

We headed back to Perth early the next day. Never saw the fellow again, but our meeting still reverberated within me for reasons I struggled to fully comprehend.

What was it about his approach that had weakened my policy of "not feeding seagulls", which was how I usually saw the act of giving to beggars?

Until now my guiding light has been the saying: *Give a man a fish and you feed him for a day, but teach him how to fish and you feed him for life*. And, that giving alms encouraged dependency, not independency. Now, I wasn't so sure. After all, the man has to survive the day first, and teaching someone "to fish" is often not quick, or easy.

But I think the main reason his appeal rattled me was because he called me *uncle*.

I am of northern European descent and so it has been many thousands of generations since the two of us shared a close common ancestor, and yet the man was correct. We were still *family*.

He had forced me to recognise that fact, and that my labelling him a beggar was a dehumanising act. No matter how much I am philosophically against encouraging begging, he was more than a label, more than the act of asking for assistance, he was simply another human, like me, but one living in unpleasant circumstances.

My initial disregard of our connectedness was probably borne out of fear, the fear of being overwhelmed financially, the fear of being swamped emotionally and, I have to shamefully admit, probably tainted by the sour aroma of resentment, (*I have to suffer the indignities of work to come by my cash, so why should he get it seemingly without sweating*). I resolved to be more humane the next time.

I didn't have to wait long.

The following Saturday, my wife and I were in Fremantle. It was a perfect day: sunny, twenty-six degrees Celsius, with a cool breeze, and hence the main street was packed with a colourful procession of sightseers and shoppers. We were shoppers, and were returning with a bag full of beans from Kakulas Sisters when we approached an old man sitting on a bench beside the footpath, next to the park, opposite the train station.

I'd noticed him on the way in. He had been leaning back, resting his large belly and chatting to a tall, slim girl in T-shirt and short shorts, which exposed a lovely pair of long honey-coloured legs. He had the chunky features of an Italian, confirmed by his accent when we had passed by.

He rested as before, but now minus the girl. We strolled closer and were caught in his lazy gaze. Two paces from him, with languid and practised ease, he held out his right hand and asked: "Can you spare two dollars?"

A Buddha had come to Freo!

But my wife tightened her grip on my hand, as a warning for me to maintain our pace. I knew why.

As a girl growing up in Yugoslavia, she had once answered a knock at her door, to be confronted by a young gypsy woman asking for money to buy food. Kind-hearted, she told her to wait, closed the door, zoomed into the kitchen and prepared a bread roll filled to bursting with salami and salad; rushed back, opened the door and triumphantly handed her gift to the gypsy.

The woman accepted the roll silently, glanced at it, with a scowl of such utter disdain you would have thought it was a doggie-do sandwich. Returning her gaze to her "benefactor", she saw the blank disappointment of shattered innocence, then turned and wandered off muttering, holding the roll as if it were radioactive. That episode permanently coloured my wife's attitude to the giving of charity.

And I, not wanting to risk domestic discord, took her cue, ignored his request and kept walking.

But driving home I felt the unease of having missed another

opportunity to interact with a fellow human, of having missed another chance to learn. As the familiar sights of the coast road slid past in semi-awareness, I took solace in a strengthened conviction that the Buddha would not forsake me. He would reappear in another guise, at another time and place, to give me another chance to learn my lesson.

Grasping the steering wheel a little tighter, I made a solemn vow to do my homework, to be prepared for the next encounter, to conquer *the art of giving*.

Note:

This essay was written in response to our revisiting Kalgoorlie, in November 2015. Things may have changed there since then.

2. Just Do It

We had arrived. Almost.

The imposing, though somewhat forbidding, immense log entry statement to the town of Manjimup – a sort of Arch de Triumph to the timber industry – was now behind us.

My excitement, kept at bay by three and a half hours of driving, shot up as my speed went down. Turning up the air-con, I sharpened my eyes and squeezed the steering wheel tighter in anticipation of the right turn that would take us to the town's centre.

The first of the houses appeared but where was the traffic? And where was the signage advertising the Cherry Festival? My mind choked on the incomprehensible thought that I'd got the date wrong. The turnoff to the main street approached. I almost missed it, "woke up" at the last second, forgot to indicate, and then took it too fast. The car lurched left.

My dear wife gave me a look of the type to blister paint, but I had to ignore her, being too busy braking to survive the next bend, a sweeping left-hander. We made it. The road straightened and normality was regained.

Approaching the next roundabout, at a sedate pace, I savoured a long calming breath and basked in the reassuring sight of footpaths teeming with people, their cars jamming the kerbs, spilling onto verges and overflowing into the parks as if a tsunami had scoured the southwest and dumped its contents upon the town. The festival was definitely up and running and the fear of having needlessly driven all the way to Manjimup for a non-event evaporated. I *had* got the date right, and by the look of things, the festival was going to be considerably better than anticipated.

But my moment of jubilation soon disappeared when it dawned on me that finding a parking spot was going to be a problem. I slowed to a crawl.

Our luck held, a small space in the car park at the back of the hotel was spotted, one flash of the indicators and moments later I was shoehorning our little FIAT 500 into the coveted sliver of real estate. Then, like contortionists, the dear wife and I extricated ourselves from the car, straightened up, adjusted our attire, and then joined the human stream flowing to where the action was: the two roads either side of the Post Office.

A companionable silence followed, occupied by my puzzling over the mad gyrations in my mood during the previous few minutes.

Not for the first time I asked myself: why are these sudden and often wild deviations from the ordinary; from gloom to glee, boredom to excitement, so unsettling?

Having read plenty of biographies, and looking back over my own very ordinary life, it seems glaringly obvious that we are all the playthings of a universe bursting with randomness and rapidly changing luck. And yet, I continue to mistakenly fret that bad times will last forever, just as much as I hope the good, would. When would I learn to accept the *temporary* and *unpredictable* nature of both?

Predictably, my philosophising was cut short the moment we turned into Wheatley Street. It had been converted into a pedestrian mall, crammed with stallholders on both sides and also running down the centre. Taking a deep breath and holding my wife's hand a touch firmer, we plunged into the bustling hubbub of humanity.

It was like entering a human anthill, one that had been kicked awake. Everyone was alert, excited, chattering, investigating all manner of things and in constant movement, though unlike ants – who at every encounter acknowledge each other with gentle strokes with their antennae – we humans prefer not to touch, instead glide past each other as though possessed of repulsing magnetic fields, with the rare collisions eliciting embarrassed, briefly muttered apologies.

After a brief discussion, we decided to circulate in an anticlockwise direction, but had only passed a couple of stalls when my nose came joyfully awake to a vaguely familiar, warm, unctuous, and utterly alluring scent. Hijacked by my olfactory senses, I gave my wife's hand a squeeze and wordlessly dragged her in search of its source.

It had been a lifetime since I'd experienced the pleasure of pork roasted on the spit, thus the connection between the heavenly aroma and the man tending the rotating carcass in the stall on our left was slow to form. I went past a few metres before the realisation knocked me to a standstill, causing my dear wife to bump into me a nanosecond later.

I turned us around and observed the scene.

It was about eleven-thirty and the man in charge of the rotisserie was clearly not yet ready for business. He was testing the meat, cutting off a tiny portion, tasting it and then, becoming aware of one of the growing numbers of drooling onlookers, sliced off another small sample, crackling included, and handed it to the surprised and grateful man, who munched the morsel with obvious primitive delight. I started to salivate.

A tug on my hand snuffed out my daydreaming; my senses again registered the sound of shuffling feet, and the hum of the crowd, which then brought the other stalls back into focus. I also became aware of the questioning, slightly amused look on my wife's face. She knew the dilemma gripping my mind.

The problem was, for health reasons, we had decided to

become gluten-free vegans, which sounds like confessing to joining a radical splinter group from a bizarre new American religion, and as such, lusting after roast pork definitely counted as a deadly sin. The increased pressure on my hand was followed by a pull sufficient to break the spell. Quietly and resolutely, she led me away from the path of temptation.

Once removed from the enticing lure of "the pleasures of the flesh", we were able to concentrate upon the enormous number of other items on display, which, like most markets, were that odd mix of trash and treasure, with cheap, poor quality or unimaginative knick-knacks and "dust collectors" in the ascendency.

Of course, that daunting ratio is the central charm of markets; the more improbable the odds, the greater the delight when one discovers the rare nugget amongst the dross.

The treasures were mainly in the form of food: award winning wines (we don't drink), olives and olive oil (lovely but we had plenty at home), cherries of course (cheaper back in Perth), magnificent cheeses (too much cholesterol and salt, and besides we were supposed to be vegans), beautiful breads and baked treats (all made from normal wheat flour and thus guaranteed to give both of us itchy pimples and diarrhoea in a day or so).

But it wasn't a total disaster. We did buy a kilo of uniquely tasty peppermint tree honey, later added punnets of perfectly plump Russell berries, and towards the end of our circuit encountered a very enthusiastic Indian fellow selling cleverly designed aerators, ideal for our kitchen tap, which we duly added to our shopping bag.

The festival of course included much more: clothing stalls, vintage cars, information booths about the region's many attractions, fast food vans, buskers and bands, but by the time we were plodding back up Wheatley Street my mind was preoccupied with the hope of finding food that we could eat.

Suddenly my nasal mucosa felt the first gentle caress from the perfume of roasting pork – in the buzz and distraction I'd forgotten we were again approaching the diet danger zone.

Mentally unprepared, my dietary resolve crumbled, but this time I couldn't call upon the strength of my wife's willpower to save me; she was as tired and hungry as I was.

With glazed eyes, and faces softened by sweet expectation, we found ourselves irresistibly drawn closer to the stall, there to stop and immerse our senses in the olfactory pleasure emanating from the roasting pork.

We stood, like zombies, silent, save for the grumblings of our stomachs, and watched the man at the rotisserie, briskly slicing up the pork before passing it to his harried offsider, who threw the meat onto plastic plates accompanied by a minimum of salad, or shoved it into buns with a few shreds of tomato, lettuce and onion, before serving it up to a long queue of fidgeting customers.

"Shall we?" whispered my wife.

Despite an almost overwhelming pressure to say "Yes", I remained mute, immobile, except for the hint of a smile that briefly stirred my flaccid facial features in response to an Oscar Wilde truism that had just stirred my consciousness: "I can resist anything, but temptation!" But quickly returned to being a flesh and blood statue when Oscar Wilde's slogan was chased out by Nike's, and my thoughts became obsessed with their call to abandon introspection and studied reason, in favour of "Just do it!".

I, who prided myself on *not* being an unthinking consumer, as one who went out of his way to avoid advertising had still been infected by Nike's emotive credo. At that moment I felt its liberating appeal and yet something about it had irked me to a standstill. Part of me objected to Nike's call to let our bodies and emotions have the deciding vote. Doing so was definitely not always a good idea. I thought of all the strife a man could get into if he followed through on every lustful thought induced by a nubile wench.

And when it comes to food our bodies can't always be trusted because they are relics of the Pleistocene. Back then we were hunter-gatherers, constantly on the move, living a life of occasional feast but mostly scrounging for enough calories to get by, not the stable and sedentary existence of today, in a world with a chronic oversupply of calory-dense foods, engineered to be tasty and so encouraging us to overeat. We all know the results: the obesity epidemic and the diseases of affluence.

I knew all this. My intellect told me the roasted pork represented giving in to the *dark side* of food, but my body wasn't convinced. It wasn't swayed by correlations, theories and statistics, it had millennia of the hard struggle for existence to draw upon. That I remained immobilised and still resisted my body's increasingly strident demands to join the queue was, in part, Taurean stubbornness, but mostly due to my intense dislike of being "pushed around".

I objected to my freedom to choose being hijacked by a coalition of unelected and unconscious forces: evolution, my absorbed societal and familial culture, and the cocktail of mood-altering hormones my body generated in response to them, not me.

But worst of all, was my recent discovery of what my microbial flora – the host of bacteria living uninvited in my lower intestine – were up to. Like hidden puppet masters they silently alter how my body uses the food I eat, influence how my immune system functions, and manipulate my moods and subsequent decisions. These gut bacteria apparently produce over eighty per cent of my body's "happy hormone", serotonin, and thus my being happy or grumpy is hugely influenced by a bunch of brainless bacteria.

That last thought insulted my male pride. Was I a man, or the servile plaything of a bunch of microbes?

In the end, it wasn't my strength of character, or my resolve to "be a man" that gave me the strength to exercise my free will and resist the *perils of roast pork*.

No, it was laziness and impatience. The queue was way too long; and we took the easier option, to eat our prepared lunch that was waiting for us in our car a short stroll away.

We drove off; found a nice shady spot away from the crowds; sat in the car and feasted on our spicy bean casserole.

As I munched, I mused upon the forces at play in my decision.

Impatience: it's a common enough human weakness, so why did I feel so embarrassed to admit to it? My lunch went momentarily untasted as I chewed upon the answer: reality had deflated my unfounded sense of superiority. The situation was especially galling because I knew well the veracity of the adage: *decide in haste, repent at leisure.*

It then struck me that the smart thing to do was to own up to my character weaknesses rather than constantly wasting mental energy denying them. And, having owned up to those weaknesses, begin to engineer my circumstances and habits to make those flaws work *for* me, not against me.

I took another spoonful; briefly responded to its unctuous titillation of my tastebuds before the pleasure was obliterated by a dangerous surge of pride. I suddenly realised that our chosen lunch had achieved just that. I had used two flaws – impatience, and laziness – to thwart another, the tendency to overindulge in the wrong foods.

Chewing mechanically, I realised my lunch was the result of the agonisingly slow process of learning that many "normal" foods were not for our particular biologic sensibilities. Once we had capitulated to *our* specific reality, we then developed a *new routine*, which involved establishing new food buying and preparation habits, one of which was to always carry our own food when travelling.

And because that new way has finally become a *habit*, it's now *easy*. It requires hardly any thinking, we *just do it*, not the impulsive and unconsidered actions normally associated with that slogan, but researched, *rehearsed* and wiser behaviours.

Lunch had been a victory of consciously created good habits over the lazy and unconsidered.

It was a victory worth repeating.

Addendum:

In the intervening six years since the above anecdote was written, our researches have resulted in modifications to our diet, via trial and error, and recently from new scientific finding enumerated in *Eat Like the Animals*, a 2020 publication by biologists David Raubenheimer and Stephen J. Simpson. That book was a *game-changer* in our understanding of what influences our *appetites*. It gave us the missing knowledge needed for better control over our food choices.

3. How Depressing

When assessing the human world with cold rationality there are innumerable issues to get depressed about.

But being depressed doesn't feel good. It is depressing being depressed. It's dreary and life-numbing. I don't like it when I'm there.

Choices. That's what it all boils down to.

Incessantly we have to decide what to do, but we can't until we decide which way to think: is the glass half full or half empty?

For each observation, we must allocate an emotional spin. Is it positive, neutral, or negative?

Things get out of hand when we shove everything into the negative bin, when in reality most things are neutral.

When I find myself in a negative state – generally in the dark early morning hours – and want to return to the healing safety of sleep, my solution is to exorcise the issue on the pages of my journal. Scrawling words onto paper may not always resolve the issue but it generally lowers its impact enough to allow me to return to bed and snatch a few more precious minutes of sleep.

Sometimes, before writing, I flip through the pages at random to see what bugged me on past occasions – perhaps as a way of putting the current issue into a broader perspective, and possibly in the hope of finding encouragement through uncovering past issues that have become less of a problem, or better still, have been happily resolved.

Recently, I found encouragement when I reread the following entry in my current journal.

"4:10 a.m. Friday 27 May 2016

Been awake for an hour, been here in the office for 45 minutes sipping my hot lemony water, just thinking: about the team building seminar at work yesterday, thinking about [a friend's] depression, thinking about depression in general.

Everything still boils down to two images of the same thing: CHOICE.

The image of a circular doughnut.

The image of a glass half filled.

Do I choose to ignore the doughnut and dwell upon the hole?

Do I choose to see the drink, (water, wine, or whatever) or the nothing above it?

What do I choose?

Why do I choose? Is it from habit or a lack of belief that I have a choice? Or is it lack of practice in seeing that there are choices?

Perhaps it is lack of energy to make any choice, and then <u>do</u> it.

Our physical body is a marvellous thing that we take for granted because most of the time, for most of us, it just works, in the background, unconsidered by our conscious mind.

When we are physically ill from a virus or bacterial attack or physical injury (fallen over, hit something, got cut or bruised) depending upon the injury the body commands us to <u>rest</u>, <u>be quiet</u>, in order to allow it to rearrange its resources to fix the problem and having fixed/contained/lessened/ adjusted to the problem, allow it to regain its immune/repair abilities.

The same happens with mental trauma: we feel drained of mental energy, it's hard to think (in order to reduce the negative thoughts and so prevent making things worse), have reduced physical energy (so that we don't do something stupid like kill ourselves).

The downside of that reaction to depressive thoughts is that, in preventing further damage, it also hinders finding a way out.

It takes energy to overwrite the negative with the neutral truth. That's where friends and kind relations come in.

But the trouble is, either they don't know, or you don't know, or refuse to say what the problem is (you enjoy being miserable, you're used to it, don't want to risk any change from fear of the unknown).

It's hard for these others to say the key phrase/point of view/analogy or whatever it is that collapses the fabric of lies and half-truths that holds up the gloomy thought's edifice.

"Always look on the bright side of life ..." the song from Monty Python's "The Life of Brian".

At work, [a colleague] was watching the final scene from the movie on YouTube and wanted to send the link to his daughter who was having an unhappy time moving house.

Can you laugh your way out of depression?

I don't think so. Laughter requires a sense of proportion, a sense of the ridiculous, both of which are lost in the depressed mind. Regaining them is the task to be done.

Perhaps that is why, in the past, I would play Leonard Cohen's music and feel better, because he sounded more depressed than me!

They say the best way to beat the blues is to help someone worse off than you ... it helps by restoring your sense of proportion ... you get to see what's important and what's not ... your sense of humour comes back ... even get to laugh at yourself hopefully, that is the goal.

When you come to recall all those stupid negative mantras and contrast them with the <u>neutral</u> reality you will see how silly you have been, have a good laugh and again enjoy the warmth of the sun, enjoy the attention of loved ones.

You may be a bit player on life's stage (one never knows whether one is significant or not) but does it matter? <u>No</u>.

Just realise that you are here, briefly on the planet, make the most of it, enjoy it, being negative is a hard way to spend the journey.

If all else fails, read Schopenhauer, the old misery guts, he'll perk you up."

4. Big Hands

Early in 2016, I attended a short story writing seminar. The female presenter began with an unusual approach to introductions, not, "Tell everyone who you are and what you hope to gain from the seminar", instead she asked us: "Describe who you are, in <u>one</u> word!"

To condense a personality and a life into a single word seemed an impossibility.

There were only ten of us and all too soon I was under the scrutiny of nine faces and eighteen eyes. I blurted out the first word from a long list, was vaguely aware of a ripple of acknowledgement before attention moved to the next "victim".

I am probably being a bit harsh here, because, as a getting-to-know-you exercise, it was a good one. It kept it short and immediately focused our writing minds onto how to meaningfully and accurately describe a person with a minimum of words.

It also made me aware that before one can describe a character, one must first know them with some degree of intimacy. It is a difficult and often slow process with fictional characters and even more so with real people.

Most of us think we know ourselves well, until we eavesdrop on people talking about us, and find discordant, or, overly generous assessments being expressed. And what of the other people that populate our daily lives, such as friends, relations, colleagues and spouses? How well do we know and understand them, and they us?

The presenter's challenge awoke all manner of questions that I had wanted respite from — questions mostly to do with my inadequate ability to understand and engage with the rest of humanity.

Later in the session, we were given the task of plucking three images from the ether in response to this line from *Killing Mister Watson* by Peter Matthiessen:

"We live many things, we remember some, and we die."

That last word dug up a vision from twenty years back, of my father lying in his coffin, his pale, emaciated face twisted by the cancer that killed him.

In the days since that seminar, YouTube-like visions and snap shots of Dad peppered my waking hours.

As a child, I am standing next to him as he relaxed in the lounge chair, our eyes level, my small hand trying to encircle his upper arm, white like cooked fish, in my futile attempts to hold back the rolling wave of muscle disappearing up his shirt sleeve when he slowly flexed his biceps.

During my late teens, he would wangle me a job at the airport, where he had a second job as a baggage handler. We would push the baggage trolley out to the Fokker Friendship where I would pass the bags and cases up to him. Some of the suitcases were huge, seemingly loaded with lead bricks or dead bodies, and I, with my puny arms, struggled heroically to lift them into the plane only to be humbled as my father effortlessly snatched them up and shoved them into the curved confines of the luggage compartment.

But mostly it was still-life's that remained.

A picture of him in his overalls, white, but grubby from assisting me to build a shed in the back garden of the family home.

Standing in his gumboots, gloved hands holding a spade, caught in the act of tending his veggie patch.

Preparing for the dog's daily stroll, he is standing at the backdoor, equipped with walking stick, his sweat-stained broadbrimmed hat perched at a jaunty angle and his pipe clasped firmly between his teeth.

During the days prior to writing this essay, I struggled to comprehend how could it be that a man so important to me could be reduced to such a tiny, silent collage. And where were the feelings to go with them?

The peeling paint on the sill of our kitchen window provided a clue. I've looked upon it too many times for it to any longer move my conscious mind, so maybe his influence, and my regard for him, have become such permanent fixtures that I no longer recognise them.

As an explanation it didn't seem sufficient to cover the vast extent of my amnesia so I searched for other reasons. I needed justifications to quell the growing disquiet it had induced.

My logical side concluded that the past is too big a place to be squeezed into the limited space of anyone's braincase and that being able to fully recall feelings would be evolutionary folly; we would be paralysed by memories, great and small, of each moment of fear, anguish and pain, or forever lost in the bliss of reliving those rare moments of ecstasy.

And yet we can, to a degree, generate and hold onto past emotional responses. It happens whenever we find those peculiar circumstances that remind us of those significant others no longer in our physical presence. Feelings of love, and hate, can be rekindled under special circumstances. But what are they?

Finding ways to revive, restore and relive our human connections can only occur if they were there to begin with. Of all the passing parade of people who have entered upon the stage of my existence, how sadly few I became strongly connected with. Was it me? Do I possess some bizarre socially indifferent genetics, or was that lack of connection the result of the multifactorial mess my life was, and is, embedded in: my family's culture, societal norms, or perhaps it was a side-effect of the size and layout of the cities I have lived in.

Even technology plays a part. That we must drive just about everywhere precludes the regular face-to-face encounters you would have if walking to the shops or café. Mobile phones, Facebook and Skype are fantastic devices for staying connected but there is only so much time in the day and the more time spent connecting electronically means less time for that precious face-to-face bonding. It's even worse when that telecommunication is conducted in front of the person you are physically with because you send their subconscious the unflattering message that the person on the phone is more important than they are.

Whatever the causes, for the most part my relationships with my fellow humans have been ephemeral, not the intellectually and emotionally sustaining ones that I had hoped for.

And thinking back over my relationships with my father, I recognised, for the first time, that the barriers that separated us were like unbridgeable canyons, all of which made the promised land of deep mutual understanding between us barely imaginable, let alone achievable.

The simple facts of his being forty-two years my senior meant he grew up in a world that to me seems more fictional than fact.

How could I comprehend what it was like for him, growing up in a foster family in Denmark during the nineteen twenties, and then, as a young man in 1935, without a word of English, sailing off alone to an unknown life in a British colony in East Africa, when the continent was raw, black and tribal.

And of course, we were son and father, and hence players of roles. The thought that there was more to him than just being Dad never occurred to me, it was as inconceivable as looking upon the sparsely wooded hills surrounding my home town and trying to understand the enormity of time and the immeasurable scale of geologic forces that had shaped them.

I was approaching thirty before I started thinking about my interpersonal relations, before I began asking the big questions of life and became aware of a gnawing hunger for something better.

By thirty-two I had grown weary of spending too much time languishing on first base with the few women to enter my world, with the rest of my situation "a portrait of a disappointment" (to borrow words from the singer Joni Mitchell).

I found myself working as an overqualified storeman in Sydney, the result of getting my geology degree during a mining bust, and once there, I watched my hopes of normality, in the form of a place of my own, disappear as house prices skyrocketed whilst my savings graph edged up at a glacial pace.

Disappointment also stalked my attempts to connect in some meaningful way with my work colleagues. Friday nights after work I would join them at the pub, where I had to persevere until they were almost paralytic before talk would turn to the stuff that really mattered in their lives. Sadly, my regard, and being understanding towards them, was not rewarded by much reciprocity.

Disillusionment has a limit. I reached mine, and something in my soul broke. I quit my job, endured the two weeks' notice by counting down the cups of tea left to go, and then packed a bag and my camping gear and exited Sydney on my motorbike, a hollow man.

But the desire to live can cling to the smallest of things. I was lucky; at least I had a direction, west, and a whim, to see the dolphins at Monkey Mia before ... I didn't have a next bit.

My folks lived in Wagga Wagga, a day's drive west of Sydney on the Sturt Highway. I headed north. I needed time to prepare myself for their questions, and north was where I had people who I considered friends.

It was August, but I hardly noticed the cold and rain, though hitting a huge water-filled pothole in the dark just south of Coffs Harbour temporarily shook me from my lethargy, and flattened the rim of my front wheel.

After a week spent repairing my bike and tending to my human connections, I headed south. It's a long ride, Coffs to Wagga, just short of a thousand kilometres and I almost made it in one hit but baulked at the idea of meeting my mum and dad cold and exhausted, so I stayed at a pub in a village forty kilometres north. There I was joined at dinner by a farmer who, happy to find a good listener, told me of his woes, mostly to do with the depressing struggle to meet a woman to share his life with. A topic I understood all too well.

My homecoming the next morning was a subdued affair. I think my parents understood my fragility and left any probing questions unasked. I just wanted to do nothing, say nothing, and they indulged me. Bless them.

It was towards the end of my brief convalescent stay that the incident occurred.

The Bwana (an honorific we bestowed upon him in recognition of his life in Africa) and I set off to take the dog for its morning stroll. Rugged up to the eyeballs to ward off a biting cold westerly, we had reached the turning around point, an open paddock that still held out against the inexorable forces of suburban sprawl.

I am not sure what prompted my confession, perhaps the cold and grey of the day, perhaps the realisation that going back to the family home was not a realistic option. I'd discovered that life is a one-way trip, you can't go back. I think it was the disappearance of that one false hope, to stay in Wagga, to hit the rewind button and start again, that brought the tears.

Staring at the ground I tried to tell him of the depths of my debilitating loneliness and the pain I felt as it crushed life's force from me. I was being swamped, drowning in grief for the death of hope and the me that was.

Suddenly he too was crying, hugging me, and joining me in the river of tears.

He understood.

Haltingly, he confessed of his despair after being sacked and blacklisted by the European community in Mombasa for having the temerity to organise a union of Port Authority clerks. He'd had to deal with the ultimate fear of a family man, that of not being able to provide for his wife and four kids.

The tears subsided. We turned for home and in silence walked back.

Shortly after I packed up the motorbike and continued the journey west.

At the time, I was too absorbed in my own uncertainty to fully appreciate what had happened. Only now, approaching sixty, have I come to see that, after that day, Dad and I had been welded together; he was no longer just my father; he was a human, like me. The tears had made us brothers.

And the knowledge of his having survived his grim years and then had created a new life in Australia must, unawares, have given me the strength to carry on.

Eight years later, I was back in Wagga watching him disintegrate and seeing him unmanned by the horrifying certainty of his death.

His ordeal was another shock for me. Dad had always been brave and strong but now at the end he was crying like a terrified child and there was nothing I, or anyone, could do.

Death is unimaginable but dying isn't, that's where the fear lies. It made me wonder how I would face that ultimate trial of character and concluded that I didn't know. That I'd have to wait, and hope, that with preparation, I wouldn't make a mess of it.

At the funeral the blow of seeing his battered face forced my gaze away, only to receive another shock: his hands. They were surprisingly big, powerful, with strong beautifully trimmed nails. How could I have not noticed that before!

I was stunned. Not only had I lost the father that I knew, but I realised I had also lost one I didn't know, and it seemed the second was far greater than the first. My anguish exploded.

A few months after the funeral, my sister discovered a photo of my mum and dad taken just before their wedding, which she then had enlarged and posted to me. My mother is facing the camera, whilst Dad is side-on, gazing at her in that special way – the way a man does when deeply in love.

That photo hangs on the wall next to our dining table. It's there to remind me of the father I loved, and of the man I didn't know but wished I could have.

5. Thinking to the Shops

It's one and a half kilometres and a ten to fifteen minutes stroll away. Thus, it's not much of a task to walk from our place to the local shopping centre, and over the past twenty-seven years I've done it innumerable times, and yet, to date, that piece of the ordinary has left no meaningful impact upon my being.

And why should it you ask?

The philosopher in me replies: why should it not be memorable?

Our lives are mostly made up of mundane activities that leave little trace in our memories and attitudes. This is probably a good thing as who wants to be burdened with a mind clogged with intricate memories of the hours wasted doing boring work, paid or otherwise?

In this essay I wish to explore the possibility that, if approached differently, much of the ordinary may hide aspects of the pleasantly memorable, or possibly the profound.

To that end I intend to review that walk to the mall by actively collecting as many notable observations as possible, dwelling upon them and hopefully uncovering some pearls of wisdom with which to "add value" to my life. And in the spirit of efficiency – that ideal so beloved by our political masters and the corporations whose interests they serve – I aim to do so without actually leaving home.

I intend to *think* my way to the shops.

I invite you to join me on this philosophical expedition to find the profound in the prosaic.

§

I shall imagine it is nine-thirty on a Saturday morning. Outside, it's springtime, a sunny twenty degrees Celsius with a cool wind stirring the trees.

My morning chores are done, and with nothing planned for the day ahead the dear wife is having a break; she's on the sofa reading a spy thriller and I am at a loose end and looking for a change of scenery. But why?

Phillip Adam's observation: "That we fear boredom more than cancer" bursts upon my thoughts. Boredom certainly is a motivator, and, if we don't let it get out of hand, can motivate us to discover, or create, better circumstances for ourselves. Ignored until it becomes intolerable, it can have us bursting with frustration and then rushing into poorly considered decisions: we abandon the marriage for a lover; we quit a steady job for something more exciting, and find the "cure" often worse than the disease.

And, like all human emotions, boredom has a physiological component. Our brain is a continuous operation – even in sleep it's at work reshuffling, reinforcing, reworking and removing our memories. Placed in a situation of severe sensory deprivation, the brain in its desperation for something to work on is forced into making things up and we find ourselves hallucinating.

Today my boredom, my *ennui*, on a scale from one to ten, is a three. I am itchy, not desperate.

'Just going to the shops to check out the motorbike magazines. Won't be long. Got my mobile, be back in an hour or so.'

I stand expectantly at the front door.

No response from the better half.

'Shall I lock it?'

It takes a few moments for my utterances to override the "page turner". After a great effort, she drags herself from the parallel universe of intrigue and heroic deeds, slowly disengages herself from the seductive embrace of the sofa and joins me at the front door. Half-heartedly she returns my kiss whilst trying not to let annoyance leak through her lips. She then pats me on my behind and sends me on my way. I hear the click of the latch on the screen door, then the softer sound of the front door closing.

I stand, alone, outside, facing the street, and, for a moment marvel at this thing called marriage.

It's a manifestation of an inexplicable force, a sort of magnetism, a kind of invisible glue that binds two people together. An observer can't directly measure it but they can definitely see its effects upon a couple.

Unfortunately, it's difficult, especially for men, to accurately judge how to measure the "marriage field strength". It is a pity that we can't buy a "marriage meter", or a "marriage strength" app for our smartphone with which husbands could doublecheck to see if their wife is really upset or just venting. The deluxe model would even suggest remedies for returning conditions to optimum levels.

Today my innate marriage meter, otherwise known as my gut feeling, suggests that she's merely anxious to get back to her book, to enjoy her holiday from "that which must be done". Hopefully, if the book delivers on its early promise, she will be relaxed and happy on my return.

Semi-confident that I have domestic harmony under control, I stroll to the street and turn left.

But domestic bliss still engages my mind. It's a situation I'm glad to say mostly prevails at our place and yet I can't help being puzzled by it because it's more an art than a science, and being a scientist at heart I would like to understand it better.

The foundation of that pleasant state rests very much on meeting the right person, physically, not online or virtually.

Imagine that you are attending a workshop, arrive at the last second, walk into the appropriate room at the venue and find yourself facing a bunch of strangers. The co-ordinator, on the stage, on seeing you arrive then announces to all, that everyone must now pick a partner to work with, but without speaking. Instantaneously and unconsciously, you, like the rest, start milling around silently assessing the form, start sifting the possible from the rejects. How do we do it? What do we look for in another person to work with, or one to wed?

Sigmund Freud reckoned men marry their "mothers" and girls their "fathers" or words to that effect. But if we can give credence to what we read in *New Scientist* magazine and in a select few science books on the topic, then there is a grain of truth in Freud's bold assertions.

The guiding hand of evolutionary pressure is at work from the day we are born trying to ensure we have what it takes to survive and reproduce. We are social animals whose survival depends upon getting on with one's fellows and whose reproductive success requires picking a suitable mate. As a suckling infant our eyes are fixated upon our mother's face, imprinting into our psyche the image of what a mother is. The baby is also watching everyone else, learning what its tribe looks like, learning to recognise the people it can rely upon. Thus, the female child sees plenty of adult males which then influence her later judgement in selecting Mr Right, and similarly for the male child and Mrs Right.

I can't recall where or when I stumbled upon these intriguing notions or how much weight to give them, but I was breastfed, and my mother was a brunette with a squarish face and so too is my dear wife! I'm not sure if Freud or blind evolutionary forces was at work, all I can say for sure is that I am very happy with the outcome.

Being uncertain about the exact rationale behind my ardour leads me, again without fully understanding why, to consider another issue: the way in which we humans have arguments, not the fact that we have them, but the inefficiency with which we engage in them.

As an aside, this new line of thinking shows that I am not immune to the dogma of efficiency that pervades the capitalist world, which is annoying because as far as I can see the net outcome of it has been the efficient removal of power and money from the majority to the minority, and I, unfortunately, am one of that duped majority.

Back to the process of arguing: my fascination derives from the fact that argument was the force that brought my dear wife and I together.

It was lunchtime, in the mess at the mining camp, that I first saw her, sitting alone in the far corner with her back to the wall – an admirably sound defensive position to my mind.

Boldly I decided to check her out and sat down opposite. We had a conversation; we could call it an argument, since we both expressed differing views upon a topic since forgotten, but the thing that never left me was that we had a *rational discussion*. We had expressed different views amicably and then agreed to disagree. Part of the pleasure of that discussion was that my eyes were opened to another view of the world I had not been aware of. That she was a feast for the eyes also made me realise she was the dream combination: brains and beauty!

It is a source of continuing dissatisfaction for me that in most arguments each contestant treats the process as a sporting event, with too much emphasis put on point scoring and winning, rather than enjoying the interaction with another human and hopefully learning something new and useful in the process.

Why should we come to blows over whether Freud or science is right regarding mate selection. It doesn't matter. What matters is the sustainability of the outcomes. Which mode of thinking produces the most useful results is the one to go with – so long as we are clear about how to meaningfully measure those results and from whose point of view we consider it, and over what timeframe.

Sadly, most conversations, even if friendly, are about telling our story, our opinion and how we feel, without actually hearing or absorbing much of what the other person has to say.

Hopefully I will remember this point later and practise active listening when engaging with my interlocutors. But I suspect it will take a bit of effort to break old non-listening habits, but then, with practise, active listening is bound to become easier.

Having cogitated enough, I proceed to go through the walkway at the end of our cul-de-sac and find myself at a T-junction. Right or left is now the question?

It must be difficult being a town planner and getting it right. In my suburb, they have designed a network of walkways to allow pedestrians to move about without interacting with the traffic. I can walk to the shops without being rundown by a car. A commendable idea, in theory.

But when I turn to the right, I see the reality. The laneway is long and bounded by high fences and illuminated at night by rows of waist high posts with lights set in their tops, protected by a metal grid. That is the physical structure, now we add in the human component.

Psychologically, walking down a long narrow laneway with high walls that prevent escape is manageable by day, in the sun, when you are young and fit and only encounter the occasional *normal* passer-by, but...

In the back of our minds lurk all the terrible stories of murders, rapes and bashings that we are daily force-fed by the news media.

Our minds are not put at ease by the graffiti and the fact that the "nightcrawlers" have spray painted all the lights in their hatred of it, with some of the more energetic managing to tear some out of the ground whilst miraculously avoiding electrocution.

The turn to the left is marginally more inviting because the narrow passageway is shorter and leads to a park area that runs behind the houses and leads you to an even bigger stretch of open ground, which then follows the drainage canal alongside the school playing fields, almost all the way to the shops. But that way is longer.

Being bold, and wanting to maximise my magazine browsing time, I turn right and find myself still brooding over the psychology of walking these pedestrian laneways.

When walking the footpaths of suburbia, the backstreets of Perth, or alongside any road here in Western Australia I suffer a certain anxiety, an unease I did not suffer whilst holidaying in Serbia. Having recently returned from six weeks over there, two of which were spent "beating the streets" in the crumbling heart of old Belgrade, I felt an order of magnitude safer there than I do over here. Why?

That feeling of safety in Serbia is more puzzling when one considers the circumstances there. The country is a ruin. From fumbling ineffective communism, they have endured the war of the disintegration of Yugoslavia, twenty years of economic sanctions and now are being battered by the brutal forces of capitalism, especially in financing where they have gone from one government bank and almost no personal debt to thirty foreign banks all fighting to enslave the populace with easy credit. The majority of the people have insecure livelihoods, are poor and struggling, and so we would expect a lot of social unrest, and, with so many presumably unhappy and frustrated people, it should feel riskier walking their streets, but that was not the case.

Perhaps, their knowledge of their turbulent history and having had plenty of practice at enduring hardship, (Belgrade has been destroyed and rebuilt forty times in its two-thousand-year history) has made most Serbs stoics.

Enduring is a virtue, but understanding and improving the situation to my mind is the way to a better future. It is a process that requires two things for success: a multifaceted understanding of the causes of past good times *and* bad (a task not easy to achieve since it involves the foibles of being human interacting with external forces such as climate, disease, new technology and economics), and *believable hopes* to sustain the populace during the transformation process. These two ingredients are required whether in Serbia or here in Australia.

I'm not poor, live in a country not at war, have a home not mortgaged, am blessed with a loving wife, a job as secure as is possible in a capitalist economy, and enjoy good health. Hence, I find being relatively optimistic about the future (mine, our country's, and the planet's) is easier for me to imagine, here in the sunshine, breathing the fresh air of a beautiful seaside suburb, than it would be in darker, colder, poorer and less healthy circumstances such as those in much of Serbia.

I never mastered the knack that bankers, CEOs, media bosses and many politicians have of not seeing the unpleasant sides of our current societal arrangements. Unlike them I can't coldly rationalise and then dismiss poverty, massive inequalities in incomes, reduced opportunities for dignified living, or ecological degradation, as "collateral damage" unworthy of consideration. I am not blind to the circumstances of others, and the planet, and thus my hopeful outlook often waivers.

Whilst all this thinking has been going on I have progressed to the tunnel that takes you under the main north-south road and deposits you on the doorstep of the shopping mall, all one kilometre of it. I slow my pace, feeling an instinctual dread of the bright lights and the hard sounds that echo within its glass and tile hallways, but I am slowed more by a difficult to describe malaise that I often get whenever I'm in its grip.

Stopping, I wonder what specifically is it about the mall that I find so uninviting? Confined spaces, harsh sounds and crowds are aspects, but not the main ones. It is not the physical that fills me with dread but a sense of spiritual repugnance.

The average shopper does not enter those halls mentally unprepared, they have been beautifully brainwashed, bombarded from birth by the mass media's extolling of corporate wishes, telling us which attitudes to possess, which goods and services to desire, and hence the unsuspecting shopper enters thinking the choices they make are theirs and for their benefit, but I see it otherwise.

I see an uneven contest between many highly qualified, and paid, professionals toiling over many decades to control, coax and coerce a bunch of unknowing, uncritical and hence unsuspecting amateurs. The result is sadly predictable, a victory of the cunning over the naive.

We waste our hard-won dollars, our irreplaceable time and life's energy on trinkets, fads and fashions that will soon fill our rubbish dumps whilst unseen, our guided spending boosts the bonuses of CEOs, the minimally taxed bottom lines of big corporations, and to a lesser extent, bolsters the bank balances of small business owners.

I find little to hope for in that temple to mindless consumerism with its greediness and snatching up of illusory bargains. There is very little human dignity there and certainly nothing to inspire my soul.

I turn around, and what do I see?

I see the path leading back past the primary school, an institution funded by the public for the public good, a place filled with the energies and hopes of the coming generation who are guided for a brief moment by adults hoping to make a positive impact on lives other than their own.

I see that the green grass all around is trimmed and decorated with intriguing patterns from being recently mown by men that our grudgingly given council rates allow to live and work. Nearby are the few surviving trees that the vandals accidentally forgot to trample and uproot, grown big enough to withstand their further efforts, trees which magnanimously provide welcome shade, for all, when the sun's rays prove too great a blessing for mere mortals to bear.

Then past the footbridge, I see the drainage channel continuing on, brilliant green with flowing strands of algae that caress the occasional "playfully" abandoned shopping trolley, through whose metal grids wander tiny native fish that consider it a sanctuary, not an eyesore, because it provides safety from the darting bills of keen-eyed egrets and herons, whose permanent optimism has them patrolling that little manmade stream throughout the daylight hours.

As my eyes follow that artificial rivulet further, my ears become aware of the clak, clak, clak of unseen wattlebirds, then I see the flirtatious flicking of willy wagtails and get the occasional emerald flashes from parrots dashing between the more densely packed trees further down.

My eyes then focus on the distant low buildings of the combined clubhouses of the Dog Club (bringing good behaviour to dog and owner), the Pigeon Racing Club (a strange hobby where the cosseted pigeons, to earn their board and lodging, each month must fly back to their keepers from some far off mystery destination) and lastly, the rooms of the Rock Hunters, who, as far as I know, go out into the vast bushlands of this marvellous state, pick up rocks interesting to the eye, to be brought back, polished and then shaped into bookends and pendants (creating beauty from dross).

Standing there at the opening of that underpass, a moment of choice lies upon me. Do I risk being seduced by the carefully crafted manipulations of consumerism, or do I focus on the more inspiring aspects of reality that I now see laid out before me.

That tunnel leading to the mall is like looking into a telescope – to get the correct picture you have to look through it the right way. It also conjures up the concept of *tunnel vision*, a term usually negative but, like the telescope, it depends upon how you use it.

My imagined journey has reached a conclusion and my mind can return home because have I vowed to develop my tunnel vision, to improve my ability to exclude more of the negative clamourings of mindlessness, ignorance and greed.

Doing so will counteract my evolved mind's hyper-sensitivity to the negative and allow me to see, fully, *all* the inspiration and justifiable hope that abounds in this resilient world of ours.

6. Mika*

This tale begins in the back blocks of Croatia, meanders, and ends up in suburban Perth.

I met Zoran* about four years back, when, for a year or so, circumstances conspired to have us thrown together. He is around twenty years my junior, intelligent, solidly built but not fat. We soon recognised in the other a fellow thinker and became friends.

Another commonality was connection to the Balkans, mine indirectly via my dear wife, a Serb born in Serbia, whereas Zoran was a Serb born and raised in a picturesque and mountainous region of Croatia.

But, at the end of high school, Zoran's world was shattered by the war that dismembered Yugoslavia. He discovered he wasn't Croatian, as he had thought of himself, but was Serbian, living in a Serb dominated enclave, and one suddenly no longer welcome in the land of his birth.

In due course, most of his compatriots and family were ethnically cleansed and he found himself a refugee in Belgrade. There he graduated from university, worked briefly in his profession but soon concluded a better future lay elsewhere. He came over here and thus, eventually, stepped into my world.

I can't begin to imagine how such traumatic events could affect one's outlook, my own experiences of fleeing unpleasantness to seek a better life elsewhere seem paltry compared to the emotional trials Zoran must have had to endure, and overcome.

How can I understand the shock of finding out that one's country of birth despises you, your family, and your neighbour's presence on their soil, enough to expel you at gunpoint, and have an uncle, who foolishly believed the Croat reassurances and stayed behind to be murdered and his home burnt to the ground, is something I can barely guess at.

It certainly influenced Zoran, but thankfully not in any seriously debilitating way, though he has developed a fascination with trying to understand war, and, like many in his position, has an underlying homesickness that will always be with him.

Recently he returned to visit the town he grew up in. The hills, the green valley and the river running through it are still the same but the people are all new, all proper Croats, and many of the street names have been changed to expunge the least reminder of the dream of a unified home for the southern Slavs. It was a sad time for him but hopefully lessened his desire to go back. Perhaps he, like many of us, may have come to terms with the fact that we can never go back.

With that background we found much to discuss and, to my great benefit, he encouraged me to read the book at the top of his list of all-time great stories: *The Forgotten Soldier* by Guy Sajer. It's a thick book – I don't read thick books as I haven't the time – and concerns the horrors of war – I dislike anything gruesome or too horrifying – but to please him I gave it a go.

It is the autobiography of a seventeen-year-old Frenchman who enlists into the German army at the end of the war. He is sent to the Russian front and miraculously survives the retreat, and the homecoming. I read that book like an addict, only putting it down from exhaustion of my endocrine system. The cruelty of the training, the horror and madness of the battles, the unbelievable cold, the lack of sleep for days at a time whilst constantly being bombed or shot at, the scrounging for food and warmth, interspersed with rare moments of hope and camaraderie.

It is written in a simple honest style, sprinkled with brief but powerful descriptions of the vastness of the steppes, or of the sound of massed Russian soldiers singing as they waited on the opposite side of the river before the coming slaughter. Just writing these recollections has my pulse racing and tears in my eyes, tears for that man who went to hell and survived to warn us, to warn us never to join his like. Like a glutton, I read it so fast that I barely tasted it, and know I must read it again, but when I'm older and less excitable. For now, my copy awaits, sitting patiently in my bookcase, its memory forever in the recesses of my mind.

In turn, I helped Zoran. He reminds me, at times, of the comfort he has received from the book I convinced him to read: *The Consolations of Philosophy* by Alain De Botton, which I thought a concise, insightful and delightfully readable journey through the worldviews of the great thinkers, from the ancient Greeks to modern times.

After that first year he moved suburbs, but our friendship continued, via emails and monthly get-togethers, occasional walks and gossip sessions over a coffee.

Around about a year ago, his young daughter Mika* expressed the wish to join us on a walk in the park. Zoran complied, organised the time and place, and I duly met them at the arranged spot for a late afternoon stroll.

On that day, my association with Zoran, apart from friendship, indirectly and unexpectantly, added another dose of positivity to my life.

At three-and-a-half, little Mika was cuteness personified, as well as being full of life, curiosity and kindness. Strolling beside the artificial stream, Zoran and I didn't get much time to talk philosophy or even work gossip, because she demanded the full attention of her chaperones, which we, in the end, were only too willing to grant.

We assisted in her launching leaves and twigs into the water, castigated her for chasing the ducks, but then joined her in the play area and supervised her on the swings. I showed her how to play *king of the castle* on the rounded domes in the middle of the sandpit. She in turn set up a pretend shop in the monkey bars, where we paid for our invisible pizza with leaves. A great time was had by all but the sun began to set and we had to guide our steps back to the cars.

Zoran opened the back door of his car. 'Mika, give Mr Alan a hug and then say goodbye. We have to go home now.'

I squatted down to make it easy for Zoran's princess. Dutifully she gave me a hug and then stepped back, considered for a long moment, head to one side, and then, having made her decision, grabbed me around the neck and softly pressed a kiss on my cheek. The kiss of an angel!

So small, so soft and so imbued with unqualified affection. She was like a medieval queen at a jousting competition, where having chosen a knight worthy of her, anoints him to be her champion.

It was a perfectly pure giving of affection. A gift of approval, a gift I will treasure until my dying day.

And whenever my mood sags, I can seek solace in the memory of that gift, and in doing so it may remind me of all the other good things in my life that I have temporarily forgotten.

I have no kids of my own but, after that episode in the park, I now have a glimmer of comprehension as to how much Zoran must adore his children.

It would appear that some of Zoran's love for the country of his childhood has found a place in the heart of Mika, a love that will flow to those worthy enough of her affections.

Mika also blessed my life with undeniable proof that

indescribable beauty of spirit exists still in this troubled world of ours to surprise us when we least expect it.

---

* To preserve their privacy the names Zoran and Mika are fictional.

7. Tea and Chocolate

In January 2016 the dear wife and I were at a shopping centre a few suburbs upmarket, checking the bargains.

Neither of us are great fans of shopping centres but to her surprise she actually managed to locate a pair of pants to her liking in David Jones, the first store we had investigated. They were duly purchased and we then decided to continue on with a quick lap of the rest of the shopping centre before returning home.

She may have had secret hopes of finding another *must have* item but hopefully was mature enough not to put too much energy in that direction. I, knowing the extreme unlikelihood of encountering anything to tickle my fancy, was content to keep her company and be vicariously rewarded with her happiness.

In due course, we ended up in a department store, which used to have some stylishness but now, possibly in response to the gradual impoverishment of the middle class appeared on that day to have gone down market. The place was jammed with trestle tables and racks overflowing with uninspiring pieces – probably from third world sweatshops – that gave their customers plenty to riffle through but little chance of discovering anything of lasting value. The scene reminded me of seagulls at the tip.

It was all too much and I nudged my better half towards the exit.

It was whilst riding the down escalator, suffering shopper's fatigue, that I saw the girl.

She was one of three walking briskly for the exit, all similarly dressed in blue jeans and pale T-shirts. Her companions were short and struggled to keep up with her. The head girl – tall, mid-twenties – was like a luxury liner heading out of port on its maiden voyage with her long black hair gleaming with youthful vigour, trailing behind like the massed streamers bedecking such a vessel courtesy of its well-wishers, and her two dumpy companions the equivalent of accompanying tugboats.

What a craft she was!

Perfectly proportioned, with a slim waist and magnificently rounded buttocks flowing to firm powerful thighs and slender ankles, with the view of her impressive lines unimpeded by pants so tight they must have been painted on.

I floated towards the ground floor in silent male bliss, mesmerised by the rhythmic undulations of her gluteal muscles as she and her entourage navigated the twisting aisles of the perfumery. A fragment of my paralysed mind was questioning the sudden awakening of libido, and why, having passed innumerable nubile females whilst traipsing around the shopping centre was this particular young woman affecting my moribund hormones and making me sympathetic towards men who keep a mistress?

Perhaps my primitive imagination was enflamed by her determined tread – suggestive of strength and stamina – or maybe it was the fact that she possessed acolytes – implying a woman of forceful character, who might also possess deep passions that, in the right hands and circumstances promised ...

Who knows? Looking down to hop off the escalator, when I looked up again, I found that the girl and her entourage had evaporated into the scented air, leaving me disoriented, staring blankly and uncomprehending into the jumbled maze of glass countertops and makeup girls.

My Walter Mitty moment had ended, but the girl's afterimage

still fogged my mind. How could I love and admire my wife *'til all the seas run dry* and yet still entertain thoughts, no matter how brief and frivolous, for a *bit of fluff on the side*?

Was it like food?

During the working week, we enjoy eating pretty much the same thing with minor variations, but by the weekend we are itching for something different, something more exciting. We eat out and generally suffer for it.

The strange thing is, that despite the meagre rewards, the pattern repeats itself. What is it in our nature that makes us dissatisfied with what we have, and why was it so difficult to always be sensible?

I decided to stretch the lover/food analogy.

Judging from the experience of others, the new love is equivalent to discovering a fantastic restaurant, where the food, ambience and service are all top notch. We are enticed to go there again, and again, and again until ... it too becomes boring, and our subconscious starts exaggerating the tiniest faults to justify our moving on.

But this internal debate was hampering my locomotive abilities so my wife had to yank on my hand to bring me back to the task of threading through the scented stalls to gain the open space and clear air of the corridor outside. There we halted for a moment, she, to regain her bearings, me, to restore my composure, after which we jointly agreed on the way to the car park and headed off.

Circumnavigating the coffee shop in the dead zone at the intersection of two main thoroughfares, its crowded tables scattered like the flotsam at the centre of the Sargasso Sea, two things hit me: first, the desire for a cup of "real" tea, which I had given up because I wanted my behaviours determined solely by my intellect and not highjacked by drugs, even one as socially acceptable as caffeine. The second cause for hesitancy was the sight of the girl.

She was standing side-on outside a shop, waiting for someone, brows furrowed, her full red lips pursed as she killed time by fidgeting with her phone. Biologically, she was the perfect woman: young, healthy, good-looking, but ...

My nascent ardour waned. Studying her unguarded visage, it became evident that she had an imperious and unforgiving nature, which would soon negate any physical joy her flesh could dispense.

My disappointment was again manifested by reduced power to my lower limbs and again I felt the increased pressure from my wife's hand cajoling me to keep up. Ditching the last of my fantasies, I picked up the pace and together we ploughed on to the exit.

Three days later, the invisible intelligence that guides the workings of the universe, knowing I had failed to resolve the questions raised by the girl in the mall, gave me a reminder of its unanswered status.

It was Tuesday, late afternoon, and as usual, we were walking hand-in-hand along the beach, heading into the setting sun. In front of us were a young couple, obviously new to their relationship as the fellow was holding the girl with an arm wrapped around her slim waist.

At this early point in our circuit, we were walking at a moderately brisk pace and as such usually overtake most other pedestrians, but not the lovers, who, despite being joined at the hip, maintained their lead, giving me plenty of opportunity to savour the view.

The young lady was of medium height, with blonde, shoulder-length hair, wearing a very short dress of some thin floaty material, beneath which she either wore nothing, or a G-string, leaving me with an unblemished view of her firm compact cheeks wiggling in the most animated and delightful manner.

I had obviously learned something at the mall because I maintained our brisk pace, engaged in mildly licentious daydreams, and simultaneously kept up my side of our conversation – that last aspect given added impetus from the knowledge that if I was silent too long, my dear wife, out of concern that I might be brooding, was likely to ask what I was thinking and, despite much practise, I remain an unconvincing liar.

I couldn't help noticing that the girl was dressed with clothing just sufficient to prevent arrest for indecency, whilst her boyfriend's modesty was well covered by jeans and a T-shirt.

This wasn't the first time the differences in dress code between the sexes had puzzled me. I'd seen it repeated at almost all social occasions, be it a wedding, a birthday party, film debuts, or an awards ceremony. The men exposed little flesh, usually fully covered in suits, whilst the women, especially the younger ones, are practically naked.

These observations seem to imply that women, up to an age I had yet to determine, are more sex-obsessed than men. And that their nonverbal cues, in this case immodest clothing, are usually contrary to their spoken and written views on propriety, which naturally causes mass confusion in the male of the species.

This train of thought had me recalling a summation of the foundation stones of male and female success as espoused by George and Ira Gershwin in their famous song "Summertime", specifically the line: "your daddy's <u>rich</u> and your ma is <u>good looking</u>". Those lyrics seem to encapsulate the key imperatives of the sexes: for men, they must appear able to provide and protect, whilst for women, it's all about displaying physical health and a disposition sufficient to attract, and hold, a suitable mate and breadwinner.

But I was sure there was more to it than that, and since the universe appeared to be goading me into a deeper investigation, who was I to say no. I thus embarked on a crusade of reading and introspection, hoping to gain a fuller understanding of the mysterious workings of the male and female ways of being.

It was a well-trodden path and one with many dead-ends, most of which I avoided by using evolutionary biology as my guiding light, reasoning that, like all other lifeforms, humans have the same remit: to survive and reproduce. If it were not so we would have become extinct long ago. My search was made easier by recent advances in genetics and biochemistry as well as by new fossil discoveries, all of which were elucidated in a number of very readable books on the forces that made us; forces both physical and social.

I was surprised to find an argument that suggested evidence of an event that had a significant impact on humanity's evolutionary saga could be glimpsed in Bunbury, specifically, in the black hexagonal columns and blocks of the Bunbury Basalt exposed at the north end of Ocean Beach. Those rocks are remnants of the lava extruded from the bowels of the planet when India separated from Australia and began its race north to collide with Asia, pushing up the Himalayas, which in turn adversely affected the climate of east Africa, humanity's ancestral home.

That tectonic alteration to the status quo, combined with others in east Africa, induced a continuous cascade of selection pressures upon our ancestors' survivability, producing a sequence of changes that roughly went like this:

- the opening of the east African rift dried the climate on the eastern side of the continent, shrinking the areas of equatorial rainforest previously available to our simian ancestors, forcing some to make a living on the expanding areas of predator-friendly savannahs, a trend later exacerbated by the rise of the Himalayas.
- Life on the savannahs required an upright posture and

the ability to run.
- Protection from lions and other predators necessitated a group effort, likewise with food harder to find, co-operating and sharing became essential to maintaining the strength of individuals and the tribe. This in turn required even better coordination, necessitating more computing power, hence bigger brains.
- And bigger heads required females with bigger hips.
- But hips have a design limit past which walking and running become difficult.
- Nature's solution was premature babies (our babies have bodies very underdeveloped in comparison to most other mammals).
- With babies completely dependent for years, not weeks, the males were required to take more interest and better care of both females and children. Nature came up with "silent oestrus" (no external signs of ovulation) and sexual receptivity of females even when not fertile. Sexual relations became a way to bolster male-female bonds and, with a bit of female promiscuity, confused the parentage of the children enough to make males more inclined to support all the tribe's children and less inclined to infanticide, directly, or by neglect.
- Female menopause was another uniquely human invention that allowed older females time off from baby-making to help with food gathering and child-rearing, which in modern hunter-gatherer societies significantly improves the survival and health of all concerned.

Thus, by about one hundred thousand ago, our bodies had reached their present incarnation. Since then, we have had only minor cosmetic changes, such as, different skin, hair and eye colour and occasional mutations affecting our digestion of exotic foods, such as milk past weaning and a better ability to handle carbohydrates.

The biggest change since our body shape steadied has been the cultural revolution caused by agriculture. This resulted in us living in permanent villages, then towns and finally cities. We went from being nomadic people possessing almost nothing, sharing food and child-rearing with a generally more relaxed attitude to sexuality, to one where everything became owned by individuals, companies or nations. Hence our present scramble for individual wealth, our strong desire for social status, and an *increase in the male obsession with female fertility* because few men can afford, or are willing, to raise another man's children.

It was amazing how, in unimaginable ways, one thing led to another to create the society and body I inhabit. A body nature designed to find attractive the childbearing capacity of women with its promise of genomic immortality, but I was still a long way from understanding exactly why some women were more attractive than others, and why I still found my dear wife as desirable as ever despite her being well past her reproductive use by date.

The answer to the second part was easier to find than the first: genetically I was obviously more a prairie vole than a rat, or so Stefan Klein implied in the chapter on love and altruism in his book, *The Survival of the Nicest*.

Researchers examined the unusual monogamy of the prairie vole (when all other similar rodents are promiscuous) and discovered that the voles have a crucial genetic mutation to one gene. This mutation produces the biochemical and hormonal responses impelling prairie voles into a lifelong partnership with the first member of the opposite sex they have intimate relations with.

Humans have more than one gene involved and hence have a wider range of partnering behaviours, with prominent infidelities amongst celebrities and high divorce rates in the general population, suggesting our genetics are skewed more towards that of rats than voles!

Thus, biology explained my continuing fascination with my dear wife and most of my desires regarding those young women, but it failed to fully explain my willingness to overrule my libidinous desires and heed the wisdom of that dour nineteenth-century philosopher, Arthur Schopenhauer, who stated that: "One can choose what to do, but not what to want."

If he managed to resist biologically driven temptations it was due to his social upbringing and in doing so it probably saved him from various dire consequences. Schopenhauer was lucky to have the power to do so because it now seems that even self-control is influenced by genetics.

This is the conclusion suggested by the famous "marshmallow experiments" by Walter Mischel of Stanford University, in which four to six-year-olds were given the choice of either having a treat now (marshmallow, biscuit or pretzel) or two in fifteen minutes. The greater their ability to delay gratification, the better were their later life outcomes. Thus, it appears the self-control needed for success is probably more influenced by nature than nurture – a humbling thought.

Of course, the last word will never be written on the intricacies of human behaviour, but by now I had reached a point where I had learned enough to understand, and marvel at, the processes behind my continuing infatuation with my wife – a monogamous genetic disposition, social norms, need for intellectual stimulation from a like-minded soul, and pair bonding strengthened biochemically and metaphysically by lovemaking – as well as my vicarious and innate enjoyment induced by the sight of a physically attractive woman – my dear wife included!

The quest to understand desire should have ended there but

it wasn't to be.

Several months passed without further ruminations on the subject until circumstances conspired to induce a bout of the blues.

My life became tasteless and colourless. I was becalmed, wanted nothing and desired nothing. Michelangelo is said to have uttered this prayer: "Lord, grant that I may always desire more than I can accomplish.". I then fully understood his wish, because I had reached the terrible state of having nothing I wanted to accomplish.

It brought me face-to-face with an aspect of desire that few ever consider: how does one deal with *a total lack of desire?*

Fortunately, or unfortunately, it was hard to decide which; this state of despondency was not a new experience and hence, in the deep recesses of my mind, I knew I would eventually sail through it. Again, biology is the catalyst for change. The physical necessity to move is the key, be it going to the toilet or searching for something to eat or drink, anything that gets me moving is enough to alleviate the gloom. Should sufficient momentum be developed to go for a ride on my motorbike then restoration of my mental equilibrium is almost guaranteed.

Another way to normality was revealed by my drug-free lifestyle. For the last decade, I had given up the regular use of stimulants (caffeine in my case) and hence my body had redeveloped its sensitivity to them. Nowadays, should I weaken and drink the occasional cup of real tea, or munch on some dark chocolate, their energising and mood-enhancing effects are much more pronounced, and memorable.

That extra piece of empirical knowledge resulted in my possessing a chemical option to add to my array of behaviours for dissipating melancholia.

Even so, when down in the dumps, I remain reluctant to resort to drug taking, (dosing on the caffeine, theobromine and any possible other psychoactive chemicals lurking in tea and chocolate) fearing the creation of habits leading to dependency. This also applies to my motorcycling cure because overuse will also diminish its effectiveness, and with age and decrepitude motorbiking may one day no longer be an option.

It has been said that *beauty is the promise of happiness*. In regard to those lovely young ladies in the mall and at the beach, my evolved biology recognised their youth and shapeliness as indications of fertility and saw their promise of *biologic happiness*, the happiness of *genetic immortality* to be found in the children I could potentially sire with them. My *body* responded with surges of dopamine which did two things: made me feel good, and also made me more alert, an alertness that *could have* been used to fuel *the mind* into finding ways to turn reproductive fantasies into biological realities.

Recollections of my recent depressive episode again highlighted the interdependence of *mind and body* as evidenced by my bodily and mental responses to those young women.

That depressive episode was instigated, as usual, by an overly pessimistic assessment of life events by my *mind*. It got out of hand and my *intellect* threw in the towel.

No desire means no will to live, which slowly, or swiftly, can lead to the body's early demise. My *body's* innate life force then took over. It went into damage control mode by inducing lethargy, to prevent the *mind* having the energy to instigate actions harmful to the body.

Sometimes it takes outside assistance to get the two sides to work together to create mutually agreeable outcomes.

Thankfully, I don't generally descend to subterranean depths and have enough residual *mental flexibility* to start the recovery process unaided, which, as I stated earlier, often begins with recognising that doing easy mundane tasks that promote *bodily* maintenance will produce the positive biochemical and physiological changes in *my body* that will lower stress hormones, slake thirst and satisfy hunger. All of which requires movement, which then stirs the circulation, clears away waste and oxygenates the blood. Movement also lowers the body's stress hormones, eases physical discomfort, which makes for a more relaxed and happier mind with which to guide both body and soul to better circumstances.

Of the two opposing states this essay has examined, desire versus the depressing lack of it, the depressive one is the harder to deal with because it involves a lack of energy and a dearth of hopeful ideas. If recovery is too slow in arriving, seek outside assistance.

But should simple physical tasks involving movement and looking after the biological basics, or even a few hours cruising the countryside on my motorbike fail to restore normality, I have a backup plan before I need phone for a counsellor or psychologist.

If melancholia lingers, hope lives in the secret reassurance that comes from possessing two readily accessible psychoactive chemical cures that are guaranteed to perk up my body and hence my mind: black tea and dark chocolate!

For more information on the themes discussed above I suggest the following books:

Sex at Dawn by Christopher Ryan & Cacilda Jethá, *How to Think More about Sex* by Alain de Botton, *Why Is Sex Fun?* by Jared Diamond and *The Science of Happiness* and *The Survival of the Nicest* both by Stefan Klein.

8. Inside the Ride

We all experience our lives as individuals and rarely get the chance to understand how the world is seen and felt by others in a way that we can fully feel and comprehend.

Read on and I shall endeavour to show what goes on within one individual, me, on an expedition through time, space and the emotions. You will learn what happens below the helmet, under the leathers, beneath the skin and find out what goes on *inside the ride, and, inside the rider.*

§

If you have never been so captured by a piece of music that the world disappears, or made love, long, and leisurely, with shared smiles during the occasional awkward moments all the way to a shared joyful transformation, or danced until giddy with the love of life, then this tale is probably not for you.

At the risk of sounding like a telecommunications provider in overselling and under-delivering, I hope, in these pages, to impart some understanding of what it is about motorcycling that can induce a prolonged state of euphoria such as I experienced during a ride to Boyup Brook on Sunday, twelfth of March 2017.

The day started off with mixed emotions brought on by a forecast of warm weather but rain later. A quick departing wave to my dear wife and I sedately moved off heading to the service station where my motorcycle club's rides depart from. The early morning air was cooler than expected, which had me wondering if the light jumper under my "go fast" leather jacket, in white and blue Suzuki colours was going to be enough.

Due to the earlier-than-normal start time, my forecast smaller turnout proved correct – when I arrived around ten minutes to the appointed hour there was only one motorcyclist waiting for me.

He was an experienced rider on a machine twice the size of mine and, like me, was looking forward to a day in the saddle though he had to be back relatively early and hence was keen to get moving. We discussed the route and eventually decided to take turns being leader and follower.

He led the way to our first stop in the small town of Harvey, but to put more road under our wheels it involved none of the usual coffee, cake and conversation, replaced by a quick dash to the loo to answer nature's demands and wash the bugs from the visor.

Not far south of the town the annoyances of straight roads, and moderate traffic, were cast aside when we turned left into the road to Collie. There I renewed my appreciation of the truth in the oft-quoted lines from the American poet Robert Frost, who famously wrote:

"Two roads diverged in a wood, and I –
I took the one less travelled by,
And that has made all the difference."

That was where the real riding experience began: The one that compensates for the aches and pains induced by hours gripping the handlebars, the unpleasant possibility of speeding tickets, or falling off, or getting rained on and all the other negativities attached to motorcycling.

Once over the railway line and across the remains of the coastal plain, all attention was focused upon the beckoning escarpment and the sweet anticipation of the delights of its enticing curves. I was possessed of an excitement similar to that of the sailor entering the bordello.

The speed limit sign was dismissed in favour of "riding to the conditions", nothing but paddocks and hills, and hence the first right-hander was taken with knees gripping the tank and body leant forward for more control. I then concentrated on powering the bike and rider through the bends that carved a path bucking and twisting to the blue sky above.

That road can be a dangerous one for the unskilled and unaware. With good visibility through the initial bends an easy rhythm develops of slowing on the approach, changing down a gear, easing off the throttle and then once past the apex accelerating out the other side such that, as each curve is conquered, confidence soars until ... just below the crest of the escarpment the land lays a trap with a treelined right-hander that apparently curves like all the others but turns deceptively tighter on the exit, leaving the overconfident going too fast, running out of ground clearance until death awaits upon the rough-barked tree trunks that threaten like rows of gigantic teeth.

But I knew its tricks; I'd washed off speed, had changed down two gears, and had picked my line well beforehand and so leant the bike over with perfect speed and line and sailed through unscathed to accelerate triumphantly up the final slope before entering the tablelands and forests that accompanied us to our fuel stop in Collie.

By then I was starting to imagine a cup of tea and a bun, but my time-poor co-rider was keen to keep moving. He promised that the late breakfast would be all the more enjoyable with its delay. Semi-convinced by his: "It's only another seventy kilometres", we set off again, with the bikes fed but not the riders.

This time I led, as he wasn't sure of the next turnoff. It's another backroad, which again has traps for the innocent. Starting off in undulating country, it has gentle curves on full-width bitumen and thus is ideal for faster riding and yet is only signposted at 100 kph. It was a sign I responded to with a sudden attack of "number blindness". I increased the pace, with only the sky and the scattered army of grey and drab green trees silent witnesses to our transgression of the rules.

Halfway, at the shire boundary, the road narrows and counterintuitively the speed limit increases, but I eased up, knowing what was ahead of us. The initial openness of the country and the gently winding road entices the unwise to relax their guard and end up unprepared when the road shrinks down to a one-lane strip of bitumen, with treacherous pea gravel peppering the normal line through the lefthanders and an impenetrable wall of bushes on either side, making it impossible to guess where the road is going or who is coming at you.

If one survives those tests, the road has one last lesson to teach. The bushes fall back to reveal rolling paddocks and scattered gum trees, with the better sightlines through the bends then tricking some into increasing their speed only to get caught out when the road abruptly ends at an uphill T junction, with a high embankment dead ahead and the intersection strewn with a generous coating of the dreaded pea gravel, courtesy of the dirt road that is its left arm.

"Been there, survived that," and so I had made sure I was on the brakes nice and early, with my taillight alerting my companion to the hazard.

At the T junction, we headed right and shortly after "returned to civilisation" when we turned left onto the highway that leads into the town of Boyup Brook. I initially behaved myself but succumbed to temptation eight or so kilometres from the town because the road became a series of perfect sweeping curves too sensual to resist. My self-control gave way upon recalling that snippet of wisdom long ago plucked from the movie *Strictly Ballroom*: "A life lived in fear is only half-lived".

I decided to live fully and tucked my head in behind the fairing, chest squashed down against the tank bag, and then soared through those bends at maximum throttle.

The game was over at the 80 kph sign on the outskirts of the town. I eased up the speed, changed down gears and reverted to the law-abiding citizen that is my usual state in urban areas.

Once parked outside the café I had a chance to calm down; my body tingled from the bike's vibrations but more so from the stirring of my endocrine glands. Like a man waking from a dream, it took an inordinate effort to find a seat, stow away the helmet, jacket and gloves, and then force my mind onto the task of reading the menu in the hope of finding something that my body's sensitivities could cope with.

It was a very pleasant interlude. The ladies behind the counter were friendly and made us happy with good food and prompt service. But we still didn't linger because my companion remained mindful of his need to get back relatively early. After a final swig of my caffeinated, black tea, we headed off to Darkin, both knowing that this section was another of those less travelled roads that give the greatest rewards. It was not to disappoint.

My companion led the way at a leisurely pace that proved too sedate for me in my well-fed and stimulated state. I overtook him and briefly stayed in the lead until I hesitated over a turnoff and he reclaimed the role of leader, this time considerably faster than before. I then had trouble keeping his more powerful bike in sight. It became an uneven contest that I willingly took on.

We entered a magical world of rolling hills and valleys connected by a rollercoaster of well-maintained bitumen. I became mesmerised by the swaying of the curves, the joy of plunging down into the valleys and then, tucked in behind the fairing, going as fast as possible up the flanks of the hills desperate to maintain my momentum and yet mindful of the bends on the crests. The process repeated with infinite variations until I was captivated by a rhythm akin to the thrust and counterthrust of lovemaking, only there the ecstasy, though more subdued, was stretched into minutes and then hours, with each bend a mini-orgasm as man and machine fused into a single entity, a flesh and metal manifestation of the God of Pleasure.

At some stage, when in a sweeping right-hander, came another revelation, that music offered a similar magic. Into my mind, unbidden, materialised my most stirringly evocative piece of music: *Europa*, the version from Santana's *Moonflower* album.

Into my head came its unhurried introduction, then the tension built up by layers of sound from Santana's soaring guitar, counterpointed with the sonorous backwash of the keyboards, and throughout, the driving rhythm of the percussionists. It was a form of aural lovemaking; reaching its climax with a piercing crescendo of guitar work in which each note was sustained to almost painful ecstasy until; the long, slow, exhausting finale.

Europa became my mind's soundtrack for the rest of the ride, replayed with each approaching bend but truncated to fit the timing of each approach, apex and exit. Perhaps I had slipped into a new state of being that words are inadequate to describe. Maybe it was what is known as Nirvana, but whatever the name, it was a marvellous place to be.

But, like all things, it ended, when I was dragged back to the normal universe by the intrusive appearance of the 80 kph signs marking the boundary of the village of Darkin.

A quick refuelling was followed by one last dose of speed before a more subdued pace was brought on by increased traffic and greater threats of radars once we turned left onto the Dwellingup Road. The slower pace was still enjoyable, the sensation equivalent to that state of satiation after the lovemaking, where one lies cuddled up luxuriating in shared warmth and quiet togetherness.

The sun had disappeared back in Darkin and with each passing minute the clouds had built up menacingly so that by the time we had our comfort stop in Dwellingup the first drops of the forecasted rain were felt. Wisely, we donned our wet weather gear and then took it easy down the escarpment for the final stretch across the coastal plain and home.

The landscape had one last delight to give. Issuing forth from it came that warm, damp, slightly sweet and earthy perfume that is triggered by long-delayed rain. It was an olfactory consolation prize for having to endure the slippery roads.

But the wet finish failed to dampen my spirits; rather it reminded me of the temporary nature of all things and as such boosted my determination to savour and remember every drop of the good times had, and, to be consoled that the dull and bad times were equally temporary and hence endurable.

Life sometimes can seem overly filled with disappointments but, for me, one antidote to the blues so induced is at hand in the form of my motorbike, and it doesn't matter how big or small a motorbike is, the physics involved in getting one moving in the desired direction forces one to concentrate and in doing so quickly forget one's troubles.

If you develop an affinity and unity with your machine, such that each bend becomes a meditation exercise, then you too may experience the joy that I felt on that day, and come to understand why I ride.

§

Addendum.

November 2022.

It has been over five years since that amazing ride. I write these words in my shed, in my "mancave", when all now is quiet, with only the hum of the fan to bother the neighbours after they endured, whilst I enjoyed, another playing of Europa with the volume up loud.

Though quiet outside, my blood still reverberates from the excitement of both that tune and its ability to let me relive that ride in all its emotional strength. Slowly coming down from that high, I bask in the reassurance that even when I become too old, or too incapacitated, to ride my Suzuki 500, I can always relive much of the joy of that incredible experience by playing Europa on my CD player and let Santana's music carry me back to that wonderous time and place.

Of course, no experience can ever be entirely regained, the world is not like that, but that music will at least remind me that I have lived more full bloodedly than most.

In the intervening five years I have travelled that circuit a handful of times in the ridiculous hope of a repeat performance, but, naturally, it never happened; worse, the world changed on me. The road up the escarpment has become too popular with bikers and others, and popular with the police too – I lost four demerit points on those bends one long weekend a few years back. And even the sense of achievement in conquering that backroad south of Collie has diminished because it is less of a challenge now that its southern end has been widened and the bordering scrub trimmed back.

Nothing stays the same. We can't hit the replay button on our lives, which is why I wrote down my memories of that ride the day after, wanting to fix it in my memory as vividly as words can hold, words and feelings that can be turbocharged with a playing of Europa.

Not every moment in life can be a peak experience, it would kill us if it were the case, but I give thanks that I have found a way to preserve at least one. I hope you too find ways to cement your peak moments of joy and achievement into your memories.

9. The Man on the Beach

The incident happened, appropriately enough, in early March, at the start of autumn, that season for reflection, nature's antidote to the busy summer months.

It was a Monday, late afternoon, on the sparsely populated promenade at Rockingham beach. The lack of crowds, discouraged by most of the eateries being closed, meant the man, walking south whilst my dear wife and I strolled north, was going to be hard to miss.

Trim, wiry, of medium height, his close-cropped hair, what there was of it, was grizzled. Clean shaven with a hint of stubble, he was a mature man, of Mediterranean or Eastern European stock, possessing a strong face, lined, but not overly so, giving more weight to his being from Europe. A notion given near certitude by his T-shirt, which was blood red and emblazoned with a screaming yellow hammer and sickle.

In joggers and faded jeans, he approached us with a purposeful tread, staring beyond us with an uncompromising seriousness that appeared to be his default setting. In less than a minute he was gone.

An unremarkable event that caused a flurry of words and thoughts upon ideas other than the weather and after... well, my dear wife, being a practical person, forgot all about him. But not I.

It was his T-shirt of course. The man would have been pleased that it had stirred up a debate within me, though he appeared the type who considers debate a case of expressing one's view and disregarding those of others. He appeared to be a talker not a listener.

Communism. A failed ideology that, in most people, automatically induces fear, loathing and contempt, and then possibly stirs questions such as: *why would any person waste time on such a discredited concept?* and, *what convoluted thinking had induced the man to shout his allegiance to it?*

It is the automatic nature of that response that bothered me. In my advancing years I have grown wary of automatic opinions because the more I examine them, the more cracks appear in their logic. These kneejerk responses usually turn to dust when the "facts" underpinning them are closely examined. Thus, he was a message from the gods to put Communism, and my mixed feelings towards it, under the microscope.

I suspect many will stop reading around about now, since who wants to suffer the slim possibility of having to change our opinion, especially when it is self-evidently true? But is it *our* opinion, or did we absorb it unwittingly, or with a minimum of scrutiny?

Be warned, changing our opinions can have uncomfortable ramifications. We may no longer be so agreeable to our friends, family and work colleagues, and, if the changes go too far from those of the majority, isolation or even persecution threatens. Thus, the rest of this discussion will be for the brave and the curious.

The first step is to define terms – a task fraught with imprecision whenever words end in "ism" are under consideration.

From my probably simplistic perspective the difference between the only two socio-economic systems that currently exist in the public's mind, Communism and Capitalism, is that one is based upon non-ownership and sharing, the other with private ownership and winner takes all: Communism is all about *us*, Capitalism all about *me*.

Neither system can exist in a hundred percent pure form because they are implemented by humans, who, by the blind forces of natural selection, are a bundle of unresolved and competing motivations. We are split between our instinctual urge to look after number one, versus our innate need to co-operate and care for our family, friends, co-workers, our football team, our nation state, and perhaps even our species and the planet as a whole. Genetically we are both capitalist *and* communist.

On our wedding day we form a "communist cell". We become two people who pledge to *share* their lives, their bodies and their finances for the good of both, for richer or poorer, in sickness and in health, 'til death do us part.

That happy communist state begins to unravel if our selfish capitalist desires are not met. When one or both, too often find themselves asking: "what about me?" Collapse starts with separate finances, too many separate activities, a decline in conversations about shared goals, then abusing the other's generosity in time, affection, and performance of domestic duties. The friendship falters, affection shrivels until divorce seems the only path back to happiness.

Despite our high divorce rates, the catch phrase of Alexander Dumas's *Three Musketeers*: "All for one and one for all!" still resonates strongly in all of us, and if it didn't our society would collapse into the brutal anarchy of "every man for himself".

But we can only hold a strong regard for a limited number of people (according to Robin Dunbar at Oxford University the maximum number is one hundred and fifty) and when the numbers rise it is so much easier to disregard the feelings of the rest, be self-serving and callus. Which is why it is so much easier to wage war on strangers than friends.

Work for the benefit of others? It's only going to happen on the small scale, hence Communism on the scale of a state is doomed because the lucky and/or ruthless few will enslave the rest.

Nations powered by the pre-eminent instinct of self-interest, do, by dint of intense competition, encourage new and often better ways of doing things, but when totally unregulated, lead to corporate and political oligopolies or monopolies, who, to maintain power, stifle any opposition, which then restricts innovation and creates a stagnating feudal state just as the communists did. We end up in the same misery for the majority but from different starting points.

The U.S.A. and China are successful economically because they are neither capitalist nor communist but blends of both ideologies. America has numerous "private-public" enterprises that they try not to advertise. The taxpayers bail out their banks on occasions, taxpayer funded infrastructure is created for the benefit of private businesses, health and education are a mix of private and public institutions both receiving direct or indirect funding by the taxpayer. China is no longer communist but also a blend, though at this stage still with large but decreasing number of state-owned industries. Like the Americans, their private corporations also benefit from the infrastructure paid for by the state, whether it be roads and ports, or education and healthcare.

Over here it is the same, for example, our supposedly private schools, are semi-private because of huge direct payments from the taxpayer, the legislative advantage they enjoy over public schools for being able to charge fees as they see fit to secure better teaching aids and infrastructure, as well as the unappreciated fact that they exist in towns and cities with roads, sewerage, electricity and numerous other benefits all organised and for the most part paid for by the state. The purely capitalist state does not exist.

And were the unsuccessful experiments with communism in Russia, Eastern Europe, and elsewhere entirely a failure? Their free education, medical care and housing, even if of a mediocre standard, would, for many of the poorer members of our society, be a worthy achievement they can only dream of.

But the key impact of the man in the red shirt was not his call for a political debate but his *courage*. Do I have the backbone to be unpopular, to go against the herd in such a public way? Do you?

Or is the question not, do I have the courage, but what issues do I consider worth fighting for, or, dying for? And, is wearing a slogan on a T-shirt the best way to fight for such a cause?

I possess few T-shirts, and the few I have are used mostly as nightshirts, but in Belgrade a few years back I was enticed to buy one. It was black – my least favourite colour – and sported, in a red box, a red man pointing a gun to the head of a blue man with a bag of dollars, in the blue box beside it, was a blue man with a bag of dollars holding a gun to the head of a red man, underneath are captions, the first box, "Socialism", the second, "Capitalism".

I have never worn that shirt because, it is true *and* it is false. To wear that shirt in public it would need a huge question mark placed under it, because that is the issue that needs discussing. Our society is in desperate need for those of opposing points of view to *see* the other side, then debate, and then modify those views in the light of *reputable facts*, not half-truths, gut feelings, meaningless generalisations, or emotional responses.

To have that type of debate we must first become aware of how and why we humans make decisions, and that is a very humbling experience. A good place to start is by reading and thinking and debating *Thinking, Fast and Slow* by Daniel Kahneman to explain the *how*, and *Survival of the Nicest* by Stefan

Klein to shed light on the *why*.

Slogans are *almost* always black and white. Reality is *almost* always in colour, and mixes of colours, and colours that constantly change as circumstances change, as times change, as new facts emerge.

I am left wondering if this modified version (pictured below) of that T-shirt I bought in Belgrade is the one I should wear to start a *real* conversation and, am I brave and flexible enough to engage in such a conversation?

10. Aimlessness

Anything. Write anything, just start writing, start moving in some way, even if it's just randomly tapping the fingers on the keyboard, just to feel the sensation of the keys on the fingertips – now too sensitive from having trimmed the nails back too far. It may be enough to renew my interest in ... what?

Filling this empty page, in this dimly lit room, in this quiet predawn that offers few clues other than the faint gurgling whispers of the electric heater bringing the energy that I lack, but need, or feel I need to ... do what?

Even as I am now, lost in a fog of existence, I am filled with goals and wants. My bodily needs are the fuel that forces me to live; they compel me to breathe, to satisfy thirst and hunger and to be rid of metabolic wastes. But the body cannot supply the goals that satisfy a mind weary of the prosaic and unconvinced that the heroic is achievable, and thus I sit at this desk mired in ennui.

Four-thirty-four, Monday, the sixteenth day of July. A day yet to be born but crying to do so. Outside in the cold dark the wind murmurs; it is the voice of the coming day trying to encroach upon a mind unwilling to acknowledge its commands to wake, to live, to achieve.

My body ensures I am not entirely aimless. I am merely unenthused by the menu options, options that are tired repetitions, when novelty and grandeur of purpose are dreamed of. But lacking sufficient powers of self-delusion they will remain unrequited.

Is it the wisdom of advancing age that knows what is realistic and what is fantasy, or does age and wisdom corrode dreams to dust that with courage and effort could have become real?

Perhaps wisdom should guide me into choosing dreams I can live with; dreams I can still want after having achieved them.

There lies my blockage, a dearth of dreams alongside insufficient wisdom to decide which will be worth pursuing and be enjoyed once gained – assuming the dream is an end product and not an ongoing process.

Can one dream of enjoying the process and not care whether or not there is an achievable goal?

Four-fifty-two a.m.

There is still a little time to enjoy the *process* of cuddling up in the warm bed to the warmth and softness of my dear wife's body, that other half of me who lies unafflicted by bizarre waking dreams. Hers she leaves behind in the bed.

Perhaps her aura will glow bright enough to show me a way to dream that will cure me of this aimlessness.

11. Ennui

Twentieth of December 2017.

Wanting nothing is a tiresome and debilitating experience, a bizarre state that can only exist in the modern world, where all the basic needs are met and the mind says "now what?" and has no convincing answers.

Christmas is approaching in a few days and then the New Year, 2018, and then? I ask myself what do I want to do and nothing comes up. I am sure that my body will force me to move for its own survival and that I will probably continue to go to work, where another me seems to exist. That other me, who walks and talks, engages with its colleagues and customers and appears quite normal, even jovial much of the time, but then transforms into another being when it gets home and has no tasks it *absolutely must* perform.

Perhaps the real problem is that there are secret things that I really want to do but have abandoned all hope of doing them through a perceived lack of time, money and/or talent. The other part of the dilemma is an apparent deficiency of imagination to dream up achievable alternative desires worthy enough to pique my interest.

Either way, I find myself with nothing to look forward to, nothing to make me happy – since happiness apparently is mostly found in the *process* of achieving, not in the achievements themselves. How can anyone be neither happy nor sad, exist in a non-happy limbo, bored, but not bored enough to be moved to action?

I type these words with no enthusiasm. More in a state of puzzlement that such an utter lack of desire, apart from minimal bodily maintenance, can actually exist. How long must it be endured?

At least it's not painful. But then, pain would create a desire and a direction. This ennui has no feeling, not even that of feeling bored, which would nudge me into doing something. I am becalmed, waiting for an act of God to push me back into the normal world of desires and achievement, back into the world of emotion, back to the messy world of the living.

I am waiting, waiting, waiting …

§

Addendum (written on 21st July, 2018)

Once I got past the falsity of Christmas, the world turned a corner and so did my mood. They still fluctuate but the periods of slothful lack of direction have been milder.

Perhaps I have reached the point where I am becoming more accepting of these periods of ennui. They seem to be one of the consequences of being human. Thankfully, like all moods, they are temporary manifestations. And, after finding the courage to cogitate upon my insignificance, and my place in and influence on the world, I now increasingly find my ordinariness and unimportance easier to bear. But how, exactly, did I achieve this wonder?

I cheated. I made my existence *appear* more significant than it really is by drastically *reducing my perspective*, the context I measured myself against. One of those altered perspectives involved consciously enacting Jordan Peterson's advice to not compare oneself with other people, but only with one's *former self*. Comparing my present self with the clueless but well-meaning prior versions has been easy because I hold the relevant data in my brain. Thus, my claims of improvement are more likely to be real than fantasy. In some areas I am confident true progress has been made, and that some of that progress is of that rare type of achievement that is *as enjoyable* in the *having* as in the getting.

I have even found an achievable and desirable *process* to work on: practising not sweating the small stuff, like boredom, *or* the big issues, such as death and insignificance.

12. The Reluctant "Robot"

The man lay awake under the covers, staring at the ceiling, unfocussed on the quiescent lightbulb centre stage in its grey-white expanse. It was probably around 4:00 am, though the problem of temporal exactitude wasn't the cause of his insomnia. The *cause* was the problem. It lay buried in some recess in his mind, deep enough to be hard to find, but not so deep that it couldn't be felt. It was an itch he couldn't locate and yet desperately wanted to scratch.

The room mirrored his mental state. He could see, from the dull red glow seeping in from the nightlight in the distant laundry, the dimmed and fuzzy features of his bedroom, the blobs that were wardrobes, the rectangles that were pictures, and of course, the dark, lumpy ridge that hid the softly somnolent form of his dear wife, whose quiet breathing provided the only aural accompaniment to his unease. The main features were discernible but the details that carried the meaning were blurred out. Life had dissolved into a dissipated, colourless and tasteless fog. He awaited the dawn like a prisoner facing another day of breaking rocks in the hot sun under the cold and unrelenting glare of unfeeling jailers.

And yet, on paper, he had a wonderful life. He owned a house, was debt free, had a loving wife, good health, a satisfying job and a moderate amount stashed away for his imminent retirement. So why was he so unhappy? Why so sad and so unenthused about the unknown number of days still allocated to him?

Existential ennui seemed the best description of his condition. But, unlike other emotions which inspire action, his boredom fed further inaction. He felt drawn ever deeper into a quagmire of malaise with no signs of escape and, worse, no desire to make the effort to escape should a way out arise.

Suddenly he grew aware of the twittering of unseen birds celebrating the dawn, and tasted the bile of disembodied jealousy. They weren't bored. They were keen to start the day.

He'd read that boredom supposedly existed to make one uncomfortable enough to do something. But what? What goal or purpose did he find achievable and worthy of pursuing? The darkness was retreating outside, but not in him.

The world continued to turn; the planet moved a little more along its well-worn circuit. His wife stirred. Still asleep, she searched for him, was semi-waken, enough to drag him into her embrace, to have them huddle together spoon fashion, flesh on flesh, holding him close with her hand clutching his shoulder.

Satisfied, she returned to her dreaming.

The man felt the shadows of those dreams, in the twitching leg and spasmodic hand flexing as she clambered through unknown troubles. The magic of her dreaming acted like a moving magnetic field that induces electrons to move. It rekindled his life energy, shunting his mind onto another track, one that led into the light, and rebirth.

He had been a rusting "robot", battery fading, software stuck, suddenly resurrected and transformed into flesh and blood and with a mind reconnected to hope. No longer lost in the echo chamber of undirected thoughts, he had discovered a purpose: the desire to live up to his wife's trust. A trust that knew no bounds, that existed even in slumber, when in her most vulnerable state. She trusted him as a sleeping baby does when cradled in one's arms, utterly confident in its safety.

What a magnificent "burden" to live for!

13. Insignificance

The place was a small town in Europe. The time was early morning in September 2016. The dear wife and I were strolling to the central square accompanied by a distant relation of hers, an educated, mature lady with a somewhat awkward disposition, when, without warning, she calmly and sincerely asked my wife: "Am I essential to you?"

To my great admiration, she didn't miss a beat, instead replied with equal calm: "Of course!", then adroitly changed the subject. Though both thunderstruck at the time, she has wisely given the incident little further mental effort, but not I. That awkward question let loose two trains of thought that long continued to rattle my thoughts: *Why did she ask, and why were we both stunned by it?*

To my mind, we only ask such a question if circumstances are going against us and we find we can no longer fool ourselves to the contrary. The cold breath of reality compels us to reconsider our actual achievements as opposed to our delusional ones. After such an assessment we then face the difficult task of deciding what we want to do with the rest of our lives and how to achieve it.

When young, this is difficult as we are new to the process, and yet it holds more promise of a satisfactory solution because we have the time to make mistakes, recover from them, then find worthier goals and achieve them. But with age there is less time for mucking around. We have to get it right if we are to achieve something of personal significance. If this wake-up call comes late, the fear looms that, on our death bed, we will be crying: "What was it all about? What was it all for?" and go to our grave disillusioned and disappointed.

My wife's relation, having reached her mid-fifties, with both parents dead, her siblings living successful lives in other countries, no firm friends, no career, and being looked after by paid carers was stumbling to the conclusion that her life, thus far, had been underwhelming and was seeking reassurance in my wife's answer.

But, being unskilled in contemplating life's truths, she asked *the wrong question*. No person is *essential*. Air, water and food are essential. The most any of us can hope for is to have some degree of importance to others. To be essential, if it were possible for any length of time, would be such an immense burden that few but a god could, or would, choose it and successfully cope with it.

With these considerations in mind, my original thoughts were transformed into two questions: *how do we determine our worth in the human world* and, *why does honest and robust contemplation of our worthiness often produce feelings of discomfort, denial, and dread, overlain by secret hopes of a flattering and socially acceptable answer?*

Part 1: How to measure our importance?

What makes us feel important? What aspects give our lives a sense of satisfaction and fulfilment and how do we measure both? Is our worth revealed by a loving spouse and grateful children, or found in the positive regard of friends, work colleagues or even hordes of complete strangers? And what of physical evidence, such as big cars and expensive real estate? Having a successful business is a badge of honour for some, as is having one's name attached to institutions such as an art gallery, a hospital, or engineering works like roads and bridges. Perhaps the ultimate physical measure is to have a time-defying monument constructed by others in our honour, something akin to the great pyramids in Egypt.

But monuments and the adulation of strangers ring hollow in my soul. Can anyone really trust the meaning in the number of *Likes* one has on Facebook, our legions of followers on Twitter, or in the fawning admiration from acquaintances and strangers of our mansions and obese bank balances?

Thoughts of meaning and worth are usually of little concern when we are struggling to rise above a subsistence level of food, shelter and status within our society. Once survival is assured and we have managed to accumulate some material possessions and useable knowledge, then some of us desire to tackle the: *what next?* We start to question the purpose and significance of our lives, and, for the majority, it seems the answers lie in the *quality* of our relationships with our peers, and especially with our inner circle of trusted friends and relatives.

Yet even this more realistic yardstick is not entirely satisfying because the quality of human relationships is difficult to measure with any validity, and those relationships can wither and die at any moment, often over trivial and unexpected incidents. And, when put to the test by power, wealth, poverty, ill health or draconian political circumstances, who can be sure of the fidelity of those relationships? I have no reliable answers and only one guide post: *hope for the best but prepare for the worst* – by keeping my expectations low, or better still, non-existent!

From the subatomic to the galactic, the universe is permeated by the cosmic joke that the only certainty is uncertainty. Once this annoying reality is accepted, that life is not predictable to any significant degree, we can then develop strategies that incorporate this uncertainty and find ways to improve the odds of our having a happy life.

To prepare for the disappointing truth of our worth, it is wise to keep the expectations of others, and ourselves, realistic. We are human. We are a flawed product, prone to wishful and deluded thinking that we are loath to modify even in the face of a deluge of evidence to the contrary. We are never as good as we think we are, nor are those we admire. And, no matter how grand or modest are our accomplishments, we must toughen our souls to the brutal truth that in a very short time those accomplishments, and we ourselves, will be gone and in time totally forgotten. That is the hardest of all the truths to conquer, which is why it is generally left to the end of our lives, giving us the time to come to terms with it – if we make the effort.

Thus prepared, devoid of unrealistic expectations of what it is to be human and what is humanly possible, we can get comfortable with a more realistic and kinder evaluation of our importance.

Does knowing that our personality and our achievements have little enduring significance mean that we and everything we do is inconsequential? *No*. Our every thought and action has a consequence, for or against us, but the sizes of those consequences are entirely *determined by the scale we measure them against*.

If one wants to feel depressed, we measure our lives against the big scale, against *all* our peers, or the *entire* nation, or *all* of humanity, now and over the full breath of human history, or go all the way and assess our significance against our part in the evolution of the universe.

For our sanity it is kindest to choose a smaller scale, a humbly human scale, and be happy to be a grain of sand on a beach, because who can say which grain is more important than the next since all are needed to make the beach what it is.

In the end, measuring importance is an illusion, a mirage. This explains why my dear and wise wife has given such assessments little of her precious life's energy. She is a pragmatist and thus is not overly burdened by illusions of omnipotence. She concentrates on being *humane*. She appreciates what she possesses, her modest number of relationships, her accumulated and constantly growing knowledge, her material surroundings, house, garden, collected books, her walks on the beach with number one husband (me). She is content to let others worry about judging her, themselves, and others. I aspire to be like her!

Are we important? Perhaps it is best not to ask. Perhaps it is better to spend our days improving what is lacking in our life but only after carefully considering what it is that we really want, and if gained, why would we want to keep it and for how long?

To find the answers we must answer further questions: *What is it about our wealth, power, status, the admiration of strangers, or our nourishing relationships with loved ones that make them important to us?*

Part 2: Why is being important so important?

Despite intellectually recognising the futility of having a meaningful measure of my worth, I, like many others, still possess the desire to do so. I want to believe, if flattering, or disbelieve if not, the results of my efforts to rate my existence. Why?

The short answer appears to lie in the fact that Homo sapiens are social creatures who do not survive long in total isolation and, despite dissatisfactions with many of our brethren, few have a long-lasting desire to totally reject society. For all of us, solitary confinement and receiving the *silent treatment* from our peers are the cruellest of all punishments.

This desire to be a significant member of society, which involves acquiring the people skills needed to get along with our kind, has been hardwired into us by evolution on the savannahs of Africa because those that didn't, and were rejected by their group, became easy meat to the big cats, hyenas and wild dogs. With our physical survival at stake, our number one concern became whether, and how much, our peers love us, or reject us, which in turn powers our constant need for feedback as to where we stand on that continuum.

The other problem caused by our peculiar evolution is our enhanced ability to see cause and effect. This allowed our puny ancestors, by group effort, to hunt big game with pathetic weapons of sharpened sticks and rocks, and with same items, defend themselves from predators. Over the millennia, this foresight developed into our imagination and the ability to see concepts, the ability to predict outcomes, to *see* the future (e.g. if I do this, this will happen).

An unfortunate consequence of this ability is the knowledge of our own mortality, something the cow grazing in full view of the abattoir is unburdened by. We know we will die and are not happy about it, and hence most expend a lot of mental effort denying it.

Genetics has wired in the desire to be important to our fellows, to regard their opinions of us as important, and not just in the here and now but into the future. We *want to be remembered* even after we die because it makes our nonexistence easier to bear. People commit suicide when they see their lives as having no meaning because, without a sense of significance, why put up with all the struggles involved in living.

Those of us who are still living, in the usual sense, as opposed to being comatose in a hospital bed stuck full of tubes, get out of bed each morning for the meanings, consciously stated or not, that we allocate to our actions and their overall purpose.

Part 3: Conclusions

"Am I important?" needs to be attached to:

1. How do I realistically measure my importance?
2. To whom am I important?
3. In what ways and in what proportions am I important?
4. Important over what timeframes?

Everything in existence is important in some way. But who is to judge the scale and nature of that importance? Is that metaphoric grain of sand on the beach less significant than a human life when set against the scale of the cosmos and time eternal? Only a god can say.

Perhaps the Bible was correct to state that we are made in God's image because we, God-like, ultimately *judge our worth*. *We* judge *our* importance in *our* world because *we* are the person who accepts or rejects the judgements of us, but to do so we must judge against something. What is that something? The universe, past, present and into eternity? Any lesser scale brings inaccuracy.

But we are humans, not God. Limited in our abilities, we dwell in the uncomfortable state of suffering degrees of ignorance, of perpetually coping with partial knowledge and yet constantly forced to decide, one way or the other, consciously or unconsciously, to make judgements, then take actions and flourish or fail from their consequences.

To lighten our burden, to improve the consequences of our decisions, to live as usefully to ourselves and others, my humble suggestion is to practise answering the four questions above, as bravely as possible, in full acceptance of our human limitations.

If that proves too difficult, one could forget the notion of our significance altogether and instead concentrate on implementing the mantra I try to humbly live by:

Seek wisdom
Practise compassion
Live in awareness

Paradoxically, by increasing our awareness of reality, especially in regard to understanding and thus accepting our biological and hence societal limitations, we will be more inclined to act with compassion. Combining heightened awareness and compassion, with the desire to seek and enact wiser responses to life events, may then result in our having a positive influence in our world, which might inadvertently lead to us becoming more beneficial and hence significant to it!

This essay was greatly influenced by Carlo Strenger's very readable, *Fear of Insignificance*.

14. A Life in Three Acts

Note: *These three anecdotes were my response to a homework exercise for my writing group. We were tasked with writing three scenes designed to reveal some important aspects of a character, and to make it easy, we were to be the chosen character.*

The first thing it revealed to me was that all biographies are greater or lesser fictions depending on the ability of the person to recall past events, the dubious accuracy of those recollections, and the false views given to the reader by the slabs of incidents left out or skimmed over. These three episodes are real, to me, but are undoubtedly not a complete picture of the incidents and only give some indication of the sort of person the author fully is.

§

Act One

When I was a kid, "Wild Kingdom" was a must watch TV show. One Saturday morning, the presenter, a slim, old guy dressed in a khaki safari suit, accompanied by his similarly attired assistant, Jim, recounted their adventures in the South American jungle. They had gone there to study Anacondas – the gigantic swamp-dwelling pythons we love to fear. At one point in the show, Jim, a tall, strapping young fellow, demonstrated, in the studio, how to capture and handle, normal-sized snakes, after which they reran the footage of their less controlled capture of a huge Anaconda in the wild.

It was thrilling stuff and so, once the show ended, I rushed off to make the most of the remains of my Saturday morning. There was plenty of time left before lunch to take the dogs for a walk which, with luck, would lead to an encounter with a snake and the chance to put my newly acquired snake handling knowledge to the test. My younger self was of course blissfully ignorant of the adage that a little knowledge can be a dangerous thing.

Instinctively realising that every adventurer needs a witness to verify their heroic deeds, I yelled to my younger brother, 'Come on, let's take the dogs for a walk – maybe we'll find a snake!'

Strangely, he didn't seem overly enthused, but I managed to cajole him into joining me. In no time we were heading for the door, accompanied by our two dogs, yapping and jostling; they were canine clarions heralding our forthcoming adventure.

Living on the edge of a rural town, it didn't take long to escape the quiet orderliness of the fibro Housing Commission homes and enter the paddocks and dams of our adolescent "Wild Kingdom".

It was cool, sunny and springtime, and so our shoes quickly became dusted yellow from kicking through the Capeweed that fought a war of colours against the lush green of the grass and purple patches of Patterson's Curse. We headed steadfastly past the dam, where my older brothers used to go yabbying – until a dose of food poisoning subsequently dampened their enthusiasm for the practice – and then all the way to the road.

That road was our usual turn around point. But we hadn't encountered a snake, or anything else interesting and I was still itching to conquer my fear of snakes, so, with a bit of coaxing, got little brother and the dogs through the wire fence. We then dashed across the bitumen and headed to the dirt track that followed the creek to the railway bridge, which was the extreme limit of our walking world.

Halfway down the track, in amongst a cluster of peppercorn trees, were the ruins of a brick farmhouse that successive incursions by vandals had reduced to waist-high piles of rubble decorated with broken glass and the dismembered remains of the corrugated iron roof, all of which was being slowly engulfed by knee-high grass and weeds. My eyes gleamed. It was the perfect location!

Carefully selecting a stick from the bountiful selection dropped by the trees along the creek, I gave strict instructions to little brother: 'Give me plenty of room, and try and keep the dogs away. I may have to make a run for it. Got it!'

He nodded, with eyes wider than normal. I gave him a departing look, as serious as a thirteen-year-old could muster, and then stepped gingerly in amongst the fallen bricks and started poking around. There was the usual interesting stuff like broken bottles and rusty tin cans but they weren't my quarry that day. I turned my attention to a big rusty sheet of corrugated iron half-buried in the grass, which, being metal, would warm nicely once the sun got to it. It was the ideal shelter for coldblooded creatures.

'Better be careful here,' I muttered to myself to steady my nerves. I looked back to check on my escape route and the whereabouts of little brother and the dogs. All was good; he was still at the track, looking concerned, and the dogs were splashing around in the creek.

If I was to catch any snakes, I first needed to bolster my resolve. The thought transformed itself into an increased squeeze on the stick and then its careful insertion under the free end of the corrugated iron. A brief moment of concentration followed before I flipped it over with a mighty heave that launched the sheet in a somersault to crash down onto the bricks and rubbish a few metres away.

Revealed on the flattened dirt and dry grass was a metre long brown snake, not too keen on having its sleep disturbed. Luckily, the morning's coolness had slowed its movements to a groggy, slithering counterattack, which in the past would have had me making a run for it but I was older and wiser now.

In a flash, I brought my stick down just behind its head and stepped forward, all the while maintaining the pressure on the stick with an arm starting to shake. Bending down, I grabbed the snake behind its head with my left hand into which I was pumping all my concentrated willpower before releasing the stick and, with a pounding heart and a mind drunk with the ecstasy of victory, waved my captive aloft for the world, and little brother, to acknowledge.

He didn't budge. He seemed not to comprehend the momentousness of the occasion! Annoyed, I had to bring my "badge of courage" over to him in the hope of a more suitable response. The walk across the broken ground felt like I was traversing a minefield holding a jar of nitro-glycerine, but in no time the danger was past and I had reached my brother in the shade by the track.

'Go on, stroke him. He's very smooth and cool, not slimy, go on …' I said, still miffed by his lack of enthusiasm.

Dutifully, he shuffled closer, gave my prisoner the briefest of caresses and then stepped back. After a few more moments of studying my captive, I became aware that after the excitement of the hunt and the capture, I was faced with the deflation of the 'what next?'

The reptile had done me no harm, in fact I was the transgressor and, not being cruel by disposition, my only solution to the moral question it raised was to throw the snake as far as I could in the direction of some undisturbed sheets of iron, with belated apologies for disturbing its rest. We then turned around, gathered the dogs and walked briskly away from "the scene of the crime" and the possibility of reptilian retribution.

I don't recall getting into trouble when we got home; we

either kept the episode to ourselves or any parental disapproval was insufficient to dull the glory of my first "real" test of character.

Endnote:

Recalling that adventure fifty years on made me realise that death was a concept that had no meaning for me then, and even now, is impossible to comprehend, let alone come to terms with. Also, that younger siblings look up to older ones but not generally the other way around, though, at sixty-plus, I find my younger brother now has more influence in my life than I probably have in his. Overall, it seems siblings are incapable of treating each other as peers, no matter how much life experiences theoretically equalise their differences. I also concluded that Goethe was right to sum up life as: "*Wanting and not succeeding, succeeding and not wanting*", my capturing and then discarding of that snake being my first encounter with the veracity of his statement.

§

Act Two

Catching that snake had bolstered my capacity to conquer my fears but it also revealed my very human need for recognition and appreciation. A desire, that, as my life progressed, was for the most part frustratingly unrequited.

Childhood flashed by. I then stumbled into my twenties and found life was dominated by getting an education, finding employment, developing friendships and trying to define my abilities and my place in the scheme of things. But, most important of all, was the desire to find a member of the opposite sex to share my life with.

Smart enough to make the grade for university, I was lucky enough to have Gough Whitlam abolish university fees and fund a modest student income, which allowed me to take up the offer of a bachelor degree at Sydney University.

As many before me had done, university life soon revealed flaws in my character, specifically, that I had no real idea what I wanted to do. Liking Biology at school gave me a direction but I couldn't visualise the end point of the study process.

Instead, I became enamoured by the many distractions that youth and a big city can provide. My first discovery was the University Motorcycle Club, and, that if I was to fit in, I needed to drink beer.

Another early revelation was that the city made friendships hard to sustain, because you live in one suburb, they in another, and the pain of city traffic makes it more difficult to spend the time together needed to develop strong ties, which, combined with being at a stage of life when you and those around you are constantly changing in unplanned ways, friendships began and then faded seemingly without end. Eventually, it all got too much for me.

By age thirty-two, the one thing I desired most from life, a true romance, seemed an impossibility. I felt I had nothing worthwhile to live for. Hope fled. I quit my job, packed a bag, hopped on my motorbike and rode off into the sunset, to Western Australia, with the one remaining desire: to see the dolphins at Monkey Mia.

Hitting Perth, I got lucky and ran out of money. It forced me to start hunting for work. By what later seemed divine intervention, I gained employment at a gold mine. It proved a gold mine of another sort as it was there I met my wife. A little over two years later, newly married and newly retrenched, we were busy re-establishing our lives in Perth when I discovered a new emotion.

At some stage, I had retrieved a few belongings from back east, one of which was a collection of poems by Banjo Patterson that my mum had given me as a birthday gift. She had always read to us kids, me especially, and even did so during my adult years whilst studying Geology at the regional university in our home town. Hence the enjoyment of being read to was ingrained in me.

Over the breakfast table, our bowls empty and a weekend ahead of us I had persuaded my dear wife to read one of my favourite poems, *The Man from Snowy River*. The words were all very familiar to me but this time around, for reasons not apparent then, when she read the line: "… only Clancy stood his friend" I found myself crying uncontrollably. That line had tapped into an unknown well of sadness that took quite a while to get under control, much to my dear wife's puzzlement and concern.

She did her best to console me, but it was a very disturbing and humbling incident that required a lot of cogitation to understand and categorise.

In the end, I realised that grief was its name. I had secretly been holding back my grieving for the death, over east, of that hopeful young man I had once been. The man reborn in Western Australia was different, possibly stronger and definitely less starry-eyed. And yet that former me, that friendless, unappreciated stranger to society, still haunted the new one. Its ghost emerges whenever I see people being unkind and unjust to each other. The rejection of the man from Snowy River by all but Clancy of the Overflow had tapped into the unexpressed loneliness of that former self. Those tears and others that followed over the next few years finally allowed him to rest in peace.

But that naïve young man, filled with unrequited hopes and idealism, has not entirely left me – he became integrated into who I currently am, and gladly so, because he reminds me of what humaneness is all about. He powers my regard for other people.

Rather than being ashamed whenever my empathy has me

feeling the suffering of others, I am glad I am *unable* to understand or condone those who are unmoved by people being cruel to each other. I also celebrate my revulsion of those who actively engage in such inhumane behaviours.

Even today that book still has two poems I cannot read aloud without choking up: *The Man from Snowy River* and *In the Droving Days*.

And I hope they will always affect me so.

§

Act Three
Belgrade, September 2016.

It was early morning and my dear wife and I had halted at the kerbside of a busy inner-city intersection. Our progress towards the markets on the other side of the road's broad no-man's-land of cobblestones and tram tracks had been temporarily stymied by the traffic. It was then that I saw the homeless man.

The fellow was off to my right, near the wooden benches that bordered the squat stone waterspout that had provided the city's denizens with drinking water during times past, but were now mostly superfluous – superfluous to all but the down-and-outs such as he.

The ability to always remain focused on the "bright side of life", a la Monty Python's *Life of Brian,* is not something I am good at, but it appeared to have been mastered by the teeming populace striding around us. They appeared cheerfully unaware of the homeless man's presence. He was apparently invisible to them.

I couldn't ignore him because at that moment he was squatting, dark trousers around his ankles, and defecating. My scientific side noted that his output was light brown and very loose, suggestive of ill-health, courtesy of an unhygienic lifestyle. He then proceeded unperturbed to slowly and methodically wipe his bottom with a roll of toilet paper he had at hand.

All the while my dear wife, on my left, waited for the traffic to clear, oblivious to the man, and my discomfort at having my nose rubbed into the squalid reality of life for the homeless. I kept glancing furtively in his direction filled with ghoulish fascination, tinged with envy, because the fellow, who appeared to be in his early thirties, had strong muscular legs and buttocks, the type I could only dream of possessing, though his were marred by red circular patches from sleeping on a hard surface.

Eventually, the traffic cleared and I was dragged back into my world. Together we dashed across the street to lose ourselves in amongst the crowds swarming around the stalls of naturally ripened fruit and village-fresh vegetables.

On the return trip, laden with a bag bulging with blueberries, raspberries and perfectly ripe pears, we retraced our path back to our lodgings. I was relieved to see that the man had moved on as it gave my subconscious more time to find a usable response to the problem he represented.

The next morning, again early, whilst performing the husbandly task of taking the garbage to the communal garbage hopper, I again spied the homeless man. He was asleep on a bench near that hopper, and lay huddled under a covering of old pizza boxes. After quietly depositing my bag of rubbish, I made a hasty retreat down the laneway to our rented bedsitter.

My wife was still in the getting dressed stage, so it took a few moments to get her attention.

'Remember that homeless guy I told you about … well, he's sleeping on a bench near the garbage bin.'

For a few minutes, we engaged in silent contemplations upon how to help the man and what we could give him to ease his misery. But our thoughts became mired in memories of unwanted and unappreciated gifts, given and received, and our shared resolution not to repeat such past mistakes. As far as I could see, what the man really needed was a roof over his head, an income, *and* a reason for being. None of which were in my power to give.

Then I remembered the blanket. The epitome of a gift gone wrong. It was a beautiful mohair throwover a relation had expressed a liking for quite a few years back and one we subsequently bought and gave to them as a Christmas gift, only to find out a year or so later it had been relegated to being bedding for their cat. After a while, it had disappeared from view only to resurface when we visited an older female relative during our current trip. She insisted we accept that same blanket, also as a gift, and, being polite, we accepted it and still had it with us. It appeared clean but had sustained a cigarette burn at some stage and was thus in our "what do we do with it" category. We weren't keen to lug it all the way back to Australia.

'The blanket?' I suggested, though I think the idea was a result of thought transference from my wife.

'Yes, a good idea. At least now it may be appreciated,' she replied with a wry smile.

We placed the blanket into a big paper bag, the type you get from dress shops, and augmented our offering with another bag, plastic, containing a two-litre bottle of mineral water and an assortment of fruit: mostly pears and apples.

Filled with the joy of being able to help a person in need, I raced out the door, down the stairs, out of the building, down the laneway, and finally, and reverently, placed our offering on the ground near his feet.

Later in the morning, walking to the city centre, we were pleased to pass the somnolent form of our man, now comfortable under our fluffy blanket. We turned and headed up the hill with our steps a little lighter and progressed, hand in hand, towards the buzzing, growling traffic of one of the main thoroughfares that marked the start of the CBD.

The man was not there when we returned in the late afternoon, or the next day, but reappeared on that same bench on the morning of our departure. The taxi had somehow managed to make it to the end of the narrow cul-de-sac where we were staying and had done a hundred-point turn to avoid reversing the two to three hundred metres. With our backpacks safely between us on the back seat, our driver drove off slowly, then turned left into the one-way side road and headed down the hill.

At that turn, the city gave us a parting "gift": sight of *our* man, again asleep on *his* bench, this time snug in a shiny, new, green sleeping bag. Our blanket now consigned to the garbage bin of history.

The holiday, like many others, has for the most part faded from memory but the man on the bench remains a conundrum still to be resolved.

Perhaps one day I may attain the wisdom to find more satisfying ways to help such persons, directly, indirectly, or both. He reminds me that a good life requires a constant supply of hope and resources, such as an income and housing. Of the two, hope is the harder aspect to maintain whilst fully enmeshed in the real world, not a fantasy one.

At least for a few hours we were able to assist him, physically with the blanket and emotionally with the physically confirmed knowledge that he had *not* been abandoned by *all* of society.

15. Friends, Strangers, Enemies

There was a time when I would have agreed that humanity could be divided into three mutually exclusive categories: friends, strangers and enemies. And, firmly believing that I understood their attributes would have thought no more about it.

But, on the wrong side of sixty, I now realise that humans are annoyingly more complicated. This essay is my journey to understand those complexities, especially in regard to the slippery concept of friend, the category I most want to expand.

Part A: Friends

The leopard is an animal so equipped with strength and abilities its survival requires no social interactions other than the occasional act of procreation. Humans, on the other hand, are far less amazing in our physiology. We only survive as members of a society, be it within a band of hunter-gatherers or as a citizen of a teeming megacity. Being born with differing innate dispositions, we survive within our societies by the quantity and quality of the relationships we make, with friendships being the most satisfying and useful to us.

Look back on your life and try and remember all the people you called friend and then ask: where are they now, do you still call them friend, why, or why not, and, what were the circumstances that allowed those friendships to develop and then deepen or dissipate?

In my case, their numbers were embarrassing small, still are, and sadly, most proved either illusory or temporary associations tied to specific situations.

The illusionary ones were those in which I did all the work, and usually ended when they terminated the pseudo-relationship or I eventually did so.

The temporary ones faded when our lives and attitudes developed along divergent paths and we fell victim to that enemy of relationships: out of sight, out of mind.

Friendships are living things that need constant and considered nurturing to survive and grow. They are like the plants in our gardens. Some turn out to be weeds. Others are pretty little annuals whose brief lifespan makes it imperative to enjoy them while they last. Others are like the trees we plant. Though slower to fully develop, they set the garden's structure and ambience, and reward us both during their development and even more so in their maturity.

Stretching the analogy, there are some destined to fail no matter the kindnesses lavished upon them, usually for reasons beyond our comprehension. And there are others that become obsessions. They take over and shade out all the rest, clog our gutters, block up the drains and finally have us cursing but reluctant to do anything because their removal would leave a friendless wasteland.

Thus, the word friend is used to encompass many who, in the end, are not worthy of the term. How to distinguish the true from the false or temporary is this essay's prime task.

The first and most common error is not knowing the difference between a friend and an acquaintance.

Acquaintances are shallow friends with low emotional cost attached to them and hence are easily made and unmade. One can be friendly towards many people such as our work colleagues and others we regularly interact with, but getting to the deeper level required for full friendship takes time, mutual effort, and fortuitous circumstances.

Only politicians seeking election attempt to be friends with everyone; most other mortals are wise enough to know it is not possible.

To find out what makes a friend, we need only consider our current friends and see who and what they are.

They will probably be of the same sex as us, of a similar age, socio-economic strata and marital status, and those we made in childhood will be of a different quality than those made later in life, because, as children, we hadn't mastered the art of lying and thus our emotions and true natures were plain for all to see.

Though friends will be selected from a subset of society, the specific process by which we, and they, do so, still needs much clarification if we are to find better ways of locating and developing fulfilling friendships.

Lacking spoken language of any effectiveness, our ape ancestors had to judge friend from foe by physical appearances and non-verbal cues, often very quickly, if they were to avoid swift and violent responses from the other. We see evidence of those buried simian abilities whenever we walk into a space full of strangers, be it at a conference, or as a child surviving his or her first day at a new school. In such situations our biology has us scanning those present for physical signs of friendliness; unconscious decisions are made and within milliseconds we move towards the best bets. That we often choose well is cause to give thanks to the blind forces of evolution.

But you and I are more complicated than our monkey cousins; we have speech with which to express our emotions and intentions. But, in order to benefit from our brethrens' reciprocated behaviours, we also learn how to lie, to them and to ourselves, from which arises much of our personal anguish.

In the face of our deceitfulness, how do we accurately assess the quality of our friendships? How do we measure their strength, depth, reliability or determine what tasks can be asked of them? And what of our intentions towards them? Are we callously cultivating their friendship so they can be used to our benefit? Are they manipulating us? Or do we both play manipulator and manipulated depending on circumstances? Does any type of covert manipulation have a place in true friendship?

Trust seems to be the quality that underpins the answers to these questions. A notion confirmed by the most painful of all human emotions: the hurt induced by the shattering of such trust, causing within us a righteous rage for punishment of the transgressor, often with dire consequences for one or both. It is the ultimate sin, with the greater the level of trust broken, the greater the desire for retribution.

Betrayal of trust is bad on a personal level; it is even worse on a societal one because trust is the invisible force that allows us to function within a group. When we cannot trust the farmers to produce untainted food, the shops to sell safe products, banks not to gamble away our savings, judges to dispense justice equally and fairly, and politicians to use their powers for the benefit of the entire population, not just the elites, then trust crumbles and violence and misery will be our daily gruel.

That we often trust relative strangers is the miracle of humanity. We trust, to varying degrees, all those strangers that we, either directly or indirectly, depend upon to do the right thing by us, such as our mechanic, doctor, dentist, that distant farmer, or those unseen cooks in the restaurants we frequent.

We hope these strangers do their tasks fairly and diligently. The trust we place in friendships carries a greater burden because it sustains our emotional well-being. Even shallow, "fair-weather" friends can, within limits, be trusted to have some regard for our feelings; those that don't are *masquerading* as friends and these days are labelled, *frenemies*, enemies with a friendly façade.

Our time and emotional capacity are limited. It is thus imperative that we learn to recognise the people who will reciprocate our friendly intentions. There are no guaranteed methods in this quest but I offer some hints gathered from my experience and that of others.

But before we consider the process of making friends, perhaps it is best to start at the opposite end of the process, the betrayal of friendship.

The pain and surprise at such betrayal can be ameliorated if one acknowledges the possibility that *we too* are capable of dishing out such dastardly deeds, hopefully never to mortal consequences. We need to ask ourselves: what are the circumstances that would have us betray the bonds of a friendship? Gaining some recognition of our capacity for backsliding and selfishness will enable us to expect less of others, even dear friends, and hence diminish the hurt and disappointment caused by the others misdeeds.

And, if I do betray a friend's trust, can I exonerate myself by claiming I am just being human? Of course! Contrary to the belief of many, we humans are not rational beings but *rationalising* ones. Science [1] reveals that our unconscious mind reacts in milliseconds, leaving its slow, conscious twin stumbling to overrule these automated responses. Our conscious is there mostly to construct narratives justifying our reflexive actions. And being stories that *we* constructed, they *feel right*, and hence are easy to believe, no matter how flimsy others consider our rationalisations.

But how do such self-affirming stories end?

Flying on autopilot works well in many circumstances but not in all. The world is full of novel circumstances that require slow, fact-based thinking in which self-serving rationalisations will not serve us well.

Confessing to our mind's ability to justify any behaviour, including the betrayal of trust, may help us recognise the early signs of a relationship in trouble and encourage us to broach the issue with compassion. It is a tricky business, as false accusations are almost as harmful to a relationship as stating the truth. I suggest we approach the issue with a generosity of spirit and tentative statements.

How to recognise any false or disquieting notes in our friendships? There are only two ways that I know of: attuning ourselves to the non-verbal cues, such as less physical contact, less time spent talking of shared plans, as well as radical changes in fashion or hair style. The other way is to directly voice our unease in a non-accusative way: *when this happens, I feel this* ... rather than: *why did you* .... Neither of these approaches can guarantee successful diagnosis and correction of the course of a relationship because we can lie with our words and most have some ability to disguise the non-verbal cues we give off.

Another way of placing our friendships into a realistic context is to ask ourself: *how important are these people to me?* The litmus test for which is: would we place them above money? Would we refuse a lucrative new job in another city because it would impact too severely upon our relationship? After answering that, try the opposite, would our friends refuse a similar offer to remain closer to us?

When younger, the imperative is to realise our potential, especially when under the considerable financial burden of mortgages and child rearing, and hence money and career advancement may render friendships less valuable. Such financial considerations should diminish towards the end of our working life when the time left to make meaningful friendships diminishes, which consequently increases their relative worth.

I recall the adage that treaties, of the political sort, are like little girls, they last whilst they last. Perhaps the same can be said of friendships. And like treaties between countries, they can last unaltered for quite some time, but, if not adjusted, will eventually falter.

This brings us to the reality of not all friendships being the same. We are a *different type of friend to different people*. Our friendships are revealed and enacted in different ways according to circumstances and will have different expectations laid upon them.

We can go no further in our examination of friends until we look upon non-friends.

To close-off this section I offer two remarks by Nassim Nicholas Taleb from his book of aphorisms, *The Bed of Procrustes*, that may allow us to be more philosophical towards past and present friends:

"Friendship that ends was never one; there was at least one sucker in it."

"If you find any reason why you and someone are friends, you are not friends."

Part B: Strangers

If we want an entertaining bridge between the concepts of friends versus strangers track down and watch an Italian movie from circa 2016 with the English title: *Perfect Strangers*. It chronicles a dinner party between a group of old friends, mostly couples, who take the challenge of leaving their mobile phones in the centre of the dining table with the proviso that all calls be placed on the speaker setting, and all text messages are to be read aloud. The plot, though predictable, is very skilfully unveiled and makes for intense engagement by the viewer. Hopefully, it will also leave us with renewed humility in regard to our understanding of the people we call friend, who, upon closer inspection, may need to go back into the box we label "stranger".

Strangers: there are around seven and a half billion of them on this beautiful planet of ours, and almost all are likely to remain strangers. And yet their influence upon us is not zero. The mere knowledge that we are but one of such an unimaginable multitude must surely temper our tendency to overstate our own importance.

Our present situation was not always so. For most of our evolution from ape to *Homo sapiens*, and during humanity's long *societal* childhood and adolescence, we lived in small groups where all were known to each other, and those not classed as friend or kin, were enemies and competitors for space and resources. For most of our early existence our sharpened stones, then arrows and spears were not solely employed for hunting food but often used for defending our patch from our most feared competitors, not the big cats or other large carnivores, but humans not of our tribe or race.

Xenophobia, the fear of outsiders, is deep within our genetics and yet, since the domestication of plants and animals, we have managed, however imperfectly, to become more civilised and more able to live in large congregations consisting mostly of strangers. How and why did we control this xenophobia sufficiently to live with crowds of unknowable others and *actively choose* to live amongst them in our towns and cities?

The feature article in *New Scientist* magazine of 24 February 2018 tackled the possible social and biological processes involved in making us more amenable towards strangers. It was a very readable place to begin an understanding of why we are as we are.

Put simply, our primordial drives for self-preservation and the development of our unique capabilities are dependent upon two opposing urges: the desire to co-operate for the good of our in-group, and fear, mistrust and antagonism towards those outside our group, those we call strangers. Human history, in all its brutality and beauty, is the interplay between those opposing innate urges within individuals and the cultural and ecological context of the day.

Returning to our Italian movie, the friends increasingly become strangers as the incoming phone calls and messages slowly reveal their secrets, with all parties receiving shocks that irreparably damage some of their relationships.

How many of us would remain friends if we were able to hear what they say about us when we are out of earshot? The survivors in that story were the brave and *forgiving*, who entered the post-dinner world with a new beginning, one offering prospects of a *greater understanding* of themselves and an enhanced appreciation for the viewpoints and needs of their significant others.

Perhaps the cause of much of our interpersonal problems stems from our default way of measuring the world and the people in it: we assume others to *be like us* and hence think like us. In reality, they never think entirely like us. All dealings with other humans involve a greater or lesser amount of uncertainty, in thought and behaviour, which can lead to disquiet and anxiety.

Other people can drag us down as well as inspire us to greater heights. Some strangers may legitimately be feared and avoided at all costs. Others are more annoyances than threats and others still represent exciting possibilities for growth.

That all people have something to teach us is a Buddhist maxim. Sometimes they teach us *what not to do*, whilst others may shine a light on the weaknesses that we need to improve on, or the opposite, affirm our character and validate our opinions. We exist, with meaning and purpose, socially. We are *our effect upon others*, with those closest to us, spouses, friends and family, reflecting more fully who we are with their frequent positive and negative feedback, and their meaningful silences.

But our close associates are not the only sources of social acknowledgement. The broader population, like the hall of mirrors at the fun park, provides all sorts of other "reflective surfaces" that either confirm our existing status or reveal aspects of ourselves unseen or not fully recognised by those closest to us.

Strangers offer the seductive hope of having our self-image either reinforced or augmented through the revelation of previously hidden strengths. Unfortunately, strangers can also shatter carefully crafted illusions and unmask our deficiencies. Do we dare seek the judgement of the crowd?

When next we go into a new social situation involving strangers, such as a seminar, party, or a new job, and after using our internal radar to create an emotional bolthole, in the form of those who could be friends or possible allies, then, from that position of strength, consider those left over and ask ourselves why we rejected them. Were they rejected for being assessed as stupid, boring, threatening, repulsive, or, possibly fascinating but in a scary or bizarre way?

And then ask what our reaction to them says about our selection criteria. Are we judging them too harshly? Are the disagreeable aspects of them a projection of those aspects of ourselves that we would prefer to disown? Perhaps there are other perspectives and alternative ways of responding to these non-friends, perhaps they have *something to teach us.*

Remember also that we are a stranger to them. What lessons, if any, do they draw from us?

As circumstances evolve, we juggle our allocation of time and emotional attachment to other people by moving them back and forth along the friend-stranger continuum, realising with varying certitude that we can't physically and, through time, remain friends to any depth with too large a number – the maximum being one hundred and fifty according to Robin Dunbar of

Oxford University.

Our choices will always be frustratingly imprecise because we are incapable of significantly understanding ourselves let alone those around us. Our thoughts and actions, and those of others, can never be as predictable as a Swiss watch, and thank goodness for that, as the state of absolute predictability would represent mind-numbing boredom.

The sea of strangers that we float amongst can provide us with vital stimulation to ward off that boredom, because their behaviours, what they write, say and do, point the way to different ways of being and thinking. Our friends provide the theatre and props within which we safely act out our lives. Friends allow us to develop our skills and abilities but, those of us with even the smallest aspiration for wider recognition, can only have such aspirations met by strangers.

And, disappointingly, the feedback we gain from those nearest can often be skewed. Praise may be given, and received, in a subdued manner because they, and we, are aware of the whole process, the greater context, and both are familiar with our words and deeds. What we, and they do, is the usual, the expected, and hence has diminished value.

And sometimes we discount their praise because we suspect they are just being kind, or perhaps so enamoured with us that they are incapable of criticism.

But when our close associates do criticise, it has exaggerated bite, especially so if valid, because we expect them to be kinder. All of which will make us unwilling to accept the validity of their contrary views. If the criticism is inaccurate, we are hurt because we assume that they know us better and hence expect greater accuracy and compassion from them.

To keep track of our impact on the world around us, we need to counterbalance our reflected image from those familiar to us with that from the fresh eyes of strangers. Whether a budding writer, a manager of people, an actor, a sales clerk, politician or personal trainer, we seek *impartial* confirmation from strangers, the applause of the crowd, and the accolades of that section of society we identify with. Those strangers may be ill-informed, easily fooled or have little appreciation of the role of luck in our life and yet we still seek them out, in hope or dread, as the ultimate arbiters of success.

The approval from friends and family can make us a big fish in a small pond, but only the undeniable approval of the crowd, in the form of book sales, votes, or social media followers, can ever make us a big fish in the biggest pond of all, that of the entire human world.

That stratospheric desire appears particularly sought after by some, perhaps because it is the hardest to achieve and thus the most precious.

The chief benefit of strangers, and the reason we are drawn to them and fearful of them simultaneously, lies in them offering the heady mix of greater recognition and mental stimulation, spiced with the all too real threat of social punishment.

Part C: Enemies

Love, Indifference, Hate could have been an alternative title for this essay. Enemies falling under the heading of "Hate", which is usually mutual, but even during wartime can we really hate *all* of the opposing side, every man, woman and child, in every aspect of their being, always, and under all circumstances?

Our answers will vary according how good we are at hating, and some people are very much better at it than others.

And what of the differences between enemies on the larger scale, the national, ethnic or religious, versus those on the personal scale, such as ex-spouses, co-workers, or obnoxious neighbours? Is learning to hate individuals different from hating a body of people? How does indifference between pairs or small groups, or sometimes even lovers, turn ugly?

These questions offer so much to consider that we may baulk at the task. I suggest we start by considering the physical manifestations of the condition.

Hate is a corrosive emotion. Want proof? Try to imagine a person we could, or do, hate. Put some effort into it and observe our body's response: the clenched fists, clamped jaw, contorted face, quickened pulse and pinched stomach, and then try and hold that physical state for as long as possible. We will find it an unpleasant and exhausting experience, which, if practised over a lifetime, will produce negative health consequences.

Hate is a stressful condition; it releases stress hormones, such as cortisol and adrenaline into the blood, which raises blood pressure and suppresses our immune system. Out of self-interest, it would be wise to examine why we are hating and find constructive ways to defuse such a destructive emotion.

Murder, that simple solution of our primitive past, whilst pleasingly cathartic has, even for a caveman, significant social ramifications. It is like the monstrous Hydra of Greek mythology; in slaying one enemy, we end up creating a lot more (their friends, relatives, the police and the legal system).

Our lives are peppered with people we can't stand, some to such an extent that we hate them and presumably, though not necessarily, they hate us in return. We either defend our rights, our dignity, our opinions and battle with them, or submit to their disagreeableness and suffer a miserable and tragic existence.

Winston Churchill said, "if you have no enemies, then you haven't stood up for anything". But does standing up for something, even self-preservation, have to result in making enemies, hating people, and then resorting to violence to maintain our self-worth?

I see little to admire in war and violence and seek better

solutions to dealing with those we loathe.

The issues invoked by enemies are twofold: how best to respond to the *physical* presence of enemies, and how to manage their mental affect: the hate, ours and theirs.

Enemies exist not just in a location, but also exist in time. In Robert A. Heinlein's classic sci-fi story *Time Enough for Love*, the protagonist, Lazarus Long, the universe's oldest human (two thousand years old and counting – remember it is sci-fi) quipped that he rarely had to kill his enemies, he bypassed them and then *outlived* them, which gave the same result!

If our enemy is of the murdering kind, we must either fight, flee, or, by negotiations, remove the cause of our mutual antagonism. That last option offers the possibility of turning them into friends, or at least disinterested strangers. It is a task requiring much skill and resolve, as well as a neutral forum in which to hold the negotiations.

The randomness of genetics ensures that there will always be a small percentage of psychopaths in any given population. These persons are totally self-centred and devoid of empathy. They will not respond to appeals for clemency or for consideration of the needs of others. They can only be dealt with by being physically isolated from society. Everyone else is amenable to some degree of persuasion, though this becomes harder depending upon the degree to which their opinions of themselves are either inflated and/or exceptionally fragile.

There are always reasons behind the enmity between us and our opponents, reasons that, fully understood, may open the way to rational debate and a resolution that both sides can live with. The great difficulty with finding such a happy ending is that *hate is a black and white emotion*, the combatants are one hundred percent convinced that they are right, that their views are undeniable and that there are no valid alternatives.

The truth is, there are always multiple viewpoints, all with degrees of validity. The task then is to find ways to have those alternate views recognised and seriously considered, which is where the ancient Greek philosopher Socrates comes in. His approach to debate consisted of asking adroitly phrased questions to get their antagonist to supply *their facts and <u>values</u>*, which, asked in the "correct" sequence, will lead them to a logical conclusion far from the one they originally held. It will be one hard to disown because *they* provided all the "facts".

The emotional heat that exists between enemies has them stuck in the win-lose, right-wrong, all-or-nothing mind frame, where conflict, physical and/or verbal, seems the only path to resolution. For them, there can only be one winner, them, with the loser, or losers, forced to suffer the consequences of being on the wrong side.

But, as mentioned earlier, winning the physical contest or the verbal stoush will have consequences other than the obvious ones, because winner, loser and the rest of the humanity are socially interconnected, no matter how tenuously. Those connections are like the ripples in a pond; they spread out and eventually reflect back with unknowable effects.

A society, corporation or household ruled over by paranoid winners will always be fearful of the revenge of the vanquished, or those connected to the vanquished, because the downtrodden will, in either sullen compliance or open rebellion, find myriad ways in which to sour the fruits of their oppressor's victories.

In the long-term, enemies, and hating, are best avoided, or better still, resolved to mutual satisfaction. In this the animal world has something to teach us.

When most animals compete for resources, territory, food, nesting sites, or access to breeding rights, to avoid unnecessary decimation, lethal force is rarely engaged in. Other behaviours are tried first, such as prancing displays of fitness and determination. These alternative strategies are designed to convince the other side to back away from the animal equivalent of total war.

We inherited this staged response, be it between ex-spouses or conflicted nation-states. Dialogue and compromise are tried first, hopefully with some real desire to find a win-win option and so avoid violence being considered the only solution.

But violence, or thoughts and threats of violence, come readily to the human psyche and are easily justified by our mind's immense ability to rationalise any action.

Violence. We enjoy it, the dishing out, not the receiving. Luckily, in the *civilised* world, we have, for the most part, exchanged the destructiveness of incessant intertribal warfare for the vicarious joys of the killing and mayhem on the television, the silver screen, or in chase and blast video games to non-lethally exorcise our lust for violence.

But more importantly, we also live in a society with a legal and social system that punishes killing and maiming, though many would argue our sanctions are not onerous enough. Our violent nature can be kept under control via entertainment and legal sanctions, but we should be aware that even the "mouse" will bite if pushed too far. It is wise to not underestimate our opponents, and our desire for physical retribution.

Since it is currently impossible to magically reprogram the values, thinking and consequent actions of our enemies, the easier task is to reprogram our own minds, in order to encourage new ways of coping with hate, ours and theirs.

Change your mind and you change your world is easily said by someone who has never tried it, and yet change must happen if our lives are to be freed of hate and resentment. Life is much easier if our non-murderous enemies can become a non-event. That is the goal, but how to reach it?

At this point I have to confess to having had a life so unremarkable that it has generated no real enemies to boast of, leaving me somewhat bereft of personal material to work with. The best I can do is to use my passionate dislike for the ill-informed and inhumane views of some politicians and my strong disapproval of several members of my workplace hierarchy because of their mindless obsession with numbers, efficiency (generally mine, not theirs) and bottom lines, and their lack of the will or mental capacity to see the real meaning in those numbers. These chosen antagonists have beliefs and actions that revile and frustrate me, emotions made worse by my apparent inability to resolve them.

Note, in the above description, the first inklings of hate in the *global* statements, *their beliefs and actions*, not the more accurate *some of their beliefs and actions*. See how easy it is to find some hate in our heart, even in a person such as I who has lived a relatively blessed existence.

The exercise and comments above also show the easiest way of changing our viewpoint. All we need to do is write down our opinions of our opponent. Feel the hate, then step back, cool down, and, when calm, return and *edit* our opinions, looking for inaccuracies and global statements. After which, rewrite them with the template of: *when they do or say this, I feel this ...*, and be as specific, accurate and as unembellished as possible, include time frames and circumstances, and then study our edited version.

Two things will be revealed: our *values*, and the *perceived* values of those who bother us. But how immutable are these values, ours and theirs? What are the circumstances that would force us to modify a strongly held opinion, for example, on cruelty towards other humans or animals? What is cruelty? Is keeping a human alive at all costs despite obvious pain and little hope of a cure, cruelty or compassion? Would we prolong the misery of a terminally ill cat or dog in the same circumstances?

After close examination, I posit that few moral stands or

strongly held opinions are so one dimensional, so clear cut, that they hold true in all circumstances at all times. If both sides of a conflict can recognise the possibility of nuances and previously unexamined aspects of their held beliefs, then the door is opened towards more measured responses to the other, and from there reduced emotiveness and greater scope for a peaceful resolution.

Unfortunately, none of the above strategies will hold much sway over the true psychopath, or some political or religious fanatics. Escape or physical resistance are the only realistic options. Distinguishing between the two types of opponents is not always easy but it must be made.

We all act on the knowledge and habits we have *at the time*, and can rationalise all our decisions to our complete satisfaction. Questioning *our* habitual behaviours and knowledge base for deficiencies and inaccuracies is the starting point to broadening our suite of thoughts and responses towards our enemies, as is an active and dispassionate study of the possible motivations behind their actions. *What do they really want?* And are their current acts of hostility the only way that they can satisfy their desires? The imaginative combination of these two approaches may lead to ways that allow us and them to peacefully co-exist.

Enemies and hate are unpleasant and troublesome aspects of being human but they have an obverse side. There can be few pleasures as great as smiting a wrongdoer, crushing our persecutor, or seeing our workplace bully get their comeuppance. Served cold or hot, righteous vengeance is a delicious dish and hence very hard to resist.

For the body, smashing our opponent is a biochemical extravaganza. In the mock warfare of the rugby pitch, the ecstatic peak experience for the victors is in large measure due to surging levels of testosterone and feel-good hormones such as serotonin and dopamine. Our innate biochemical reactions help explain why violent conflict has been a defining aspect of human history and why finding undramatic, unheroic, peaceful solutions, is less motivating, dull, even boring, and hence harder to sell to the protagonists, though not so to those who are the collateral damage of their conflict.

In acknowledging the hormonal joy of righteous vengeance, we must find ways powerful enough to counteract it. We need to make reasoned, sensible solutions sexier!

One way to do so is by appealing to our human need for recognition and status. The granting of the Noble Peace Prize to the leaders who negotiate a treaty that ends a war is an example.

In our personal lives, the converting of enemies into people we can co-exist with can similarly be buttressed by some form of physical recognition, which need not be elaborate, something as simple as a *sincere* handshake, reinforced by the conciliatory moment being recorded, with photographs of it presented to both, to act as a permanent memento of the reconciliation.

Our enemy's attitude and actions *stimulate* us to act, one could even say they *enliven* us, even if for the wrong reasons. Think of the technological advances created by the First and Second World Wars. Consider the technologies that developed out of the space race between the USA and Russia. The fruits of such stimulation are often more efficient ways to kill people, but not always so. The aerodynamics, metallurgy, and electronic wizardry of warplanes have been transferred to civilian aircraft, making modern air travel safer, faster and cheaper.

Another side of our enemies that is rarely mentioned is their role in bolstering our in-group identity [2], which greatly enhances our ability to function as a team, and/or a nation. This is used by politicians to gain power in times of war or when the nation faces some external threat, such as terrorist attacks. The external threat forces us to see ourselves as one of "us" and less as individuals looking after number one. That feeling of belonging to a coherent group is rewarded biochemically, which in turn makes us more willing to put up with the restrictions to our rights and societal norms deemed necessary to overcome *our* foe, for *our* king and *our* country!

In the heightened emotional atmosphere of intensified "us versus them", it is much easier for *rational* debate on the *validity* of the reasons for the conflict to go unexamined, which is a bonus for those at the top of the hierarchy. They benefit from having a more compliant populace and all without them having to do the actual fighting or suffer restrictions to their freedoms and lifestyle.

At the individual level, having an enemy can give greater meaning to our life. An enemy can provide us with a worthy cause, which is why some become bewildered once their enemy has been removed because gone too is their life's main motivating force. They then struggle to find another reason for being, one with the same emotive power. Without a fearsome foe to heroically battle, normal existence can seem bland and hardly worth the effort.

I shall be flippant and leave my closing remark on enemies to *Hagar the Horrible*, the hen-pecked Viking warrior created by cartoonist Dik Browne.

Hagar smilingly remarks, mug of beer in his raised fist:

"Friends come and go, but enemies, you have for life!"

Part D: Those not mentioned so far.

Friends, strangers and enemies cover much of humanity but not all. The remainder must be understood if a better metric for finding, developing and accessing friendships is to emerge. We need to understand our attitudes to our close relatives, parents, siblings, aunts and uncles. How do they fit into my original tripartite division of humanity? And what of all the people we must take orders from and that lesser number we give commands to?

Personality and viewpoint differences with our relatives, combined with physical circumstances, such as too much or too little time together can either exacerbate differences or prevent us from having sufficient interactions to meaningfully understand them – both of which can result in them being transferred from friend (in its broadest interpretation) into the stranger or even the enemy bucket.

But can we really be friends, in the usual sense, with our parents or siblings? It appears not. Normally the *friendliness* we feel towards our relatives increases with diminishing relatedness and reduced age differences. Hence, second cousins will make better friends than first cousins, and distant cousins of a similar age will be even easier to become friends with, all other factors being equal.

The problem raised by relatedness is that we and they are, for the most part, *roles* not people.

Parents always see their children as children, even if they have transformed into a grey-haired, sixty-five-year-old successful executive. And children always see their parents as parents, not as older people they know. For siblings, we are the bossy older brother, or the irresponsible younger sister. And even if we never saw or grew up with our siblings, their role overrides any other way of interacting with them. One can be friendly towards them, even have a deep regard for them, but it will never be the same type of relationship as between two unrelated *friends*, which is not to say it can't be as intense, just very different.

And no matter how much we dislike our parents or siblings, can we truly divorce ourselves from them to the same degree that we can disengage ourselves from former spouses, lovers or friends?

For that to happen we would have had to have spent very

little time with them, have only interacted in the most superficial ways or be excessively self-absorbed, in which case nobody's departure from our life would cause much regret.

Talking of divorce brings me to the last, and most important person and *role* player to be considered, our lover and/or spouse, with life best when the two are combined.

Our biology has given us a very strong abhorrence to incest and hence our long-term lover or spouse will start off as a stranger. By various magical processes, we find them attractive enough to instigate closer relations, that, with luck, result in happy coupledom, one based upon more than physical looks and unconscious hormonal responses, which diminish markedly with time.

Again, I have to admit to a lack of experience of the many forms, permutations and rationales behind the marriage of two people, with marriage being a term I describe as an intense regard for a person, with the desire to share our life with them for as long as is humanly possible. This is a very different situation to those who are married to careers not persons. Their spouses, partners, lovers are merely appendages that supply the emotional support they need to enhance the successful pursuit of said career.

There are over seven billion people on the planet, with probably as many variations on the meanings attached to the idea of marriage. I have only personal experience of one marriage, mine, and so cannot pass myself off as an expert on marriage in general.

The mind-body duality oft talked of in regard to understanding good health, appears also to be the secret behind the health of a marriage. The attraction between a couple lasts longest if brains and biology are equally involved. We can't marry someone we find physically repulsive and likewise it won't last long if beauty of the flesh is the only glue that holds us together because we all deteriorate physically with the passing decades. It is the meeting of like minds, of those with similar thought patterns and ethics, which trumps all other considerations if the marriage is to survive any distance.

Marriages fail for reasons too many to count, often unknown to the protagonists, but I shall make a bold statement that most failures arise when the couple loose contact with the person they were attracted to in the first place and subsequently get lost in their *role playing*, at home and elsewhere. Their singularity of purpose gets lost in their multiplicity of jobs, tasks, and roles forced upon them as they navigate through the exigencies of making a living. They start in convoy and end, through lack of sufficient communication and reiteration of purpose, on opposing hemispheres without a map to show the way home.

Being constantly in the picture, those closest to us, co-workers, spouses or brethren, are easy *to take for granted* and in doing so, devalued as feeling and thinking persons. If the process is allowed to continue, they leave or disown us, at which point we rationalise their departure and say good riddance or, if of a more humane disposition, suffer chronic guilt and regret.

Knowing how it feels if people only recognise the functions we perform, or worse still, when they become blind to our work *and* our being, and knowing how we all crave fuller recognition for who we *are*, as much as what we do, and having felt the resentment when our needs in these parameters are not met, then we should treat our nearest and dearest with the same level of consideration and appreciation that *we* crave.

Perhaps our newfound understanding of the disadvantages of losing sight of the person, of merely seeing their role, is something we can use in our dealings with *all* people, be they spouse, relative, friend, stranger or enemy.

Like us, they too will resent being ignored or pigeonholed into stereotypic roles, and hence deserve a more balanced understanding of them, from which happier interactions will emerge.

Being assigned roles generally gets in the way of better understanding our shared humanity, but one aspect of our interactions with people who are not sworn enemies needs to be considered: *the giving and taking of commands.*

Not too many of us like being told what to do. Only when compelled by circumstances do we willingly consider other people's directives. The reason for this is that our thoughts feel as if they are our own, they *feel* real and *true*. So, why take the advice or worse, the commands, of someone who has either little understanding of *our* unique needs or regard for them?

In the workplace and, to a lesser extent, in voluntary organisations, we are obligated to be a role first and a human second. We are contracted to obey orders from those higher up, even if displeased with the arrangement and then expect those lower down to obey *our* directives without complaint.

Again, we encounter the unpleasantness caused by the conflict between our wants and those of others and feel either the biochemical joy of giving orders, or the biochemical discomfort of either receiving such an order or having our commands ignored or shabbily performed.

All that biochemistry and the feelings they generate is why we find it hard to be friends with our parents, who must issue orders and enforce rules in their attempt to guide us through the dangerous world of our innocence and ignorance.

Similarly, our siblings cannot be our friends because they readily tell us what to do, and we do the same to them, often with reluctance or rancour in both directions. Their orders are discounted, delegitimised from our living with them, in line with the adage: *familiarity breeds contempt*. And one cannot be friends when contempt walks in the room. "Who are they to tell *me* what to do?", as a thought, is not one to induce positive regard.

Thus, one can be friendly towards parents, siblings, work colleagues and authority figures but never friends *with* them. Enemies, yes, friends, no.

Likewise, intimate partners, spouses, and long-term lovers are not fully covered by the usual meanings given to the words: friends, strangers, enemies. Physical intimacy seems to irrevocably add an extra dimension not found in other relationships.

Conclusions

Understanding friendship was the prime motivation for this exploration of human relationships. Disappointingly, I still find myself puzzled and perplexed by the concept. There remains a dissonance between how other people define the term "friend" and my stubbornly, different and hazy ideas. I hope you have fared better.

It hasn't been a total waste. I have a fuller appreciation of the worth of strangers and enemies. This gives me some hope that one day I will be more comfortable with the slippery multifaceted nature of those I tentatively label 'friend'.

I am grudgingly coming to accept that I can't be friends, by my foggy definition, with my siblings, close relatives and people with authority over me, or to those I must give commands to. I can still have positive relations with them but true friendship appears only possible between relative equals. And "equal" is also a rubbery concept.

I consider my dear wife as my equal and she considers me likewise. Our regard for each other is equally strong, with that equality founded on acceptance of our human limitations.

We are not equal in our worldviews, though very similar. She is a woman; I am a man. Biology makes us see and feel the world differently. Despite our differences, we are not afraid of them, though there are some that we agree not to pursue in recognition of our human cognitive limitations. All of which is why my wife and I, like everyone else, need true friends to talk things over with.

I had hoped for more certainty in regard to friendship but the universe apparently offers little. My task, and perhaps yours, is to be brave enough to accept that we will never fully know who our "true" friends are.

Walter Winchell appears correct in stating that: *a real friend walks in, when the rest of the world walks out,* that we will never know who they are until that fateful moment arrives.

But we can improve the odds of judging the true worth of people if we make the effort to first understand our wants and needs, and second, better understand those of the people we interact with, especially those of our friends and spouses.

---

[1] *Thinking, Fast and Slow* by Daniel Kahneman explains the humbling truths of human cognition.

[2] *Survival of the Nicest,* by Stefan Klein, examines this and many others aspects of being human.

16. Knowing When

I had an incident at work yesterday* that I could have handled better but didn't – an all-too-common occurrence.

The episode reminded me of the wisdom, difficult to practise, espoused in the chorus lines of the song *The Gambler* sung by Kenny Rogers:

"Know when to hold them,
Know when to fold them,
Know when to walk away,
Know when to run ..."

Whilst his advice was pitched to a professional poker player, the song's theme resonates with our lives in general, which is perhaps one of the reasons behind its great success.

As a driver assessor, I am exposed to all sorts of incidents and my all too human reactions to them. Yesterday morning my seventeen-year-old driver provided me with one.

He was in the process of turning around to drive to a car park for the parking exercise. It was a relatively quiet suburban street and, after moving off from the kerb, had chosen a driveway on the left to do his turnaround. It was a good choice because it was wide and the house was a fair distance from the front fence line. There was a black car in the carport, tinted windows with no signs of occupation – as in no activation of brake lights or reversing lights being evident.

My driver decided to reverse in and come out forwards, which was a good choice for the circumstances. I glanced down at my tablet to record the method used, he started to reverse in, after having a look around, but no sooner had I looked up to see how he was going than we banged into the black car reversing out. The two drivers obviously not looking properly and the guy in the black car going way too fast for the circumstances. I told the kid to get the details and check the damage. There was little to speak of, the owner of the black car was obviously in a hurry and suggested we forget all about it and be on our way. I noted his number plate and the house number as he drove off and we then returned to the licensing centre, my candidate knew he had: *failed to meet the standard*.

That was when the fun began. His instructor was one of those argumentative amateur lawyer types who expressed the opinion that the fellow ran into the kid so his client should not have failed. I stated that both were in the wrong and that my decision would stand. He asked to see the manager. I obliged him and left her to sort it out.

Five or so minutes later, I joined our manager in front of the desk of her second-in-charge, who was chatting to one of our Compliance guys (the people who audit us assessors to keep us "up to the standard"). He was there on another errand but decided to investigate the outcome of the manager's chat to the instructor. I was not enthused about the discussion to come.

No one likes being told they have done something wrong and I am no exception, and hence took umbrage at the general consensus that I should not have been looking at my tablet for the few seconds that I did, and that I should have intervened to prevent the collision, which would have been difficult as it would have involved me hitting the brakes telling my driver to get into first gear, for him to look and then move out of the way. At the pace the other driver was moving there was insufficient time, or distance, to do any of these preventative measures.

Two things about their negative assessment of my actions,

and non-actions, stoked my rising indignation: their lack of acknowledgement that *to err is human*, that we mortals don't possess divine powers to *totally* predict the outcomes of *all* situations, and worse, was the implication that *they* could have done better.

The advice giving continued in a circular way with me feeling the red mist developing, but inexplicitly that Kenny Rogers song popped into my mind. Was it luck or perhaps the divine intervening? I don't know, but I took the advice and walked away.

I was proud of myself in that moment because in the past, when I've had altercations with disgruntled drivers, parents and/or instructors, I have wasted my time in trying to express, logically, and calmly, my viewpoint to no result apart from inflaming the situation. This time, I realised, a little late perhaps, that I had zero chance of modifying the opinions of those around me and did the smart thing by departing the arena.

The hardest aspect of being accused of a wrongdoing, or error of judgment, is the anger at oneself when some, or God forbid, all, of the offending accusation is substantially true, which wasn't the case in this instance. The truer the accusations, the harder they are to admit to, and the easier they are to justify diverting that self-anger onto those close at hand, preferably people less powerful and/or more forgiving. I cannot recommend such a policy as it is likely to lead to dramas later on.

Perhaps yesterday's early acceptance of the pointlessness of further attempts to defend my view, to accept the realities of both the ambiguity of the incident and the unforgiving and implacable judgments of the others, was a hopeful sign of my developing some semblance of wisdom.

I can only hope that such a mental augmentation persists and develops.

* The incident occurred sometime in May 2017.
In regard to the hoped-for development of greater wisdom and self-control, and the satisfaction it brings, here at the end of 2022, I fear such a state will be episodic at best and yet I still consider it worth pursuing.

17. The other side of Sunday

I was planning a motorbike ride for Sunday, fourteenth of April 2019, and was studying my map of W.A., searching for a destination when my eyes fell upon Kulin – a tiny wheat-belt town about two hundred and thirty kilometres southeast of Perth. It was a place I couldn't recall visiting, which seemed reason enough to make it my ride's focus.

The day arrived, with a forecast of temperatures to the mid-twenties, moderate north-westerly winds, but with showers developing later.

But, as Alain de Botton elucidated in his book *The Art of Travel*, the journey would be more than: *we started at eight-thirty a.m., rode about five hundred and fifty kilometres in total and returned home shortly after five p.m.* Though likely a true, if bland, summary, it would hide a mass of prosaic details as well as a possible scattering of profundities.

Of the innumerable motorbike rides I have been on, few have had a lasting impression on my memory, and those few are mostly remembered as mere fragments of sights, sounds and feelings.

This essay is my attempt to heed Alain de Botton's suggestions regarding travel and how to gain greater value from it. I approached that particular Sunday for its restorative qualities but also with the hope that, with greater mindfulness, the day would acquire more meaning and last longer in my memory, an endeavour which may make it easier should anyone, myself included, threaten me with some of life's bigger questions, such as: *What do you have to show for your time on this planet; what would you have done differently and why?*

A bold and perhaps bizarre endeavour, one I made more difficult because I wrote this recollection a month after that ride. In a way, the delay was a blessing because the trivial had evaporated leaving behind a smaller pile of the prosaic, which made the few pearls of wisdom easier to find.

One such pearl lay concealed within the statement "We left at eight-thirty" because the journey actually started well before then. It began with my preparations for departure, not the showering nor having breakfast and organising the bike, but the tricky task of getting my dear wife's blessing for the day ahead.

She doesn't like motorbikes. It is an opinion she can back with a multitude of quite rational facts. But she has never piloted one, has only been pillion a few times, reluctantly, and hence she sees only the *external aspects*, the wearing of all that restrictive safety gear, the sitting for hours in an uncomfortable position, the being bounced around, risking life and limb, suffering wind, cold or heat and speeding tickets. It seems she asks herself: where is the up side; where is the pleasure? Why does he do it? Apparently with no suitable answers arising.

Hence, these monthly rides of mine almost always have a frosty start and finish, because not understanding is seldom an option. Our minds insist on obvious reasons for behaviours; failing that they seek the less palatable ones, and in our house my "irrational behaviour" seems to induce fear, specifically the fear of rejection, because if motorcycling has no pleasures, then my reason for wanting to go for a ride must be to get away from her! A notion contrary to all the words and deeds of love and affection from me throughout our many years of marital happiness. Psychologists might say my rides created *cognitive dissonance*, which in the vernacular means: confusion, suspicion and unhappiness.

I have tried on several prior occasions to explain how biking has meditative qualities that dissipate negative thinking through forcing me to concentrate on mastering the physics of motorcycling, which involves constantly negotiating and responding to the bike, the road, and the traffic.

Those rides in the countryside also help by placing my existence and my troubles into a bigger context. Petty anxieties melt away as the hours pass and I immerse myself in the landscape and I feel my smallness against the unthinkable vastness of the sky above. The road adds to that sense of smallness, from its constant presence beneath me and its countless junctions both implying that it has no end, that if I were to keep going, I would reach eternity!

Riding my motorbike is one of the few places that offers respite from woe. But alas, thus far, my explanations of the reasons I ride seem to have been as ineffectual as describing sight to a person born blind.

But motorcycling isn't totally about rebalancing my thinking; it is also one of the few aspects of life that can still provide a *peak experience*, (as discussed in a previous essay, *Inside the Ride*). A day conquering the bendy bits is like a rust remover that makes the world shiny and new again. And though only temporary I find it still worth the effort.

Before setting off I had another go to explain the process to her and received encouraging indications that my words had found some purchase in her psyche, giving me the hope that this one schism in our togetherness might finally be resolved.

Thus, I arrived at the service station where our rides commence in a buoyant mood not dented by there being only one rider waiting to join me. Thankfully, he too was looking forward to a day off from the daily grind to enjoy a day exploring the countryside, and possibly more so because he had a new motorbike that he was keen to get more acquainted with.

So, after a brief discussion of the ride's specifics, we made our escape from the city's smothering embrace.

The next philosophical moment emerged at our morning tea stop at the Tanglefoot winery and café on the northern approaches of the hamlet of Wandering. It was a case of same place but very different result. The dear wife and I had a morning break there a few weekends before, but she, not being a dog lover and also one for scrupulous cleanliness, was most upset by the owner's dachshund wandering around the tables, and insisted it be shooed out. Our enjoyment of the tea and gluten-free cakes was then diminished by her overactive thoughts on the bacterial contamination from dog to our plate. We didn't linger.

In contrast, my riding companion was a dog owner, and I was raised with dogs and cats. This, combined with men having greater "flexibility" towards hygiene, had us less troubled by the presence of the furry little ankle-biter, and so our morning tea on the verandah overlooking the valley proved convivial. Same place, same food, same staff but a very different outcome, an outcome predicated upon the attitudes brought to the situation. It was a lesson worthy of further thought.

After filling up at Pingelly, I led the way to Brookton, specifically to enjoy the rollercoaster backroad from there to Aldersyde, which consists of a wheat silo and a few houses. That road is a challenge. It is bumpy and bendy, with many bends on crests and the latter half of it reduced to a single lane of bitumen, which adds spice in the form of oncoming traffic. I put my head down and, bearing in mind my modest capabilities, took up the challenge. Upon reflection, that road, like many others, can be regarded as a physical manifestation of the Taoist concept of *yin* and *yang*.

The symbol for yin and yang is a circle bisected by a curved line, one side black, and one side white, with each side having a small dot of the opposing colour inside it. The symbol represents two snakes entwined head to tail attempting to devour the other. The colour black for chaos, white for order, with the eye dot in each representing the seed of the opposing force ready to turn chaos into order and order into chaos.

Apparently, the path of maximum happiness and meaningfulness lies in travelling along that knife-edge separating chaos from order.

When I ride sedately, behave myself and stay safely in the white of orderliness and obeyance of the road rules, I get some enjoyment. If I go ballistic, move into the black of chaos, I come unstuck, fall off, trash the bike and kill myself, or get away with it only to cop a massive speeding fine. Travelling the line between the two, as stated earlier, is not just where maximum happiness is found but it is also where peak, positive and negative, experiences live.

I did my best to travel that philosophic battle zone separating yin from yang, by riding the physical one, the bitumen strip laid across the land. I rode to the best of my abilities and survived each bend, crest and dip. I had a great time until the lack of my companion in the rear mirrors forced me to stop and contemplate whether to backtrack for fear that he'd fallen off.

A few minutes passed and he duly turned up. From our brief chat at the start, he appeared to be an experienced rider, and probably bolder and better than I, and should have had no trouble keeping up, but his new motorbike, though twice the capacity of mine, was proving underwhelming in the handling department. The bike looked great; had heaps of go and terrific brakes but when he caught up, he explained that its suspension was too harsh; it didn't soak up the bumps and hence failed to inspire his confidence in the bumpy bends we encountered.

It was analogous to discovering a new friend, or lover, one

who is physically attractive, smart, capable, seemingly an ideal companion but when encountering one of life's often mundane obstacles a serious shortcoming is unveiled. A situation that gets us wondering about the wisdom of our choice, whilst reluctant to concede an error because we have invested too much in the relationship, such that abandoning it would involve a painful loss of face. The foolish deny the problem and try to live with it or work around it. The wise see it for what it is and try to fix it. If that is not possible, they cut their losses and move on. It was a dilemma my co-rider now faced.

We had to turn down the speed once we returned to the highway leading to Corrigin, which reminded me that our supposed *free will* is very much prescribed by society's invisible chains, though on this occasion any frustration was mollified by the lower speeds allowing me to soak in the glorious immensity of a cloud speckled sky lording over a gently rolling ocean of paddocks.

After filling up the bikes in Corrigin, I led the way south to Kulin. It was a main road, though lightly travelled, and so I "embraced the black serpent of chaos" by increasing my speed in the sweeping bends before returning to the white of orderliness by backing off on the straights. It was a compromise strategy that kept my companion in my mirrors, gave me the spice of "pushing the envelope" and still allowed for interludes of relaxation.

Kulin was a pleasant surprise, neat and tidy, showing evidence of a Council that was making an effort to keep the place alive, in contrast to many wheat-belt towns that have an air of terminal neglect about them. Stopping outside the Post Office, we took photos to give proof of our arrival. I was hoping for a café with interesting food but the only one open proved to have unappealing options.

A moment of disappointment was shared.

After a few minutes, we made the decision to have a meagre lunch in the carefully maintained park in the main street. Luckily, I had packed a sandwich and my companion had the foresight to bring a snack.

While eating I was reminded of the central tenet behind most of the contemplative practices of Buddhism, namely the task of reducing our suffering, a large part of which involves *learning to deal with disappointment*. Lunch thus included a meditative munching upon the causes and cures of disappointment. I also reminded myself that life is lived, and hopefully enjoyed, mostly in the journeying, and less so in the destination.

My riding companion was happy for me to continue leading and so we set off on the first leg of our return: via Narrogin to our fuel stop in Williams.

By then the sunshine was slowly being defeated by a gathering army of darkening clouds. I ignored the signs and pressed on as before, fast in the bends and slower on the straights. The level of risk towards my driver's license increased twofold because we were approaching the bigger police presence of those larger towns and the increasing hilliness of the land, which produced more bends to entice me to disregard speed limits and poorer sightlines to give warning of approaching patrol cars. A case of motorcycling mimicking one of the fundamental laws of economics: *more risk, more reward but also greater threat of ruin*.

One could say that my riding with awareness had opened my mind to the yin and yang of Taoism, to Buddhism's call to learn to deal with disappointment, as well as to act upon a fundamental law of Economics, the relationship between risk and reward!

Strangely, at our refuelling stop in Williams, my companion made no mention of similar revelations! About the only thing of consequence discussed during our brief chat over the bowsers was who would lead the next section to our afternoon tea stop in Dwellingup, via Quindanning.

He led the way, which gave him a chance to set the pace, and me time to relax a little. By then the clouds had overwhelmed the sun and were growing darker and more threatening. Again, we ignored the warnings and pressed on, but by Quindanning the intermittent light rain was getting hard to rationalise away, and no amount of ducking down behind our fairings was going to make the rain give up.

I at least had choices, having brought my wet weather gear, but my companion had none and only a tiny handlebar fairing to shelter behind, so his risk of a soaking was far greater than mine. Yet I still resisted the sensible – to pull over to the roadside and put my weatherproof gear on – electing instead to push my luck and keep going even as the first inklings of dampness in my trouser legs were making their way up my nerve endings to a brain in denial.

No matter how knowledgeable, educated, or experienced we are, why are we humans so reluctant to use our intellect and heed the warnings early? Why is denial one of our favourite resting places? Then, as now, my only answers lay in the delight to be found in pushing one's luck *and winning*, coupled with our tremendous ability to concoct stories that shed the blame for our mistakes onto others, such as Fortuna, the wilful goddess of luck.

My crouching down behind the handlebars hoping for any serious rain to hold off until Dwellingup was not without its compensations because the heightened awareness required to cope with roads turned slippery also made me more aware of the vision splendid of the mist alternating with intermittent shafts of late afternoon sun turning the bitumen from patchy black roughness to a blazing silver metallic ribbon, a ribbon that was the lifeline I had to follow or end up devoured by the surrounding forest, reduced to a grey, green and black striped blur in my peripheral vision.

We made it to Dwellingup and tromped into the warmth of the Blue Wren café relieved to be only damp around the edges and further delighted to find a bunch of our motorcycle club acquaintances inside. Our time was then spent drying out, sipping our hot drinks and enjoying a bit of biker gossiping.

My new friend, grateful the clouds appeared to be dissipating, volunteered to lead the way home. But before following, I, having come under the influence of the white serpent of order and logic, had done the sensible thing and donned my wet weather gear. Naturally, the rain stopped and the clouds thinned. The sun eventually strengthened enough to end the day with a burst of late afternoon bravado. It left me thinking how true to form the situation was, listening to my good sense *after* the danger had passed, not before it. At least it proved beyond doubt that I was eminently human!

The frivolous fairyland of escape and adventure faded with my stepping through our front door. I braced myself for the possible frosty reception from my motorcycle-allergic wife when, to my pleasant surprise, she seemed pleased to see me and that our home radiated its usual glow of domestic harmony.

It appeared my explanation, before the ride, of the reasons for my motorcycling, using words borne of much thinking and philosophising and delivered with a desire to resolve the issues with sincerity and compassion, had helped reduce her needless suffering *and* mine. In a way, that chat was the most valuable philosophic legacy the day had to offer.

Later on, I realised that I had unwittingly put into practice one of a series of wise sayings posted by my wife over her graph of our monthly finances that hangs in our lounge room, there to remind us of the mostly happy state of our monetary fitness.

It was from Charles Handy – a sort of philosopher to the business community – who said: "Change the *words* and you begin to change the way you *think*. That in turn changes the way you *behave*."

It was a process that my pre-ride chat had demonstrated in a somewhat jumbled order. My act of considered *thinking* upon her apparently misguided conclusions regarding my monthly motorbike rides, changed the *words* I used, which in turn modified, for the better, the thinking and *behaviours* of the receiver, my dear wife.

That successful application of received wisdom boosted my already considerable awareness of the power of words to grow or wither relationships. It pushed my resolve to choose the words I utter with care into a state of permanent high alert, because, once let loose, the effect of unkind words can never be fully undone.

End Note:

I can report that as of December 2022, the mutual understanding of my monthly motorcycle rides continues. Its apparent permanence vindicates my philosophising ways and feeds my great respect for the immense power hidden in words and ideas.

18. The Wife

'Remove, "the wife", the rest is fine.' – or words to that effect – was the only memorable response of a female relation to an essay [1] of mine on the vexing issue of giving.

I was disappointed because I'd hoped the essay would encourage a conversation about charity from which I might learn to view the topic differently. Instead, I was stuck with a brief admonition of a descriptive of my better half.

Being male and still very much wedded to my dear wife, I was peeved by that criticism of the term "wife" and mentioned the incident at my next writers' group meeting. There were a few new faces, younger than the rest of us and female, who upon hearing of my puzzlement over the apparent lack of esteem for the term "wife", reacted with much vigour and emotion. It seemed I had stumbled onto a sensitive issue for many women, especially the younger ones.

A few years later, the matter, still unresolved in my mind, resurfaced when reading page seventy-eight of *Factfulness* by Dr Hans Rosling, a 2018 publication that dispels many of the myths we harbour about the current state of the human world – its message was that things are better than most think. In the book, he mentioned an incident when attending a banking conference in Hong Kong and seated next to an eminent banker, a lady in her mid-thirties. He, a medical doctor concerned with human well-being and also a family man, to make conversation during the dinner, asked if she planned to have a family. Her forthright response was that she thought about children every day, but it was the *idea of a husband* that she couldn't stand!

I realised then that it wasn't just the concept of wife that was problematic in modern society but also that of husband. In fact, the whole notion of marriage seemed under a cloud.

Defining marriage, and more importantly what it entails in everyday life, causes the same difficulties as asking people to come up with a satisfactory definition of "friend", one sufficient to cover the diverse range of expectations of those we label so. It appears the confusion and angst surrounding the obligations and roles encompassed within the word "married" has progressed to the point where the words "husband and wife", due apparently to their sexist connotations, are increasingly uttered only on the wedding day. It seems the newer generations can only bear the term "partner" to describe the person they exchanged rings with.

It appears that much of the disquiet associated with marriage lies in semantics. Maybe somewhere on the globe a culture exists which has words that better describe the roles and expectations taken on when two people get hitched, akin to the fabled twenty or so words Eskimos use to describe snow. Sadly, I know of no such people. English speakers are stuck, for now, with husband and wife and the unfortunate history behind those nominatives.

And the words we use are important as they set the scene for future events because of the associations we attach to them. Even the currently popular label "partner" has its downsides. According to law, the term invokes financial obligations between people engaged in business, with each partner – and there may be more than two – equally liable for debts incurred by the others.

When two people call the other "partner", not "wife" or "husband", what are they saying to their gullible subconscious about the nature of their union? I suggest that they are unwittingly training themselves to see their relationship as a temporary business arrangement, with monetary obligations the key consideration. If so, I predict such a marriage, or should I say "enterprise", will be short-lived and devoid of much affection, intimacy and the generosity of thought needed to be forgiving of misdemeanours.

I am not aware of any men who object strongly, or mildly for that matter, to being referred to as Jane's or Bridget's or whoever's husband. I for one am proud to be my wife's husband and she is proud to be called my wife because we both agree upon what *we* mean by those words. They are our badge of our one hundred per cent commitment to the other's physical and mental well-being. We are happily co-dependent because we *like* 2 each other, not just love the other, and every day we celebrate our pact for the internal strength it gives us. It is the enduring commitment that forms the bedrock of our happiness.

It appears women are those most unhappy with the connotations attached to the words: husband and wife. And you don't have to look far for the reasons.

Throughout history, most men have treated women as property, not persons. It is an indignity that has deeply penetrated the female psyche. But for some time now, in Western nations, things, legally, have changed for the better. Women are no longer chattels but have the same legal rights, and obligations as menfolk, but …

The problem both men and women face is that in love and marriage we still think and talk in terms of property. The bride is "*given* away", "do you *take* this woman", "you are *my* man" is said with pride, "you *stole my* man" with hate. When the divorce comes through what do they fight over, *possession* of the kids, the dog and the house.

The sad prevalence of divorce is another reason for both sides to be less enthusiastic for marriage and the roles and names attached to it. A niggling fear of divorce has the tendency to become a self-fulfilling prophecy because it brings to the marriage a worm of uncertainty that gnaws away inside, especially if our expectations of the day-to-day realities of living together are out of sync with what is humanly possible.

The unfortunate reality is that we are all too prone to see the shortcomings of the other but not our own. And if there is a mismatch in the levels of self-awareness, forgiveness and commitment, then the relationship quickly rots and dies.

Perhaps another more deep-seated reason behind the reluctance to admit to the "married state and our being labelled so lies in the differing biological fates evolution has bequeathed to males and females of our species, Homo sapiens".

Girls, you can curse evolution for making you a mammal not a fish! Imagine the delight of being a female fish. At spawning time, generally only once a year, you find a spot to unload your eggs, the pestering males are fighting for their chance to fertilise them, you select the best of the bunch, let him do his business and then calmly swim off to enjoy a carefree life cruising around the coral reef, leaving the "children" and "husband" to fend for themselves. Has this become the modern woman's dream?

I don't think it is for most women. And if it were, is it achievable? And if achieved, does it lead to a satisfying life with a happy ending?

I suspect women have less trouble with the concept of marriage than the apparent disadvantages biology has dealt them. Women have breasts and a womb because nature has allocated to them the role of life nurturer. It is a vital but heavy burden. Sadly, for most of human existence, the adult female has spent life either pregnant, breast feeding and/or supervising the few children that survived past weaning, a situation that thwarts any ambitions in other fields. And being physically smaller than the males makes it harder to carve an alternative role by brute force.

As *Factfulness* reminds us, things have improved. Women's legal and social status, and hence opportunities to fulfil more of their inborne capabilities, has been revolutionised by modern medicine and the control it gives over their fertility and the survival of their offspring. They are no longer completely ruled by their ovaries and wombs. But, male or female, we are all slaves to our biology. This essay is concerned with finding a more comfortable accommodation with our biological constraints and motivations.

Unlike fish, producing the next generation of humans requires a huge and sustained effort and thus evolution selected for humans with an urge to form lasting and mutually supportive relationships with members of the opposite sex. It is an arrangement that worked best when concentrated upon one person, not several simultaneously.

But modern society allows us to couple without the rationale of reproduction. We can opt for having no children, which brings into question the evolutionary purpose behind pairing up. The glue that holds the couple together is now less biological and needs reformulation if it is to satisfy both members. This brings us back to *wife* and *husband* and negotiating "modern" meanings to be attached to the words and roles.

Even if today's younger women can only admit to being Jack's *partner*, what does that label mean to her and to any third parties? As a social creature, we are constantly trying to understand the role and status of our compatriots, and as part of that process we attach labels to them, for better or worse. The words: *wife, husband, partner, mother, father, lover, the ex, Mr. Mrs. Ms.*, are attached to us as much as our job titles: *C.E.O, teacher, cleaner, Mayor or General Manager,* and all carry clues to our status in society. Labels are things we are forced to use, and live with.

When my wife-to-be blessed me with the answer *yes* to my request to formalise our union, my joy was qualified by my uncertainty over her response to my next question: "Will you do me the indulgence of changing your surname to mine?"

Why was I fearful of a no?

In our long evolutionary struggle, men, to provide for and protect their families and tribe members, probably needed muscles first and brains second. And for greater reproductive success they needed a higher social status within the tribe. Those primitive desires are still there, though muscle power has been eclipsed by socio-economic standing in granting social and biological success. We males like to feel useful and needed by those around us. It is the cornerstone of the edifice that is the fragile male ego. Should that edifice crumble in the face of a barrage of inconvenient facts then the man can spiral into depression or infantile rage.

Those archaic desires for power and status amongst my fellow males were behind my desire for my wife to wear my surname. I wanted other males, upon learning she had accepted my surname to be impressed because it implied that I was the *head of my household* and possibly that my wife understood the fragility of the male ego and was prepared to placate at least one of her husband's silly insecurities.

On the surface, it was a trivial point but a piece of trivia that sets the tone of the relationship. But when the girl does consent to change her name, she needs to firmly and regularly remind her husband, and herself, of the Serbian proverb: *the man may be the head of the house, but the wife is the neck*. And that it is the *neck* that directs the head!

And if she does retain her maiden name, are they, in their minds, wedded as husband and wife, or still boyfriend and girlfriend, or partner and partner? Again, we come back to the psychological importance of the labels we attach to others and ourselves.

Humans are forgetful creatures, which is why friendships rapidly fade if too long out of sight and why we should think of ourselves as Gracie's *husband* or Darryl's *wife*, and why we *wear a wedding ring*, and why most of us *have a wedding photo*, or one of the two of us together somewhere *on display* in our homes. All are symbols and physical ways of reinforcing our memories of our commitment to the other.

And society at large, male and female, adult and child, is very much attuned to the power of labels and symbols that show our commitment to one another. Think of our attitude on learning that a man or woman has never married. Immediately and unbidden, we ask: why? Were they unattractive to the opposite sex? Are they incapable of resolving differences such that they can live harmoniously with other people? An unmarried presidential candidate is unlikely to succeed because of those same questions. Voters conclude: if they can't handle marriage how can they govern us with any mutual regard?

Children of unmarried parents will ask them: "When are *we* getting married?" They instinctively know that marriage symbolises commitment, and understand that a commitment from both parents gives them the best chance of survival and a good life.

And why do non-heterosexual people clamour for the right to a legally sanctioned marriage? Their actions surely suggest that marriage is a valued state of being. I have even heard such couples refer to each other as husband or wife and seem happy using those labels.

And why do most women seem to desire a fancy wedding, with an elaborate and expensive dress, reception and ceremony? Is it driven by their unconscious desire for the reassurances provided by a *public* demonstration of the strength of commitment of *her* man to her, and hopefully of her commitment to him?

What are the reasons for romance novels being so popular with women, and to a lesser degree with men? Why do women, and men, like to read stories of two people meeting and, after a few struggles, making a loving commitment to the other, our commonly held idea of a happy ending?

All these questions and situations seem to state that marriage is a fundamental desire and an arrangement that is *worth doing well* in order to maximise the benefits to the couple, their children and society at large. Its requirements need to be more fully discussed and clarified by the couple, and by society, to make the breadth and depth of that commitment understandable and workable. Such a task requires *words* to describe the special roles taken on, with "husband" and "wife" being those traditionally used.

There are men who baulk at formalising their married state, who are reluctant to attach "husband" to their body. But male or female, in the eyes of today's legal system, irrespective of the label you attach to yourself, you are treated as married if you have been cohabiting for an appreciable length of time. Not admitting to being a husband, or a wife, carries no weight with the law, or government departments, so it's best resolved sooner than later. And long-term *non-commitment* is a slow-acting poison that will inexorably degrade and ultimately destroy most relationships.

Returning to the female disregard for the term *wife*, ladies, if it still irks you to distraction, teach me a new word to describe the *exact state* of your relationship, a word that is kind to both of you. A word that shows to others the level of your regard for your most significant other. The same, of course, applies to the male side.

Until that word emerges, I and my dear wife will do our best to demonstrate, in our speech and behaviours, our *affection* for each other – not just lust, but *an unconscious liking* – and by doing so, show that the old-fashioned and battered titles "husband" and "wife" can be worn with pride.

[1] The essay referred to was *The Art of Giving*
[2] *Liking* is a much more *sustainable* emotion. Love is essential but too many confuse it with lust, which is wonderful but episodic and prone to fading.

19. Forgive and Forget

If you have lived a normal existence then at some stage you have either given or received the advice: *to forgive and forget*. Such advice is usually a well-meaning attempt to allow the receiver to recover from, and thus move on from, a painful incident that is poisoning their enjoyment of life. But is it possible to implement such advice?

My motivation for this exploration is the aftermath of a disastrous reunion with people I had, for decades, been on good terms with. It still rankles more than two and a half years later. I am sure you, dear reader, can find a painful episode to work with, so let us begin.

The first hurdle is the neurology and biochemistry of memory. All remembering requires repetition; think of the tiresome effort required to remember our multiplication tables in primary school. Memories of people and our interactions with them also need the extra impetus of some emotional attachment if they are to last. We may have a friend whom we have known for many years, but do we remember every word of all the conversations we have had with them and all the details of every minute in their company? Of course not! To do so our brains would need to be the size of a whale. Instead, our brain actively prunes, rehearses and edits our experiences, but, do so biased towards making new experiences coherent with previous ones. When there is a desire to remember, they are also lazy; they seek the gist of the event and discard the finer details. This editing and pruning results in the few old memories left to us often having minimal resemblance to actual events [1].

We are unreliable witnesses, though when strong emotions are involved, memories can be vivid and accurate, in most details, but we still *do not have all the information* to fully understand any incident because *we do not truly know the thoughts and motivations* of those who wronged us. Even discussing the hurtful incident at the time, or later when we have calmed down, is no guarantee of getting to the truth and then a resolution, because most of us have timid and fragile egos that find admitting to errors existentially painful.

And neurologically we find it difficult to actively erase an emotionally charged incident from our memory, though I suspect some would claim to have that power. I certainly don't, which leaves only one path to a more accepting attitude to the hurt. We must try to get more facts, not speculation.

In a way, getting more facts on the issue, from the safety of time and physical distance, is akin to the process by which phobias are conquered, or at least lessened. The fear-inducing object or situation is studied from afar and in safety, we then move gradually closer to the fearful object or idea until we can face it, close up and dispassionately.

An almost impossible task as we humans generally only have the ego strength to admit to palatable facts, those that support *our* existing views. But more information is better than less. Information and *a broader perspective* on the matter are the only guides to salvation I can offer.

If we can have a conversation, in a safe environment, face-to-face with each antagonist, useful information may surface, especially if we use the classic counselling approach of: *when you did this*, or, *when you said this, I felt this*. Hopefully, by breaking the incident down into small *specific* parts, it will be less threatening and hence easier for the other side to respond more truthfully.

Trying this process by phone, or letters, or emails doesn't seem to work, or at least it didn't for me with my selected issue and protagonists, all of whom live a day's flight or a week by car away from me.

What do we do if the people or person at the centre of our unhappiness are not physically available, or if so, refuse to discuss the issue in any depth?

The answers to that lie in the level of pain we continue to feel and how badly the issue affects our overall level of happiness.

I admit to having made mistakes at the time and then compounded them by trying to downplay the issue, probably from overdeveloped politeness. Logically, the divergent viewpoints and their attached emotions were not insurmountable, but I, and they, are human, and rationally assessing facts is the last thing we are capable of in emotionally charged situations.

Having failed with long-distance communication and not much prospect of resolution from making the effort for a face-to-face encounter, I was left with only one avenue to pursue: to modify *my* attitudes and assumptions regarding the incident. In directly examining those assumptions and expectations, and indirectly theirs, we soon realise that disappointment will always result whenever assumptions are untested and when expectations of behaviours are *unrealistic*.

My antagonists are all older than I and hence were assumed to be wiser than I. Two have tertiary educations and much experience in the area of human relations, the other has decades of working in managerial positions as well as years of studying philosophy on the side, all of which foolishly heightened my expectations of them. But I should have known that education and experience are no barrier to foolishness, pride, and blindness to seeing their errors – all of which are explained in detail in David Robson's brilliant book, *The Intelligence Trap*.

Expecting a higher standard of empathy and understanding was my first mistake. My second was not recognising the hole I was digging for myself at the time. In hindsight, maybe things would have been different if I had looked upon them, and myself, as being oversensitive, rationalising, and affection-craving dolts! But at the time we all seemed too scared, too polite or too blind to encourage the awkward truth to rise to the surface.

Another consideration is my and their egotism. We all think we are more important, smarter and more deserving than we probably are. "I" is everyone's favourite pronoun, so why should they hold *my* feelings sacred? Why should they care much about me? Do *I* really have a huge regard for them, or is it just the ego stroking of their good opinion of me that I desire?

A lot of unanswered questions, which will only be answered once I decide how much further I wish to exhaust myself in searching for the truths of the situation.

There is a sad, hauntingly beautiful song sung by Shirley Horn called *The Man You Were* [2]. When I examine my chosen painful incident, and from there my history with those involved, I realise that I am pining, like Shirley, for the people I thought they *were*. Were my relations with them real or mere illusion? If false, why should I grieve for the loss of an illusion?

I am reminded of a piece of contentious opinion from Nassim Nicholas Taleb, from his book of personal aphorisms, *The Bed of Procrustes*: "A friendship that ends was never one; there was at least one sucker in it."

The sad facts of my case are that those three persons, in response to my heartfelt entreaties, have shown an almost total refusal to seriously discuss the matter, with all attempts to broach the topic being on my part. Their lack of desire to communicate, their wall of silence, should be shouting the obvious truth at me: they don't care, so why should I?

But I do care and hence haven't given up all hope in regard to those now severely damaged relationships. The universe is an unknowable place and odd and unexpectedly good things happen as much as the bad. Perhaps one day they will be brave enough to generously and truthfully examine the episode; information may be exchanged, and a truer understanding of the situation from both sides may emerge that will make forgiveness, in part or whole, possible.

But *I shall not forget.*

To forget is to learn nothing, and forgetting leaves us open to repeating the same tragedy with others.

For now, I must conclude that my expectations of them, and of my abilities to resolve the disappointment, have been overly optimistic.

I must resign myself to that fact and concentrate on enjoying my relationships with those people currently in my life with whom my regard is genuinely reciprocated. At least then my good wishes and humanity will find fertile soil to grow in.

So shall it be!

---

[1] For more information on how our brains create and store memories read: *The Ethical Brain* by Michael S. Gazzangia and *Thinking, Fast and Slow* by Daniel Kahneman.

The song and lyrics to *The Man You Were,* sung by Shirley Horn on the *Loving You* album can be found on the internet.

20. Intimacy

Back in my late twenties, I overheard a brilliantly brief summation that encapsulated the absolute essence of a person I knew well. The comment was that the person had spent their life chasing and grooming "a thousand <u>intimate</u> friends" with the rest left unsaid; the bit about "and no real ones!" It was a remark that has resonated within me ever since.

That judgement disturbed me greatly at the time because it forced upon me the unpleasant realisation that I had *neither*. Of the few people I had called, and those I still labelled *friend*, all were acquaintances when measured against my probably unrealistic idea of *real* friendship. The consequence of that quip was that I could no longer paper over my unrequited craving for deeper relationships, for the safe haven of intimacy with at least one person – being unsure, at the time, if such a state was possible with more than one. It is a situation that persists even now when in my sixties.

Though it took a painfully long time to find, I did get lucky and was eventually blessed by such a truly intimate relationship. I was thirty-two, working in a small mining town, where the ratio of single men to marriageable women seemed like a million to one, and yet, against those odds I miraculously met my wife-to-be. But perhaps living in a small community had advantages over the big city, because there the choices of potential friends and/or future spouses are fewer and hence easier to locate, and once located, there are fewer distractions to spending time with them.

Unappreciated at the time was my luck in having been previously unlucky in love, because when it finally arrived, I was all the more appreciative of what I had stumbled into. I was also lucky by then to possess a yardstick against which to measure the reality and strength of a romantic relationship.

Physical attraction was important but not enough. The other essential ingredient was a philosophical harmony such that even differences of viewpoint could be aired, discussed, and accepted, even if only to agree to disagree. Such a person is one that we can be ourselves with, one who will forgive our trifling differences and whom we deeply respect, and in turn receive the same from them. They have a type of magnetism that attracts us and is of a type that has us "glow" in their presence.

Wanting to be with them physically finds its ultimate expression in lovemaking, which for most is done whilst naked, because in shedding our clothing we symbolically remove our external persona and join together in mutual need and regard as who we really are, not as who we pretend to be. It is a rare time of social and physical vulnerability.

Making love changes everything. But loving it is not enough to maintain the heightened state of intimacy that it enables. Intimacy is a living thing that needs constant nurturing and sadly this is where the hectic pace and distractions of modern living take their toll. It is not just our lifestyles that interfere, but also our differing genetic predispositions that can push us into valuing or devaluing relationships.

If our spouses are to remain so, we need to recognise our genetic weaknesses and be frequently reminded of the benefits of our other halves, which is why we wear a ring, scatter photos of the two of us around the house. We also need to make the commitment to the other and consciously choose to spend much time together, and talk of things other than groceries, work or the weather.

Which brings me to something I should have started with, a definition of what intimacy is and what it requires. My dictionary reckons *intimate* equals a close or warm personal relationship, which is a very insipid description of my idea of the regard I hold for my dear wife. For me, intimate is not merely close, it is a hundred per cent regard for the other, such that one would unflinchingly give one's life for them.

It is most commonly possible between married couples but exists, in different forms, between long-standing true friends, or comrades-in-arms who fought together and survived the horrors of war. It is a state of trust that allows us to discuss the most sensitive issues without fear of ridicule, and one in which our unguarded self can feel the deep relaxation unavailable in almost any other circumstance.

The downside of intimacy is that the deepest hurt we can suffer is to have such trust and regard betrayed, which I suspect is why so many shy from intimacy. Theirs is a very real fear because humans are weak-willed; we are prone to see the worst in others, but naturally not ourselves, and we barely understand our own motivations let alone those of others and hence can easily misunderstand situations, to disastrous results. Since there is plenty of room for things to go horribly wrong in relationships some would caution us not to *overinvest* in them. Are they correct in their thinking?

It appears that human relationships mimic the arrangement in the natural world whereby plants and animals, when it comes to reproducing, have two strategies, either nurture and carefully guard a few offspring, or have hundreds or thousands that are cheap to create, and abandon, all in the hope that though almost all will fail a few will survive. Similarly, is our human strategy of either thousands of acquaintances or a few intimates. There appears to be no middle path and no guarantee of success in either.

This brings us to the different reasons for wanting acquaintances versus intimate friends, or spouses – those special beings forged on the anvil of physical *lovemaking* as opposed to *just sex*. Our attitudes regarding our desired style of relationships seem to lie in the divergence between our public persona and the murkier, hidden, internal being, a creature barely perceived or understood, filled with confusing and competing desires, and with expectations often at odds with reality. All of which can have us careening unexpectedly between prideful arrogance and a crushing fear of inadequacy.

If humans didn't need other people for physical survival, then there would be little need for a divergence between the external persona and the vulnerable, hidden, internal one. Being little more than instinct-driven "robots", cockroaches have no imperfections they need to hide or be ashamed of. They also have no need of trust and hence can never betray each other.

But to get food, shelter, and social status we must get along with many others, which requires us to quell our initial infantile egoistic responses, be it punching an overbearing supervisor in the nose or ravishing the shapely new girl in the office, and all that quelling takes its toll.

We eventually need a break from playing who we *have to be*, to just being who we *are* and that's where friends and intimates come in. We seek friendships partly because they will be people who are similar to us and hence will be easier to get along with because they will require *less pretending*. But more importantly, they give us a safer environment in which to express embarrassing or fear-inducing difficulties and/or hopes. Admitting to these requires a much greater level of trust and mutual regard if they are to be aired. If not dealt with, these same suppressed emotive issues will clamour for resolution and "leak out" in peculiar ways, producing *out-of-character* behaviours, often at inappropriate times and usually with negative consequences.

The more polite, or more competitive a society is, then the greater the need for an antidote to all the suppression of true feelings and opinions that such societies induce. Thus, such societies have a greater need for intimate friends and/or spouses. And yet our crowded, busy city lifestyles, whilst giving more people to select our friends from, offer *less* opportunities to develop and maintain those friendships or marriages because we are too busy working, too busy commuting, too tired when we get home – a situation made worse by the people we want to be with being in the same boat, in the same frazzled and time-poor state. That any meaningful relationships can survive in the modern city is a wonder of itself!

And most city dwellers know something is wrong but have either not figured out what it is, or having done so, found no acceptable solutions. But solutions have to be found because our happiness and mental health depend upon good relations with our fellows in general and, more so with that smaller group of close friends and spouses who underpin our motivation for getting out of bed in the morning.

One of the main barriers to developing such a close supportive group is the cultural brainwashing of our capitalist cult of individualism. We are told in many subtle, and less subtle ways, to place *our* personal fulfilment above all others. *Our* aim is to pursue *our* dream, to become self-actualised with little mention of our role within society. And if we don't succeed, it's all *our* fault.

But how is success measured by this credo of individualism and competition? What is the purpose of all our capitalist economic and social efforts? It appears to me that the purpose of a good capitalist, otherwise known as Homo economicus, is to accumulate and consume as much money and stuff as is humanly possible. Success in our society is thus hugely skewed towards becoming wealthy and to be adored for it. But, are such measures of success really worthy and *satisfying?*

Personal growth is essential but equally so is the ability to have some regard towards others, to have a meaningful and positive impact on society, and if those parameters are not substantially achieved, then our life will have no more meaning than that of the scurrying cockroach, a life of mindlessly eating, breeding and dying. Such a constricted lifestyle is not for me.

This essay, in trying to understand why the concept of a thousand intimate friends seemed absurd, forced me to more fully appreciate the preciousness of the intimacy, in mind and body, that I share with my dear wife, and the happiness found in the company of those few friends with whom I can speak freely.

I hope it encourages you, dear reader, to join me in being walking, talking exemplars of the benefits of valuing intimacy and friendships of depth. Doing so will provide a much needed and powerful counter argument against those who consider relationships not worth the effort.

Perhaps, by setting a good example, we can steer society towards a more humane future, even if it's at the pace of one happy relationship at a time.

21. Snobbery

I am sure snobbery had been lurking in my midst for quite a while but it only grabbed my full attention about five or so years ago when we took a visitor on a tour of our suburb's principal attraction, its beaches and coastline. In a playful mood I, with my dear wife as an impartial observer in the back seat, drove to *our* beach, to show off "our" weekender, a grandiose two-storey statement of wealth, resplendent with Corinthian columns, filigree wrought iron fencing and a fake sandstone finish. It has stood there for well over ten years, and, despite our frequent visits to that stretch of beachside development, appears to have been occupied only on a single occasion, over a few days one Christmas.

Our guest was born to humble circumstances but had been fortunate enough to receive a tertiary education, then steady employment in his profession. He was also "blessed" with the desire to better his financial and societal position. That betterment duly arrived and was mostly evidenced through a series of houses that he had bought, tidied up and then sold. In the decade before his retirement, he had kept himself, and his wallet, busy by slowly restoring an older style home to its former glory.

By the time he retired, that house had been transformed into a stunning showpiece. Naturally, it was sold to move to an even better location, a town with an upper middle-class clientele, which was also closer to his spouse's family. Their new house is modern, possibly more efficient even if somewhat lacking in character, but it is *bigger*, having five bedrooms, two or three bathrooms and a beautifully *big* garden to be proud of, and maintain.

I, unfortunately, was late to twig to the importance of money and hence live a more modest lifestyle, in a working-class suburb but one close to the beach. My circumstances may be modest but they do allow me the pleasure of a daily stroll by the seaside and, once there, to enjoy the vicarious titillation of viewing the grand houses that line the foreshore.

But grand is the wrong word because most are like our modest brick and tile bungalow but simply more of it, having more rooms and/or a second storey. They almost certainly possess little that is technologically superior, such as double glazing or underfloor heating, and certainly have very little outstanding beauty or uniqueness of design to make them worthy of preservation for future generations to admire.

All this inspired my desire to play a little joke on our guest. As we slowly cruised past the beachside houses, I asked him to check out *our weekender*.

Upon sight of it, his features revealed the momentary horror that his poor relation was apparently far wealthier than he! An agonising moment of dismay that I all too quickly ended with my explanation that it wasn't really *ours*, merely a mansion we had grown so attached to that it seemed as much ours as its mysterious true owner's.

That aghast reaction, which he of course strongly denied, was the last piece of evidence to tip him into the bucket labelled "snob", and motivated me into thinking more on the subject of snobbery.

One of the curious features of snobbery, the desire to rise above one's lowly origins and then proudly display the fruits of one's success, is that few will admit to it – a denial probably induced by society generally denigrating snobs and snobbery.

But why the social disdain? Surely, the sentiment that underpins snobbish behaviour is the same motivation that has driven much of humanity's progress from unwashed caveman, to the villager slaving in the fields and living in mud huts, to the cleaner and healthier living of the present-day average Aussie suburbanite. Rather than disparaging snobs and snobbery, society should be erecting statues glorifying the great snobs of history, but we don't, which brings me back to not only why not, but also to, who, specifically, is doing the denigrating?

Looking at my own motivations I conclude that the disdain of snobs by the less well-off, such as myself, is driven by a certain level of envy, but more so by the repugnant implication that they consider themselves better than I. They proclaim, and justify, their self-assessed superiority through displays of wealth, such as big houses, flashy cars, trophy wives, or proofs of their perceived place in the ruling classes, such as exalted titles held and social honours received.

But it is not only the poorer members of society who have little respect or regard for snobs. They also receive condescension from those on the highest rungs of society's ladder, probably for similar reasons as those lower down.

But envy and condescension are corrosive emotions to embrace and, if left to fester, can produce nasty and cruel behaviours: think of the French revolution and scenes of the envious and angry mob guillotining the gentry, all the while secretly wanting the lifestyle of those they despised.

The *have-nots* hating the *haves* for what they themselves want is a ridiculous situation, as is the disdain from the mega-rich, and it's not good for the snob either because they presumably display their achievements in the hope of admiration from their chosen reference group. But how many of their number get that admiration, and is such admiration worth society's disdain? I don't know, but suspect an honest and accurate answer to the question will be hard to come by.

Logically, it would appear that the desire for betterment is something to be encouraged if a population is to make the most of its human capital, and from there provide civil living conditions for *all*. But, like all forces of nature, we need to understand it to avoid being bitten by it, or risk handicapping our efforts to create greater societal happiness from not fully utilising our desire for something better.

Getting more comfortable with the seeking and displaying of success may become possible if we develop a greater and more widespread understanding of the realities that constrain success, coupled with a better grasp of the qualities by which successfulness can be deemed universally worthy of praise.

I suspect that a greater appreciation of the undisclosed realities behind any person's success will temper our envy towards them because we would fully understand the price they and others paid for their fame and/or fortune, as well as their consequent struggles to hold onto that success.

Perhaps that greater understanding will have us poorer folk more appreciative of the lesser number of possessions we have, and a comfortable house certainly beats living in a tent, but more importantly, we may learn to more highly value *our intangible assets*, such as living in a civil society and the nourishment we receive from our close relationships, though even the most distant people have some relevance to us now that societies are increasingly interconnected.

The main reason that most people, rich or poor, dislike snobbish displays of wealth, status, and/or knowledge (with intellectual snobbery being as hard to bear as the big house syndrome) is the previously stated implication that snobs consider themselves better than the rest of humanity.

That arrogance irks us because we *all* are humans, and hence, no matter how knowledgeable or wealthy, are equally fallible and prone to stupidities. It is a fact that inescapably binds us together, that makes us equals, and to hint, or brazenly shout otherwise, is the acme of hubris *and* ignorance, and hence universally disparaged.

Our anti-snobbery angst is possibly a vestige of our hunter-gatherer past, which relied on group effort and the sharing of resources equally. Any tribe member who got too sure of themselves and demanded a bigger share of food and/or regard, was knocked down a peg or two to remind them they were the same as everybody else. This inherited disposition also results in an unfortunate urge to mediocrity. Here in Australia, we call it the *tall poppy syndrome*, where we downplay the achievements of those "standing taller" than the rest of us.

And yet we *all* want to be recognised as being in some way important and useful to society, or a significant section of it.

It is a dilemma that appears unsolvable until we find better measurements of success and how to display it. Society needs worthy achievements recognised *and* encouraged. Success, in its multiple guises, will find universal praise an easier task if it is defined broadly enough, such that the majority have some real chance of attaining some measure of it.

Such universally approved definitions of success will probably require some widespread acknowledgement of the role played by our evolved genetics, our social circumstances, and the influence of uncontrollable external factors, such as, where and when we live, local and world economic circumstances, the vagaries of the climate, unexpected wars, recessions, as well as barriers to educational opportunities and the overarching role that luck plays in our lives.

If we, as individuals, admit to the multitude of aspects influencing our lives and achievements, then we will find that much of our pride in those achievements is unfounded, because those successes were not fully ours. To console us is the knowledge that the *same can be said of those others* that society deems successful.

With this more nuanced view, snobs and the über-rich will become less irksome against the backdrop of our truer vision of reality. Hopefully too, that bigger view will allow us to praise a more humane and livable definition of success, and clarify our reasons for wanting recognition of it. Doing so may help us find more fulfilment value in our newly measured achievements.

For me, the place to start that search for a more conciliatory attitude towards success, its recognition *and* encouragement (society does not benefit from encouraging the *lack* of achievement) can be found in reading and contemplating Ralph Waldo Emerson's thoughts on the matter:

> *"What is success?*
> *To laugh often and much:*
> *To win the respect of intelligent people and affection of children;*
> *To earn the appreciation of honest critics and endure the betrayal of false friends:*
> *To appreciate beauty;*
> *To find the best in others;*
> *To leave the world a bit better, whether by a healthy child, a garden patch or a redeemed social condition;*
> *To know even one life breathed easier because you have lived;*
> *That is to have succeeded."*

22. Enslavement

Slavery in any significant sense doesn't exist in Australia. Right? And even if it did, there isn't much you or I, as individuals, can do about it. Right?

I shared that opinion until recently. As an issue, it was something I had long been intellectually aware of, but it never seemed *real* enough to stir my emotions. However, the practice of *forcing* people to do things against their will became more real after reading an article on *Human Trafficking* by Clarissa Sebag-Montefiore in Issue 23 of *New Philosopher* magazine. Her essay forced me to recognise the sneering face of *modern* slavery. It is a sneer that I wish, in my small way, to help dispel – a face that we, the unthinking, uninformed and distracted, need to see if we are to combat it.

That we don't see slaves, or slavers, in our midst is due largely to our image of both being stuck in antiquity; we think of galley slaves chained to the oars, flogged into action by the master welding the cat-o-nine-tails. But humans can become enslaved and remain so, by more than whips, swords and muzzle-loading pistols.

In the ancient world, slavery was considered natural. The survivors of the battle lost were enslaved and sold as a matter of course, and any slave who annoyed their masters too much was killed to maintain the fear that kept the rest docile. But then, in those days, people of all classes were "slaves". Back then, everybody believed their lives and actions were not entirely their own, but "knew" they ultimately lived and died according to the fate allotted to them by the capricious gods.

Even in mediaeval times, the serfs, merchants and nobility similarly believed their lives were ruled over by the supernatural, then reduced to a single all-powerful God. And when free will was seemingly exercised, God got most of the credit. Their achievements, whether success in battle or composing a piece of beautiful music, were deemed to be the result of God working through their hands and minds. Naturally, anything unpleasant was divine retribution for human sinfulness, which originated when Adam and Eve were cast out from God's paradise for their sin of eating from *the tree of knowledge*.

But throughout history some of the sinful continued to nibble at the fruit of the tree of knowledge, which had them applying logic and astute observation to phenomena and consequently discovering more about how the physical world works. In other words, they started practising science, which led them to develop better explanations and ways of doing things.

This process was slow to begin with, gained momentum, and then, in the last three centuries, grew exponentially until God's will is seldom invoked to explain why the photocopier isn't working. And when we get sick, we no longer pray or consult holy books, we seek science-trained doctors and use medications that are the products of scientific research by pharmaceutical companies.

All that accumulated science also led to the reinforcement of the notion of *free will*. These days *we* make the choices, not fickle gods. We endeavour to use *our* free will to engineer a good life for ourselves here on Earth, with a heavenly afterlife now merely an optional extra that fewer people consider worth the expense in time, money and restrictions to their lifestyles.

With an enhanced belief in free will came an increased abhorrence of slavery, since it involves the curtailment of *our* right to decide, to choose and fulfil *our* destiny, to develop *our* abilities and to live *our* lives, hopefully with dignity and meaning.

But how much free will do we really have?

How often are we unwittingly enslaved by others? How often are our thoughts and actions not wholly our own but strongly affected by the blind forces of evolution, which created our physicality and our emotional responses, and the invisible hand of our cultural context?

Since everybody's proclivities, histories and current circumstances are unique, I am unsure how best to explain the enslavement process at work in today's circumstances. The only solution that came to me was to describe the path I took in reaching my currently expanded view of the forces producing enslavement and our capacity to negate them by becoming masters of our thoughts and actions.

My first unwitting step towards this greater understanding was taken in my twenties when I read a short story by one of the legends of science-fiction, Robert A. Heinlein. Written circa 1954, it was called: *Logic of Empire* and was the last story in a collection titled, *The Green Hills of Earth*.

The plot starts with a fellow drinking in a bar and arguing with a friend over whether slavery existed in their advanced society. Next morning, nursing a hangover, he finds himself on a rocket-ship bound for the colony on Venus. He protests, but all the paperwork is correct and the only legal way of returning home is for him to pay for a return ticket. Unfortunately, he finds he has no money, and with no means of support, he is promptly arrested as a vagrant and is then "contracted" to a plantation owner, as an *indentured worker*. He became a slave, in all but name, and would remain so until he could save enough from his miserable wage to buy a ticket home.

Two things stayed with me from that story. Firstly, his fellow slaves, to gain temporary relief from their terrible reality, spent all their meagre wages getting high on the local moonshine.

Though technically having the means to free themselves, their need for some respite from their horrible lives ensured that they remained enslaved.

The protagonist was made of stronger stuff. He escaped and joined a band of escapees scratching a living as fugitives in the steamy swamps that surrounded the plantation. He was eventually rescued when his friends from Earth managed to track him down and pay for his ticket back to Earth.

The second, more startling, aspect of the story was the revelation that the plantation owner, the slaves' cruel master, was also unhappy. He too was stuck in that hellish jungle, forced to browbeat a bunch of recalcitrant workers. He was *compelled* to keep doing so by his desperate hope of earning sufficient profits to send his daughter to a good college back on Earth and thus give her a better life than the miserable one he was living.

Later on, I discovered Peter O'Donnell's Modesty Blaise novels. Modesty was a sort of female James Bond. They were terrifically entertaining page-turners and as such seemingly unlikely sources of intellectual stimulation, but wisdom lies in odd places and in all manner of people, real or imagined.

Last Day in Limbo, came out in 1976, though I read it in the early eighties and last returned to it in 2004, hence my recollection may lack accuracy. In essence, Modesty gets caught up in a bad guy's scheme to placate his mad old auntie. He allows her to live her fantasy as the queen of a slave plantation in the Central American jungle, with her slaves recruited from unwary foreign tourists.

They are mostly wealthy so their change from the privileged class to the lowest of the low makes for fascinating reading. Modesty is *saved by outside help*, (a recurring theme), in the form of her trusted lieutenant Willy Garvin. It's an action-packed story but the aspect that most impressed me was that once the slaves had given up hope of rescue, they radically edited their expectations and attitudes into new ways of seeing things that then allowed them to find scraps of happiness in their scant leisure time as an antidote to the drudgery of their daily routine. A similar situation to Heinlein's story but the implication stressed was that people can adapt to, and normalise, any situation, no matter how atrocious. The normalisation of "the way things are", especially when they are unjust and degrading, was a revelation I found scary then and more so now [1].

More recently I stumbled upon *A History of Nations: How Their Identities Were Forged* edited by Peter Furtado. It was a collection of essays, by locals, on aspects of their country's identity and the issues resultant from their history. It was a book that left two lasting impressions relevant to enslavement.

The Indian author noted, with a hint of dismay, how easily and for how long the British ruled India, with oh so few men, a few hundred thousand controlling hundreds of millions. The British did so by their studied use of the old *divide and rule* principle, aided by the help of millions of local *collaborators*, rich and poor.

The essay by the fellow from Ghana raised the embarrassing admission that the transatlantic slave trade was only made possible by the *complicity* of the leadership of his country's warring tribes, whose conflicts supplied the European slavers with their "human resources".

Finally, within the last year and a half, I came in contact with science-based insights into how the slave mentality can be induced, maintained and also *overcome*, courtesy of books by Daniel Kahneman [2] and Yuval Noah Harari [3].

It now seems to me that induction into modern slavery is through ignorance, naivety, isolation, timidity and lack of a strong, long-term vision. In short, we get conned into the slave-master arrangement.

We stay there from ignorance of palatable alternatives,

combined with a fear of retribution if we try to escape, fear of shattering our self-respect if we admit our mistakes, and the shame felt if our weakness and folly were to be revealed to friends and family. We are stuck unless trustworthy and non-judgmental outsiders arrive to help us break the chains, mental and physical, that enslave us.

Despite that article in *New Philosopher* and my sensitivity to the issue from books read, talk of slavery in Australia still seems unlikely to move many to action when so few of us feel it under our skin. Or perhaps we do feel it, but fail to recognise the feeling, or do but actively deny it.

Aussie workers may jokingly call themselves *wage slaves*. Unfortunately, it isn't a joke for the majority because very few of us are of such independent means that we can choose to work for free, work just for the pleasure, work simply to keep our minds occupied, or work because it is the only thing that gives our lives meaning.

It would appear that we are all to some degree complicit in our own economic subjugation. The sad thing is that so few of us use the means available to us to break free. Money and knowledge are the keys to doing so and, as an employee, we have access to both. Money is power but so too is knowledge.

We all have some choice, no matter how small, in how we choose to spend our meagre incomes. With each dollar saved, the boss's power correspondingly weakens. Increasing our knowledge, especially of the money-generating kind, can be bought at tertiary institutions or acquired *free* from colleagues, libraries, the internet, and from intelligent friends and strangers, who may be physical or found in the pages of books, fiction or non-fiction.

Just as freedom from alcohol addiction comes first in *recognising* the choking grip of the booze, so too is freedom from enslavement. Like the alcoholic, we too must first recognise that we are addicted to a dead-end job, abusive relationships or a failed idea.

Living requires doing. It is the nature of our doing and the thoughts we use to justify what we do that are critical. Sleep takes up about a third of our existence. Paid work, and the commuting to and from, takes up at least another third, though often considerably more. The remaining hours left are eaten up by things we *have to do* such as showering, personal grooming, dressing and undressing, going to the loo, procuring, preparing and ingesting food and drink, shopping, home maintenance, and so on. Hence, there is not much *free time* to do the things we really want to do, like socialise, surf the internet, relax, go on holidays, listen to music, pursue a hobby, go for a stroll, read a book and perhaps, do a bit of serious thinking.

The portion of life *not* taken up by sleep and work is where enslavement in its many guises can be fought, and won, because that is where we have most freedom of movement.

Enslavement in the workplace, in all its subtle forms, is harder to admit to and overcome because we need the money. And work, to varying extents, gives us meaning and status. This is especially important for men, who have an unconscious understanding of the social power that comes with being successful and *a good provider*. Women folk are apparently particularly favourable towards the good providers!

If we desire proof of the importance of work, and the money it provides, all we need do is ask a colleague to join the union, or, God forbid, help start one in the workplace. There is an indescribable silence and blankness in the face and eyes, which communicates a vivid tale of their *fear* of upsetting their bosses, their chosen slavers.

Their attitude is understandable after decades of media campaigning denigrating unionism so that today most employees accept the seeming truth of: *if you don't like it here, quit and get a better job*, and reject the veracity of the unionist motto of: *united you bargain, divided you beg*. The ruling elites, working through our bosses, are controlling us just as the British did in India, with the tried-and-true strategy of *divide and rule*.

So don't be fooled, we are *wage slaves*, whether blue-collar or white, with the white-collar slaves the harder done by because, being on salaries, they have the joy of overtime hours being "unpaid". And no matter how much we enjoy our work, and I am one of the lucky ones who does, mostly, if we are not of independent means then we *work because we must*. We are *forced* to work by the invisible hand of economic necessity.

And like the plantation owner in *Logic of Empire*, even the rich and mega-rich often fail to break the chains of that *compulsion to work*. Rupert Murdoch still runs his media octopus at eighty-eight. He apparently can think of no better ways to spend his time and billions. Many millionaires and probably most billionaires are drunk on wealth, and the power and status it gives them.

Sadly, the world suffers because they are reluctant to *go on the wagon*, to rein in some of their *slavery to prestige*, and do something kinder for themselves, their families, their employees and the rest of humanity. Even Bill Gates' tremendous philanthropy has little impact upon his status as one of the richest persons on the planet. Many other wealthy people give generously, but, like Bill Gates, it is usually done publicly, with the unstated agenda of gaining societal kudos. And few wealthy philanthropists actively campaign *against* the structural inequalities built into our laws and social attitudes that allow the few to unfairly command the resources of the many.

For me the most sinister aspect of the hidden slavery in our lives was flashed across the silver screen in the James Bond movie, *The World Is Not Enough*. In it, the central character, the heiress of an oil billionaire, resumes her life after being kidnapped and held for ransom by the bad guy. She then creates havoc because she is secretly enamoured to her kidnapper and former persecutor. The movie hinges upon a sickening aspect of the slave-master interaction known as the *Stockholm syndrome*, in which the slave comes to love their cruel controllers for the memory of the moments when their pain and suffering was eased by them.

The syndrome is an evil manifestation of humanity's flawed method of thinking, from the lazy use of the *peak-end rule* first elucidated by Daniel Kahneman [1]. In summary: we do not remember all that we experience, we remember only our highs and lows, with pleasant feelings not as memorable as reductions in pain. And recent memories are more influential than older events. Thus, the kidnapped girl forgot the pain of her long imprisonment and maltreatment and only remembers the peak experiences of the lessening of pain, especially the last action, when the bad guy releases her.

Those two pieces of memory obliterate all rational measures of her experience, which was ninety-nine per cent terrible and attach the crumbs of non-pain to her tormentor, making him the man *who stuck by her* and who caused the end of her torture. She then blamed her pain on her parents and the authorities for not ending it earlier.

In a way, most of us have a *mild* case of the *Stockholm syndrome* because we identify with the ethos and ideologies of our rulers. We have swallowed uncritically the current dogma that *individuals* should be *free* to exercise their *free will* in *unfettered* free markets as the *only* way to heaven on earth.

We are not encouraged to see that our free will is mostly proscribed. It is easily hijacked by our flawed mental architecture and the influence of cultural pressure. That establishing a profitable business is only possible so long as it is not a threat to bigger competitors, once so, it is crushed or swallowed.

We are not reminded that *unfettered* market forces created the African slave trade in the past and the banking excesses that created the GFC, which still haunts us ten years on. Or that the slave trade was brought under control by *group action*, by governments *responding to society*. The current economic malaise lingers because governments and economists, mesmerised by free market fundamentalism, lack the will to think of alternative ideas and hence more effective remedies.

And in all stories of success, whether of a fictional hero, or in a true-life *rags-to-riches* biography, what is emphasised is the *individual's* brains, intelligence and/or strength, not the part that random luck played in their lives. As readers, we are complicit because we don't like to learn that those success stories were mostly down to luck because such an admission diminishes *our* own sense of control over our life.

The dogma of individualism is a corrosive fraud.

In reality, we exist in a society of *interdependent* individuals, who must respect each other's needs as much as our own, otherwise, the social contract that binds us unravels and results in the anarchy of every man for himself and winner takes all.

We have the power to see the reality of how the economy operates, to recognise our flawed decisions, to know we are going in the wrong direction, to know we are being taken for a ride by marketing managers into spending our hard-won cash on stuff we don't really need, cash, that accumulated, opens the gate to greater financial independence.

We all have the capabilities to recognise enslavement in others and ourselves. If we examine our relationships, fearlessly and honestly, we can develop the awareness to see the wrong thinking going on and thus find an escape, or renegotiate a mutually beneficial understanding. The same goes in our workplace.

Old style slavery is still with us, think of sex workers in

brothels, but our eyes need to be opened to the *shadow slaves*, such as workers on 457 visas or similar, and workers too scared to join a union. Outside the workplace, we have some options for improving life for those on the inside. We can change things by voicing our concerns about their situation, by spending our money so that we don't support inhumane businesses, and by voting for politicians with more enlightened views on employment.

It is in the realm beyond the office block or factory that the greatest gains can be made to reduce enslavement, especially our particular brand of it. It starts when we become aware when we are thinking: *that we must not upset others, that we must behave, that there are no alternate ways of doing things.*

Must, should, I cannot, I have to, there is no alternative, externally or internally, are the internalised *words of enslavement* that bend us into compliance. Only once we learn to recognise and question these incantations will we gain greater control over our destiny. Once free of these words we can face unpleasant truths, work within the realities of being flesh and blood humans, and from there have a better chance to enjoy a life in which we truly exercise the limited free will granted by biology and culture.

Gaining relative freedom requires *work* of a different kind. We need to work on our knowledge base, on our understanding of how we think, of who benefits from our attitudes. We must recognise that freedom from enslavement can be gained with the help of outside forces but it will reoccur if we don't develop the knowledge needed to more fully and more wisely exercise our free will, which, with practise, we will use to better effect.

§

After thoughts:

In the weeks since finishing the above essay I realised there were other aspects to slavery that needed consideration.

Slavery, in all its normal forms, is a *parasitic arrangement* in which the slaver, whether a person or a thought pattern, lives off and controls the *host's* mind.

There are many parasitic arrangements in the natural world that appear to shed new light upon the human form of parasitism.

Ebola virus could be considered the ultimate slaver. This mindless chunk of protein and nucleic acids, by chance circumstance, wheedles its way into a victim, man or ape, highjacks the cellular biochemistry and unleashes a hell of haemorrhaging, fever and then death. It doesn't care. It gets what it wants, reproduction, and then moves on to the next unlucky host.

There are many other such disease-causing microbes whose wish is to abuse our bodies for their own unexamined life's purpose: reproduction. But it is in the interests of both parasite and host to come to a more sustainable arrangement than the deal offered by Ebola, because killing the victim lessens the chances of further reproduction. Keeping the host-slave, alive and functioning is better for both and evolutionary pressures generally lead in that direction. The result is that less drastic arrangements eventuate, the bacterium or virus uses the victim, gets what it wants, reproduction, but with the bonus of the victim surviving to become a vehicle of contagion and available for re-infection.

And there are some parasites, like hookworms, which, though causing a little anaemia, are mostly a minor problem in healthy individuals. On the plus side, they benefit their hosts by stimulating their immune systems to such heights that they gain increased resistance to further hookworm infections with the bonus of greater resistance to a wide range of more dangerous infective agents. Thus, overall, the hookworm, actually makes most of their hosts healthier!

I recently learned in a news bulletin about a particular strain of the cold virus that induces an unexpected and wonderful response. In fighting the cold virus, the immune cells gain the ability to recognise some types of cancers previously unrecognised. Those cancer cells are duly attacked and the cold victim becomes the *victor* over their cancer!

These developments and others had me thinking that I may have missed the possibility that enslavement, in its many forms, isn't *all* bad, *all* the time.

In *Survival of the Nicest* Stefan Klein suggests that sustainable societies need a small portion of selfish, uncooperative and predatory or parasitic persons in them to "immunise" their members from incursions by predatory rival societies or the birth, amongst them, of practitioners of new anti-social schemes and scams.

Perhaps, if we find ourselves enslaved, as a wage-slave, an abused spouse, or obsessively attached to an attitude that is poisoning our relations with the majority of society, we might think of our situation as being equivalent to being afflicted by a parasite.

The next step is to decide whether we are up against Ebola, hookworms, or a strain of cold that offers a cure for more pressing insecurities and worries.

If we face the human incarnation of Ebola, our only chance lies with getting outside help. That is where we must place our every waking thought.

If we face lesser parasitic people or ideas, we have more options, and more to gain from the things we learn during our resistance efforts, which hopefully will lead to an easier form of enslavement, analogous to the hookworm situation, or a complete release from it in the same way the cold cured the cancer.

Once our form of enslavement is fully comprehended, we can then start asking ourselves the questions that will lead to a better future, questions such as:

Are there any benefits accruing from my time as a wage-slave in my current job?

Am I learning anything that can help me escape and find a less onerous way to finance my life?

It is in the best interests of a parasite to keep its host alive. That fact gives some leverage to the host (wage-slave) that can be used to manipulate the parasite's (boss's) behaviour, so why not investigate how best to use that fact to quietly push back and possibly gain the upper hand?

Is the lifestyle I seek, realistic, sustainable and truly one that is worth the toil? If not, are my foolish wants contributing to my enslavement? Can I change my wants into what I really need and, in doing so, find greater freedom of movement?

Biology shows us that enslavement has its nuances.

We need to see them, learn from them, and then use our fuller understanding to reduce or escape our subjugation and live a better life.

---

1   This issue is the focus of my essay *That's Just the Way It Is*
2   *Thinking, Fast and Slow* by Daniel Kahneman
3   *Homo Deus* and *Sapiens* both by Yuval Noah Harari

23. Understand

A few years back I reflected upon the aftermath of attending my father's funeral in an essay entitled: *Big Hands*.

I liked my dad. Very much. During my twenties when I returned home to study for my degree, I was privileged to have been able to share time and ordinary tasks with him. I was even dimly aware of my appreciation of our time together.

Later, in my early thirties, back in Sydney but in the process of escaping that life to head west to face a new and uncertain one, I, during that escape, was momentarily back home and in the briefest of moments, in an empty paddock with the sky as our only witness, my dad and I shared the rarest of events: a father and son, stripped of roles by tears that momentarily dissolved all barriers to understanding. We were for that briefest of time *brothers*.

Decades later, and several years after his funeral, I wrote *Big Hands*, but whilst typing the word "brothers", a ripple of uncertainty had passed through me. It was ignored and then forgotten. Until recent years.

Sadly, I should have written: *like brothers should be*.

Listening to other people's stories, and knowing my history with my siblings, it appears *fraternity* is a mostly bankrupt concept – that brotherly and sisterly love seems too often destined more to strangers than siblings.

Don't get me wrong, all my siblings are decent people. People I have attempted, over the decades of separation, to keep in contact with. In some cases, I spent years either happily cohabiting or enjoying time in their company. Thus, my relations with them have been better than most.

But as they will probably attest, all those minor quirks of character that in earlier years were easily ignored or forgiven, seem to have grown ever larger and more bothersome with age and practice. The end result is that family relationships often wither or turn sour.

When I look in the mirror each morning to inspect the ravages of time, who do I see? It's certainly not the person most others see.

One of the tragedies of being human is that we see and judge others, but rarely fully see or truthfully judge ourselves. The person I see in the mirror is like a résumé: all the good bits remembered and the weaknesses downplayed or denied.

As the years tick by, we develop our characters and perhaps achieve some level of self-awareness. Hopefully too we learn who and what we are, what we can and can't do, what we want and possibly what it is we need to do to ensure a happy ending to our life.

The same process occurs with our understanding and possible appreciation of the people we spend our lives with. But too often we are disappointed. Those people, who seemed interesting at first, usually turn out to be as ordinary and flawed as everyone else. We face two responses to this disappointment: understanding and acceptance, or dismissal and then an endless and futile search for perfection.

True friendship takes time. It only arrives when we realise that we substantially know the person, and *still like them*.

I currently have troubles with several of my siblings caused largely by the seduction by the peak-end rule [1]. They remember a recent disappointment, and being human and innately more sensitised to the negative, that recent disappointment overrules a long and mostly happy past.

I recognise the ramifications of the adage about choosing our friends but not our relatives, and yet still believe family members should endeavour to make the effort to get along. I have in my bumbling way attempted to do so and will continue to do so in spite of recent setbacks. I find it a sad embarrassment to have to admit to not being on speaking terms with anyone, let alone my close relatives.

Perhaps our culture's individualistic indoctrination hinders kinder interpersonal relationships. The U.S.A. has *e pluribus unum* emblazoned on their Great Seal and their one-dollar bill. *Out of many, one,* with the implication being, *in unity there is strength*. A strange dichotomy for the land of the rugged individual.

What a shame it is that our current societal attitudes, heavily infected by American-style individualism, no longer seem to encourage family members to see the benefits of sticking together, of seeing the benefit of acting as one. I was sensitised to this disappointment when I recently read about a family that did stick together: the Rothschild clan. They are one of the wealthiest extended families in Europe. In reading their history we see the dividends to be accrued from a majority of siblings, cousins and other relations putting aside their differences to work for the collective good.

When family members go their individual ways, successful lives often will result. And, in some family cultures, this is the only option because they impede rather than nurture the positive development of our potential. But one wonders how much wealthier and hence easier people's lives would be, if families worked together to build a collective inheritance, instead of each generation starting from scratch.

Money isn't the measure of all things and doesn't necessarily equate with happiness but it certainly gives us more options and lessens the grip of enslavement to employment.

Perhaps the cult of individualism has gone too far and has

reached the point where its ubiquity encourages us to inflate the value of our opinions and disparage those of others.

I remember once being openly accused of being *opinionated*. Two things struck me at the time: one, was that I was unsure which opinion in particular they were complaining about, and two, that they had just passed an *opinion* about me and could not recognise their own hypocrisy.

The thing is, we constantly make opinions. It is how we make sense of the world. We see, hear, feel, remember and think about what is happening, and then, despite lacking all relevant information or an infinite capacity to understand, produce an *opinion* as to how to respond. Affront often happens, not because an opinion is made known, but because it is not *our* cherished one!

With regard to my strained relations with some of my siblings, Georges Simenon, through his character Detective Chief Inspector Maigret, has provided me with a possible solution. Maigret tries to espouse a creed I find worthy: <u>understand</u>, *and judge not*.

Understanding my own attitudes and from there my actions and expressed opinions is my first task. From lack of access to honest dialogue, it will be harder to fully comprehend the attitudes of my temporarily estranged siblings. But hardest of all will be the not judging. I suspect I can aim for no more than to judge with greater kindness and humility.

I also believe that, like most other aspects of human behaviour, there are some deep biological underpinnings to the rivalries and antagonisms between myself and some of my siblings. Two ideas have recently occurred to me.

Genetically, incest leads to bad outcomes. The Pharaohs of ancient Egypt and the Inca kings of Peru, and probably others, thinking themselves gods, got the notion that they shouldn't dirty their purity by mating with the common folk and at one stage deliberately practised incest, with disastrous results.

Our evolved history wisely gave us a strong revulsion to intimate relations with siblings and close relatives. So, perhaps poisonous sibling rivalries are an aspect of an overactive incest taboo?

The other bit of information stumbled on was that pelicans lay two eggs, one always hatches before the other, and if it survives and grows, having a head start, it becomes bigger than its sibling. Food is scarce for both parents and offspring and so, in a matter of days, the firstborn pushes its rival from the nest to die, and in doing so assures its own survival by being better fed. Do we humans have some pelican genes being expressed when we see and feel sibling rivalries?

Competition for the attention and affection of our parents is very real, especially before puberty, after which we are more capable of looking after ourselves. And once independent financially, our parents are no longer essential to our survival. Like the selfish, first-hatched pelican, we can safely eject them from our lives.

I am probably being simplistic and unkind to my siblings, myself, and my fellow humans, but I wonder by how much?

Like my siblings, I am not all-seeing or all-knowing. I am human as they are, and probably suffer from a few "pelican genes" stoking my annoyance with some of them.

But I cannot directly rewire their brains, or anyone's, for enhanced interpersonal regard. I can only rework my mental software to ease my disappointment and perhaps reach the point where I can be like Detective Chief Inspector Maigret and *understand* to such a degree that I can leave praise or condemnation to other powers.

[1] For more information on the topic read: *Thinking, Fast and Slow* by Daniel Kahneman (in detail) and *Homo Deus* by Yuval N. Harari (in summary)

24. How Few

At work, on my tiny patch of the bench stretched along the window overlooking the street and park beyond, are a handful of objects.

Two take pride of place: first, is a photo of my wife, taken at Green's Pool on the south coast; the other is an A4 colour poster I created back in the nineties as an antidote to an unforeseen personal drama, which had forced my wife and I to seek answers to how best to live our lives thereafter. Using the premise that, *if you do what you have always done, you get what you always got*, we modified our lifestyle and tried all sorts of things, one of which was meditation, which then led to a brush with Buddhism.

Buddhism aims to end suffering. The framed A4 poster on my workbench was a Buddhist affirmation, there to remind me of the way to do so, it reads: *seek wisdom, practise compassion, live in awareness.*

Naturally I have given those three directives much thought and realise they are better undertaken when the order is reversed.

The first step to the happier life is a greater and more accurate awareness of reality. This increases our knowledge base to the point of being more able to be compassionate to others because we better understand the causes of their and our behaviours.

Increased knowledge, and the compassion it induces, then makes wiser attitudes and actions more attainable.

It is wise actions that are the tricky bit.

If finding and using one's wisdom is the way to end suffering in our life, and hopefully in those around us, then the great philosophers, past and present, should all have led pain-free and blissful lives. But it doesn't seem to be the case. This poses the question of whether wisdom, in whatever form, is sufficiently achievable to be worth the effort.

In my previous job, I covered the walls of my shabby office overlooking the rear car park with the above-mentioned poster and a host of others, all with similar inspirational themes.

One of that collection had, as a backdrop, a sunny beachside scene, early morning, with a few joggers to give it a human focus. The caption at the bottom, in bold flowing script, was provided by England's first poet Laurette, John Dryden (1631 to 1700) and read:

Look around the habitable world, how few, know their own good, and knowing it, pursue.

My current tripartite workspace poster's exhortation to live in awareness also reminds me of John Dryden's observation of human nature.

We are born a blank slate, bursting with many potentialities. We get an education. The institutional side allows us to make a living. But how to live within the restrictions of a human body and get along with other humans is left to chance.

And chance is an inconsistent teacher and hence our wisdom, like science, is never complete. It is always a *work in progress*. We thus live frustrating lives having to make decisions constantly on the basis of incomplete information, from which our faux pas, our soured relationships, poor investment choices and a myriad of other suboptimal actions arise.

Wiser answers to our dilemmas are best found in a sceptically examined awareness of the external world, as well as regularly re-assessing the "facts" underpinning our own viewpoints. The relative wisdom of our actions then rests upon the quantity, breadth and *quality* of our acquired knowledge.

If we start the quest for truth earlier, are brave enough to ask the difficult questions earlier, face the unsettling answers earlier, then the sooner will our actions display greater wisdom and guide us to a more satisfying and purposeful life.

The wisest keep in view human fallibility and consequently have life purposes that are stated simply to make them easier to follow and hence achieve. Being a decent human being is my life's goal.

Over the years, my efforts to become more aware of reality have led to greater compassion and episodes of greater measures of wisdom.

These days I am beginning to see myself as *one of the few*, who, *know their own good and knowing it, pursue*. But one who knows that my "own good", my happiness, can't be bought at the cost of other people's. That the "good life" I pursue will be a symbiosis between myself and the many people I impinge upon.

25. Responsibility

Typos, mangled spellings and missed words are the bane of every writer and proof-reader. We do our best, but to err is human and thus errors slip through – mistakes that I embarrassingly have to take most of the responsibility for. Most, but not all.

Dear reader, I plead that there are mitigating circumstances behind my *written* errors, number one of which is that English is inherently difficult to spell. I blame the French for that.

Though sadly for me I can only half exonerate myself because half of my ancestry hails from Scandinavia. My father was Danish, and the Danish, Norwegians and Swedes collectively were known as the Norse, who made up those raiding and pillaging Vikings of the Dark Ages.

Some of those Norsemen settled on the northwest coast of France, in an area appropriately named Normandy. They settled down with the natives, took up the local language and that would have been that, but for William of Normandy deciding to become William the Conqueror. In 1066 at the battle of Hastings, he defeated the English king, Harold, whose forces had been wearied from battling other Norsemen further north. William and his nobles moved in and started running the show. Which is when the spelling dramas started.

William and his cronies spoke and wrote French, which is a language whose spelling, in my opinion, has only the barest of connection to how it is spoken. Now I'm no linguist but most of those hard to spell words that we all struggle with are usually inherited from William the Conqueror's lot. I'll give a couple of examples: ron day voo (rendezvous), on ree (Henri).

If we'd stuck to our Anglo-Saxon roots, to the language of the peoples from northern Germany, then we would be spelling as the Germans do, who, having settled upon an agreed sound to be allocated to each letter, stick by the rule of spelling as it is spoken. Hence, they have few problems with their written language, apart from the ridiculous length of some of their words.

The French spoken by William's ruling elite and their successors infected our language with silent letters, strange letter combinations and even stranger sounds indifferently attached to them. Their influence has given us the mess we have to write with today. Thus, at least a sliver of the responsibility for my spelling errors can be unloaded onto William the Conqueror's shoulders.

But that's the slippery thing about responsibility. How does one apportion it in any meaningful way. For instance, who is responsible for the typo in the latest version of Australia's fifty-dollar note?

Some sharp-eyed coin collector spotted it, to the left of Edith Cowan's shoulder in the shading under the picture of our *parliament* building (parl*i*ament being a French-derived word spelt with an unnecessary "i"). That shading is not shading but our first female parliamentarian's maiden speech, in tiny letters. At end of the first line of it, the word *responsibility* is missing the last "i". There were forty-six million of those notes put into circulation, which makes it one of the few times that a typo can be given a precise dollar value, in this case fifty multiplied by forty-six million!

It was a mistake I only found out about when discussing, over the breakfast table, the changes in the new fifty-dollar notes I'd obtained from the ATM the day before. My wife immediately consulted her iPhone, to find any news items about the changes, and came across the article exposing the embarrassing typo. An error that I hope the Governor of our Reserve Bank – the man responsible for the quality of our currency – had a good laugh over, before undertaking some kind-hearted measures to correct it in the next printing run.

Which brings me back to responsibility.

How much responsibility do we accept or shirk?

How much of the good things in our lives can we honestly take the credit for and equally, how much of our misery do we truly own?

And how should we respond to the perceived successes and failings of others?

The answers to all the above lie in how aware we are of the biological, physical and cultural restraints upon our freedom of thought and action.

Suffice to say, the more we look at those constraints, the humbler we become of our achievements and those of others, and, hopefully, the more forgiving we are of our shortcomings and theirs.

In regard to those in charge of the printing of our currency, I trust they too have a well-developed understanding of the constraints upon perfection, and consider that typo on the new fifty-dollar bill as both something to be learned from and lived with. That, rather than instigate an unnecessary $2.3 billion recall, they allow those notes the blessing of being forty-six million potential collector's items!

26. Cogitations on Entertainment

In the olden days, on Friday evenings, my dear wife and I would go to the local video shop in search of entertainment to cure the malaise brought on by the grind of the working week – something engaging, but not too hard on the brain. It wasn't an easy task.

There was so much choice, and yet, so little.

Almost all their selection was churned out by Hollywood's dream factories, with a smattering from the British, the occasional Aussie movie and rarest of all, foreign movies with subtitles.

The imbalance in the origins of their wares was equally reflected in the genres. The vast bulk of the video covers displayed, in garish colours and weaponry, the violent nature of their contents. A distant second were comedies and romantic comedies, mainly American and hence mostly forgettable. The rest was a smattering of kiddie shows, cartoons, documentaries and plain romances, a small segment of which dropped much connection with love in favour of unadorned biological reproductive activities.

The video store owners were in it for the money and hence needed a good understanding of what their customers wanted.

On reflection, my curiosity was piqued by two aspects of the videos they offered up for rental. Firstly, had they got the mix right? Was the video store's collection a true reflection of the hierarchy of human motivations in regard to what we find entertaining?

Secondly, if they were correct, what did it say about us, and what can we do with that challenging truth? Does our entertainment menu read: violence (overt, threatened or its aftermath) as the main meal, with side dishes of laughter and bonking?

Robert Ardrey hints at the origins of our violent nature in his book *The Social Contract*, which can easily be confirmed by considering the prominence to which violent events are given in our newspapers and news programs. But most convincing of all is an *honest* look in the mirror. How often have thoughts of violent retribution for being wronged passed through the mind of that creature locked safely behind the glass?

Ardrey argues that our forest dwelling ape ancestors did not start hunting to compensate for less leaves and fruit when their forest lifestyle was upset by the drying climates of the Oligocene and beyond. Apparently, our distant ancestors became hunters whilst enjoying the lush climates and vegetation of the previous epoch, the Miocene.

Why did those distant forebears take up the hazards of hunting? His suggestion is that the nutrient density of meat wasn't the primary reason. They started killing mostly to cure boredom, *for entertainment*, for the buzz, for the same hormonal exhilaration felt by today's crowd at the football match when victory is near.

Directing our violent cure for boredom outwards, towards rival bands or prey animals, provided us with both improved nutrition *and* helped strengthen internal tribal bonds. That enhanced bonding then greatly improved our co-operation and hence effectiveness at obtaining and sharing food, as well as defending our territory from rivals.

This use of violence against others to solve boredom also worked with other frustrations. Its broader application can be glimpsed in the untrained behaviours of toddlers, who resolve their disputes most often by brute force, pushing and shoving first, failing that biting, kicking and punching. Unsupervised and given weapons, who knows what would be possible?

Our violent adulthood is revealed by the statistics on violent death in various societies [1], with a violent end much more likely within the rustic charm of a hunter-gatherer's camp than in a modern city. This is true despite the news media bombarding us with items showing humanity's worst side, which, if were the *whole* truth, would have us paranoid from the *perceived* likelihood of being bashed to death in our homes, or mugged walking to the shops. Whether here in Australia, or in a foreign inner-city ghetto, few people are forced to constantly go armed and in company, no matter how bad a city's reputation.

Civilisation and civil behaviours arose and then flourished when our violent inclinations were significantly domesticated. How was it done?

Large cities can only exist if huge numbers of strangers can be made to forget their fear of those not of their tribe or reference group. Not just forget that fear, but actually co-operate, however grudgingly, with those strangers, for the collective good.

It seems to have been achieved through evolutionary pressures modifying our genetics that then allowed for the development of cultures that over-rode the fear of those not closely related to us – culture being that invisible anthology of laws, customs, religious beliefs, shared taboos and social expectations, all of which must be enforced if hordes of disparate humans are to function together in any lasting way.

The key word is *enforced*. If the rules, however manifested, are not enforced then that invisible social glue breaks down and we find ourselves reverting to a prior state: the savagery of every man for themselves. Without sufficient *group consciousness*, the family, the workplace, the city, or the nation eventually collapses.

We need to fear the thrill-seeking murderous ape-man lurking within our DNA even if it's not something we particularly want to own up to, but denial is a poor option.

The first step is early recognition of anger, then learning delaying strategies, one of which is questioning whether we have *all* the facts, which is unlikely, and if we do have sufficient information, have we explored *all* the possible responses, to cover the immediate situation *and* the long-term?

Again, it's not necessarily easily done, but with practice we can more effectively use our minds to find better ways to use anger's energy to fire our imaginations for solutions that benefit us and the rest of society. Taming our internal savage is very much achievable.

So, it would appear that video store owners have got it right: action and violence is what we find *entertaining*! Is it similar to our fascination with fire? We fear it but are still fascinated by it, perhaps because we realise that wisely directed the use of fire opens up a range of beneficial possibilities – in fact commanding fire is what made civilisation physically possible because how else would we have invented pottery, bricks, mortar, metalworking and everything else that flowed from those inventions.

It remains humbling to admit to being entertained by news footage of a brawl in the crowd at the basketball or the football match. That, of our collection of DVDs, those we watch and enjoy the most are *murder* mysteries, *action* movies and TV shows, be it James Bond or our current viewing: *The Professionals*, an action TV show from the late seventies.

But as I have mentioned in other essays, this vicarious violence possibly has its upside as it seems to exercise our aggressive side in the controlled safety of our loungeroom, rather than finding its expression with physical violence towards an annoying supervisor, or engaging in the catharsis of a bit of road rage against the guy who cuts in front of us at the lights.

But, like most things, action shows, movies and games can be overdone. Too much can desensitise us to the consequences of real-world violence. And if too much time is spent in the virtual world, then it becomes more difficult to distinguish fantasy from the reality. And, there is nothing pleasant about being on the receiving end of actual violence.

I am lucky that my inner homicidal maniac is a relatively puny and manageable beast. But what of the other adult passion hinted at in the video shop, our sexual urges?

There are sound evolutionary survival reasons why fornication is fun [2]. It certainly seems to be the bedrock upon which much adult male thinking rests.

As a young man sexual desire was always annoyingly and often embarrassingly close to the surface of my waking thoughts. One of the few benefits of age is that the sexual obsessions of youth subside to allow other thoughts to dominate for longer, which is great for productivity. And yet no man wants the mind of a eunuch, no matter how potentially peaceful or productive. In fact, men of any age with very low testosterone levels complain of being listless, depressed and lacking the joy of living.

Young men are not the only ones keen on copulating – the young ladies are as well, but their enthusiasm seems more often expressed in circumspect ways, and appears to fluctuate in sync with the rhythm of hormonal tides.

Being a reproductive woman seems to be a rollercoaster of moods that must be hard to bear at times. I wonder if the ride is too often disappointing or overly embarrassing. Do the heights compensate for the lows? Are postmenopausal women happy or sad at their lessening of libido? (Someday I may be illuminated on these topics but at present I must guess at them from my limited experiences and research.)

Sexual desire is nature's way of ensuring the species mates and reproduces. It need not be joyful. In many animal species it can be downright painful. Luckily for humans it *can be,* and one hopes, should be a shared ecstasy, with the biochemistry of those *peak* moments [3] helping to reinforce a couple's regard for each other, which hopefully extends towards any children they produce.

Pornography is all about the *bodily thrill* of the chase and the climax, whilst romance concerns itself with the discovery of attraction, physical and *psychological,* and culminates in a happy and mutual commitment. As far as survival of the species, of the couple and of their progeny, romance is the genre that needs to be encouraged because it engenders consideration of the other, of the spouse, of the kids and perhaps extends its harmonious reach towards work colleagues and the public at large.

Bonking, doing what comes naturally, needs little further instruction or encouragement. It is thus pleasing to see that romance is more plentiful in the video store than pornography, but disappointing that it is so outnumbered by murder and mayhem. It is also noteworthy that it was undoubtedly the ladies that hired out the romance titles, not their mates. Men seem either naturally, or through socialisation, reluctant to show their romantic side in public, which in my mind is a pity because I suspect society would be the better off if this were not so.

That men publicly appear insensitive to romance is probably fixable. But in our current culture, other men, and women, expect men to be men. Apparently, few women want a wimpy mate. She secretly selects a male capable of defending her physically if the need arises, to have the "go" to be a good provider, and yet paradoxically wants him gentle enough to be manageable at home. It is difficult task, to be tough and gentle, given the burden of male hormonal responses and socialisation, which is all the more reason why romance needs to be encouraged in the male with constant but subtle training.

Louis L'Amour, my favourite writer of Westerns, in a way does this with his action-packed stories in which the guy gets the girl in the end. The critical thing is that their relationships are always about a *strong* woman and a strong man and, most importantly, of their mutual respect for each other. His stories end with the couple going off *together*. And if the man leads the way, it's because the lady lets him. His women are not doormats, they are powers to be reckoned with. That's what I like about them and, with book sales of over two hundred million, it seems plenty of other men agree with me!

But, when one looks at the statistics concerning sexual crimes, one wonders if my Y chromosome wants me to be a violent sexual predator. That I am not I can thank my lucky stars for not possessing such a Y but one muted by other genes and a civilised upbringing. But as a man I have to consider its possible thuggish nature and use its power for "good not evil" as they say in the comic books.

Though we mustn't joke because we do not know in what extreme circumstances our primitive instincts may find expression, in ways regrettable and unforeseen.

But women murder and do cruel things too, so no one is exempt from the need to be vigilant in regard to controlling savage responses inherited from our evolutionary past. We all must learn to recognise when they attempt to hijack us into doing things against our long-term interests.

This brings me to the other genre, underrepresented in the video shop and elsewhere, and that is laughter, preferably *with* people not *at* them.

I don't like people laughing at me. It's a form of bullying, a mental mugging, and as such can only be endured. It certainly should not be encouraged because it kills respect for, and any future co-operation with, the perpetrators. Revenge will rear its ugly head and trouble will be on the cards. And like most behaviours, if one doesn't like being on the receiving end, one shouldn't dish it out.

Healthy humour seems to be confined to those rare circumstances when both sides of the transaction have the flexibility of viewpoint to see the joke, to see the ridiculous side of the situation.

Zealots of any persuasion can't laugh much and never at themselves. And it's not just zealots who don't smile with kindness. Those with fragile egos and unexamined opinions that break under questioning also find it hard to see the absurd.

Laughing at overinflated ideas that don't stand up to scrutiny is one way society avoids the calamities resultant from delusional and dogmatic thinking. Laughing at our shared human foibles, at our *serious* regard for *trivialities*, at our fumbling mistakes, is a healthy way of keeping our feet on the ground when our glorious self-image ascends into the clouds.

Sadly, it seems recognising all the silliness in the world is becoming a lost art. I for my part am making the effort to see my ridiculous side and that of the world around me. It's a pity fewer people appear not to be doing likewise. Where are the modern-day Monty Pythons? Has the humourless credo of overblown political correctness become a terminal state of mind?

A flexible and forgiving outlook that engenders innocuous chuckles is also the mindset that reduces violent solutions from springing so readily to mind.

Lovemaking with gentle humour for when the timing is off, or awkwardness happens, is a lot more forgivable and fun than taking the whole embarrassing business too seriously. Loving a person with mutual good humour is hence a more sustainable pastime than loving someone with a fragile ego and little regard for any but themselves.

The frustrations of living combined with our propensity for choosing the easy violent solution to problems will continue to make vicarious violence a favoured pastime. Vicarious violence lessens the need for the real thing, which is good. But I suggest this is not enough; it needs to be tempered with a bigger serve of romance and good humour.

In our house, action movies are definitely countered by generous doses of romance and humour, practised daily. Maybe that's why, even in our advancing years, we retain that sparkle in the eye for the other.

Hence, for a happier life, we need to massage our attitudes, to lighten up, to loosen our death grip on opinions and dogmas, to admit that no one knows all the facts or all the reasons. Recognising these imperatives will not guarantee an end to misunderstandings and ill-informed offence being needlessly felt or given, but it provides much needed strength to our ability to be and act as civilised beings.

Seeking a fuller and more balanced understanding of reality is my suggestion for gaining the broader context needed for us to see the ridiculous side of things, as well as the appalling, in the *correct measure*.

An example of the benefits of that wider view of reality was stumbled upon when I read *The Continuum Concept* [4]. The book recounts the author's visit to the Yaquina Indians in the remote jungles in the mountains of Venezuela. The part that best demonstrated the outcomes of differing viewpoints was revealed in the author's description of their arduous journey by canoe to the Indian's village, which involved many portages where they had to manhandle the laden canoes up and around rocky sections.

The Americans cursed and swore at getting, muddy, wet, bruised and scratched each time they fell, which was often, but their native guides, suffering similarly, were laughing and joking at their own painful stumbling. They had a very different attitude to the same experience. Perhaps they realised that pain and suffering were a normal part of existence and chose to laugh not cry. That dichotomy has stayed in my mind ever since. Their lighter and more flexible viewpoint is one I believe worthy of emulating.

In Australia, for most of us, most of the time, life is pretty easy in comparison to many places on the globe. Though the difference between *us* and *them* is clarified brilliantly in Hans Rosling's book [1] with its cogent demonstration of the improving reality for most of humanity. There are still plenty of problems, socially and environmentally, but he opens our eyes to the truth of how the world is now, not thirty years ago. It provides us with an expanded worldview based upon facts not hearsay.

That broader, more accurate outlook gives scope for better outcomes, for seeing the silliness, for *kind* humour to flourish, from which happier and more forgiving interpersonal relationships have a chance to bloom.

Returning to what entertains us and why …

We have to live with our evolved motivations and mental architecture, and vicariously venting our frustrations and sexual desires through reading, or watching shows on the screen, has proved one effective strategy for keeping us civilised. But it is the broader, more realistic, honest, and factual view of the world that, if encouraged, has the greater value. More informed and kinder attitudes then dominate from which better decisions flow. Best of all, it also leads to more laughter in our lives.

In homage to this spirit of informed generosity and fun perhaps we should occasionally revisit Monty Python's *The Life of Brian*, or at least YouTube the last scene where, in the face of death, they start singing: *Always look on the bright side of life…*

It is a heroic song that I hope I am able to sing when I face, "the final curtain".

[1] *Factfulness* by Dr. Hans Rosling

[2] *Why Sex Is Fun (The Evolution of Human Sexuality)* by Jared Diamond, *Sex at Dawn (The Prehistoric Origin of Modern Sexuality)* by Christopher Ryan & Calilda Jethá and *How to Think More About Sex* by Alain De Botton.

[3] *Thinking, Fast and Slow* by Daniel Kahnemann (for detail) and *Homo Deus* by Yuval N. Harari (for the Peak/End rule summary).

[4] *The Continuum Concept* by Jean Liedloff.

27. The Wedding Photo

On my bedside table sits a time machine, though to the unimaginative it is merely a wedding photo. That framed six by four inch print is a time machine because through it I am able to travel back in time to a place twenty-nine years away. Unfortunately, the trip from there back to the present seems to have gone via a faulty matter transporter, a la *Star Trek*, because the present-day incarnations of the two people bear little resemblance to the prior versions. Increasingly I ask myself, who *are* those people? Where did they go? What connection do I have to them? What is left of them?

These questions are asked fleetingly and with good humour because both their present manifestations, though older, are still in pretty good shape. And since I know their histories, it's always the last question that lingers, the 'what is left', more so, 'the essence of what is left'?

The answer should be easy but the principal impediment has been my attempts to describe my wife's essence because of the *Mona Lisa smile* she wears. There she sits, frozen like an artist's model, watching me, pen in hand, micro-seconds before signing the marriage certificate. The photo allows the observer infinite time to study her features and capture the meanings of that moment.

As an aspiring writer I have pretentions of having some command of words, but an adequate description of her smile has, to date, eluded me. All I know is that, when I'm in bed, pillows plumped up, ready to read a few pages before sleep and I glance at that photo, my dear wife sitting beside me, also supported by pillows, is intrigued by my odd looks as I study it. Her usual response is to ask: "How is your girlfriend?" I turn and see the present, the sagging cheeks, the silver hair, the mischievous glint in her eye, and, reply truthfully: "Wonderful. She's still got it!" Smiles and sometimes kisses are exchanged, after which we stick our noses into our books and companionable silence prevails.

On some occasions, I have wondered if any thirty-year-old male could comprehend the idea that that silver-haired lady would be able to stir his male heart with romantic notions and admiration. How would that thirty-year-old react on seeing the present her stroll past? Would he notice her? Would he find her attractive?

These strange cogitations are driven by my continued puzzling upon the vexing topic of what forces rule over attraction and repulsion between people? Specifically, how do we choose our other halves, and which traits are the most endearing and enduring, the ones that keep us together, hopefully more from happiness than habit.

These are not easy questions to answer because interpersonal relations involve many variables that interact and change according to the specifics of the situation and hence are probably unanswerable with any accuracy. That said, I will be bold and suggest that biology is the area most likely to provide the best clues.

As we develop from child to adult and then into old age, at each stage our biology dictates the overriding emotional imperatives that direct our behaviours. Our desires at ten, twenty, thirty, forty et cetera are different, even though all will involve the needs of security, identity and stimulation [1] (as discussed in other essays).

Within broad parameters, we *act our age*, an aspect of which is that we prefer the company of people *of our age*, again within flexible limits, limits that expand and contract over the decades and differ between the sexes, for example, women tend to marry older men and men prefer younger women.

Back to the young me versus the old one. The younger version's biology finds procreation its core motivation and hence a female with baby-making capabilities is what his hormones want. Silver-haired, old ladies are not on his shopping list.

But once biology has narrowed the field, the specific causes of attractiveness get very complicated because our emotions are modified by innumerable factors that are usually situation-specific and affected by current mood, recent events, our history and our current physical state, whether healthy or hurting, all of which make understanding of our emotional response to people very much a mystery. Perhaps it's just as well, because that mystery adds spice to our life and stops it from being boring!

And yet I still wish to have some grasp of the essence of what lay behind my wife's enigmatic smile, eternalised in that wedding photo.

After much thought, I have reduced the magic of her expression down to three words: *amused, intelligent affection*.

When I look at her in the photo and then cast my eyes onto the present version, I give thanks that she had, and has, the intelligence to discern that most issues in our collective lives are small potatoes in the grand scheme of things and not worth sweating over. Instead, with a broad enough perspective, they should induce tears of laughter, not tears of disappointment, with the most important laughing being directed towards our own sillinesses. That attitude has prevailed throughout our marriage and enabled us to quickly iron out the scattering of dramas that befell us.

In fact, it was her logical presentation of a contrary viewpoint at our first meeting in the canteen at the mining camp that was the spark that had me contriving to see more of her. After that first chat, I walked away a little dazed, my mind wobbly from its stunning conclusion: "Wow! Here at last is a person I can honestly talk with and, even if we disagree, will remain on friendly terms with."

Later I found that her fact-based logic was coupled to a generosity of spirit that was happy to allow others to be as they are, so long as they caused her no harm, a grace that granted her another equally endearing quality: good humour.

Our life together has had few rough moments, mostly sparked by some misdemeanour or clumsiness on my part. All were resolved by my one hundred percent commitment to her and our combined ability to discuss matters civilly, even when the right words proved difficult to find.

Thus, our decades together have been filled with smiles and laughter, a kind-hearted laughter not possible in people whose egos and beliefs are so fragile that differing viewpoints are seen as threats, not wakeup calls for investigation and/or reassessment.

Armed with the ability to laugh, to see the other side, she seems to understand that we all get things wrong, and hence we need to have a more generous attitude towards our mistakes and those of others if we wish to live together amicably.

Looking back, I increasingly realise that having fun together was as important as our joint study of reality, be it in the books we read, or our discussions of world events and human relationships. That said, in writing these words, I now conclude that a sense of innocent fun is the more precious commodity.

If I were forced to write her obituary it would be short and concise: *she was intelligent, kind, <u>and</u> fun to be with*.

All of which explains why she became the sparkle in my eye,

why she remains so, and, I am quietly confident, why she will continue to be so until my last heartbeat.

---

[1] Motivations explained in *The Social Contract* by Robert Ardrey.

28. The Red Hibiscus

Having an inquiring mind and plenty of years under my belt to use it, I have unfortunately accumulated much knowledge that feeds my pessimism. One only has to watch a news bulletin or read a newspaper to keep the negative side of life fully charged. Now that I have retired and no longer suffer the frustrations of working for a large organisation, I have less *personal* exposure to the negative sides of humanity and hence am more able to absorb the positive. The rebalancing of my outlook received a leg up today (18th December 2019), for which I am most grateful.

Checking the scant offerings of our letterbox I discovered a Christmas card, which then combined later on with a surprise from a spindly young Hibiscus bush in our back garden, which, combined, instigated this essay of gratitude.

The Hibiscus had a troubled start. Initially placed too close to the shade of the back fence and next to a vigorous Grevillea, it suffered from a drastic lack of sunlight. The poor *photovore* starved. It barely survived. I moved it forward, trimmed the monster beside it, then manured, mulched and watered it until, *lo and behold*, it revived. And now at long last, it has begun to prosper.

The reason I was particularly keen to save that bush was due to its endearing habit of producing brilliant red flowers *one at a time*, and for one day only, after which they fell off and you had to wait, with delicious anticipation, for the next one.

In *The Science of Happiness*, Stefan Klein's investigations concluded that happiness is mostly found in anticipation and hope of achieving a desired goal and considerably less in the actual possession of our goals, giving scientific backing to Goethe's quip that life is "wanting and not succeeding, succeeding and not wanting".

If one needs further proof of our need for the anticipation of rewards, consider how we feel if we have nothing achievable worth doing, to having nothing in our life to look forward to. When that happens depression sets in, and, if no worthy goals can be found, a terminal decline of regret and dour resignation becomes the only anticipated outcome.

In contrast, that bush's occasional gift of a single magnificent red flower gives me the joyous anticipation of waiting for the next one and, equally important, the plant has reminded me that rare and precious gifts are valued in proportion to their scarcity and our physical and psychological need for them.

For us humans, living busy lives, usually separated in time and space from our friends and family, it is time and loving attention that are the rarest commodities we can give and receive, with time and attention one-to-one and physically touching being the most precious of all.

That Hibiscus's sparsely given floral gifts also allowed me to more fully see the gift of the time and effort taken by the sender of that Christmas card to firstly, buy it, then inscribe it with kind words, and finally, drive to a Post-box and post it.

So, on Christmas morning, when I go out to the backyard to water our garden beds, even if the Hibiscus has no flower to share, its being there will be pleasure enough. It will remind me of all the other aspects that bless my life, and, being human and ever forgetful of good events whilst loath to give up the bad, that plant's gift of appreciation is thus precious beyond measure.

§

No sooner had I been moved to write of the wisdom inspired by my Red Hibiscus than it gave me more to contemplate.

The next morning when I wandered out the back to perform my garden watering ritual, expecting to see it minus its single flower as was its usual custom, the plant surprised me. It sported two!

Was the bush laughing at me or setting me another riddle?

It certainly caused me to smile. Just when I thought I had something figured out, the universe provided a new permutation to tarnish my freshly minted but apparently flawed moment of wisdom.

Proof perhaps that God has a sense of humour? Or that the Deity dislikes pride and hubris and is determined to have me practise greater humility? Or was I simply being sent my next lesson?

I decided it was all three. Humbled, I reminded myself than life is for learning. The lessons never cease. All knowledge is a work-in-progress, just as I am a work-in-progress. Who I am now is not the man I used to be, nor the one yet to come. I am who I am right now. I make the most of my body's current abilities, limited as they are, and my current knowledge and attitudes inherited, absorbed and developed to date.

It's an annoying truth that I have great difficulty being comfortable with. My impermanence, my gradual, and sometimes not so gradual, physical and mental changes can at times be all too much. It is as if I am a shapeshifter in a sci-fi world populated by other shapeshifters where recognising and understanding my own changing shape and motivations is as difficult as recognising and understanding those in others who, likewise, are constantly morphing into someone else. Life appears to be like wrestling a greased pig – when we think we have a good grip upon understanding life's rules, it soon proves an illusion, and certitude of thought again slips from our fingers.

All very discouraging. But that appears to be our fate. Though it is a fate that need not be gloomy. Unlike the mythical Sisyphus, condemned for eternity to roll a boulder up a hill each day only for the boulder to roll back down at sunset forcing him to incessantly repeat the arduous task, we have some choice in the nature of the boulders we must struggle with, those problems life gives us to deal with [1].

Which brings me back to the problem imposed by the meaning to be gleaned from the appearance of two flowers.

The occasional single flower had reminded me to be more appreciative of rare and hence precious gifts. Two flowers? The thoughtfulness induced by the extra bloom had me glancing away from it only to be accosted by sight of the next-door neighbour's Apple Blossom Hibiscus. It is a huge bush encroaching onto our side of the fence, a bush decorated with masses of large pink blooms that *I take for granted!*

My bush was telling me I only had half the message. A good life is built around more than being appreciative of our special blessings, be they rare events or gifts, but more importantly, *all the good things* in our lives that are constantly there but are taken for granted, until the day they are gone. We then weep for having not appreciated them.

I looked at the neighbour's bountiful floral display, then to the clear blue sky heralding another day, then turned to our house, a humble but comfortable abode, inside which my dear wife was working on our breakfast. All these I experience every day, with variations, but how fully do I appreciate them?

For the most part I appreciate how lucky I am. My young Hibiscus was reminding me to review and expand my efforts in appreciating the many good aspects that form the backdrop of my life.

For that, once again, I give thanks to it.

[1] *The Subtle Art of Not Giving a F**k* by Mike Manson has more to say on the subject of choosing our problems. The book may prove useful, if you can stand the constant f word.

29. Für Elise

I'm no expert in assessing the quality of literature, art, or music. I measure their worth by their effect upon me and I prefer experiences that stir my emotions such that they move me forward, ones that stimulate my senses and engage my mind. Experiences which, when mulled over, create a wiser appreciation of that piece of encapsulated thought and its place in the tapestry of my existence.

A rather wordy, fuzzy introduction that will have to suffice until better words materialise. The reason for this missive?

Für Elise.

A three-minute bagatelle by Beethoven, written as a gift intended to win the heart of a lady. She rejected it and him. Consequently, that piece of music was not played until rediscovered forty years after his death. It is now considered by many to be an essential part of one's collection of classical music.

I stumbled upon it by accident. Doubly so.

Not having a huge budget to spend on music, most of my music CDs are sourced from op shops, which is where the CD containing *Für Elise* was found. That track was on a collection of Beethoven's shorter works on a CD made in *West* Germany back in 1989. It proved to be in good condition and was easy on the ear.

I enjoyed listening to it for many months, mostly as background music whilst reading, and in all that time failed to really notice track six, *Für Elise*, being more enamoured to track one, the *Violin Romance in F, opus 50*.

At some stage the heavenly spheres turned and the stars and planets aligned in a mysteriously unique way and I found myself in a music store. I was there to make the first move to scratch an itch, my then incipient and uncertain desire to play the piano – perhaps to emulate my dear mother's piano-playing ability or from the unrealistic hope of musically impressing some guitar playing friends of mine with my keyboard prowess. It was a flimsy motivation that has, to date, had one wonderful consequence.

The girl in the shop, noticing my interest in the rack of electronic keyboards, came over and offered her assistance. I felt rather embarrassed to be wasting such a lovely young lady's time – but she insisted – and having a little time to spare, though not much, because my dear wife was waiting impatiently upstairs wanting to go home. After a little struggle, the salesgirl got my chosen keyboard, the most basic, simplest one, plugged in and turned on. All I wanted was some idea of the quality of the sound it could produce. She obliged.

Her pale hands hovered above the keys for a moment then dropped, seemed not to touch them, but fluttered like a bird over them to produce … the heavenly sound of the introduction to that Beethoven bagatelle I knew of but could not name.

The girl's feminine graces, the incredible clarity and sweetness of the sound and the floating magic of its first few bars overloaded all the pleasure centres in my brain and I had to insist that she stop. It was as though I had slipped for a moment into aural heaven and found my emotions not strong enough to cope. I made a hasty retreat but the experience burned my soul for weeks after, and still does, for which I feel blessed.

Once home, I eventually discovered the name of that magical musical moment, the introduction and main theme from *Für Elise*, but this time I concentrated on *actively* listening to the entire tune.

I have played that West German CD many times since and now hit the mute button when *Für Elise* ends, so as not sully its reverberations from the distraction of hearing any other sound. I want the silence to frame its ending and cement its glory into my brain. I want nothing extraneous to overwrite my short-term memory's grasp upon it. I want it to always remain fresh and clear in my memory. I want it to be like my love and admiration for my dear wife; immeasurably large, full, rich, and eternal.

This morning I played that CD in the shed whilst varnishing a woodworking project. When track six arrived I fast-forwarded to the next. When my work was done, I took possession of my recliner and, armed with the remote, selected *Für Elise*, pressed *Play*, cranked up the volume and sharpened my ears and, of course, hit mute when it ended.

In studying that track I realised it seemed to be a musical rendition of the perfect life. It starts with the wondrous and lively main theme that then finds a mellowness but one peppered with odd quirky notes thrown in to pique our interest, to have us unsure if they were an accidental stumble or a deliberately playful one. Next, arrives a strange change of mood, perhaps representing the enthusiastic explorations, achievements and setbacks of our twenties or a reflection of Beethoven's deeper more troubled thoughts mixed with manic exuberance. Midway we return to the joy of the main theme, perhaps alluding to the thirties and forties when content with life, steady employment and a comforting home life, after which he departs with another excursion, perhaps prompted by the doubts of the fifties and sixties upon seeing the end of our life approaching. The interlude concludes with a dramatic flourish as if to say: "To hell with death, whilst I have breath I shall make the most of life!" The tune ends with a return to the main melody, implying the enjoyment of our old age and its ending with a peaceful acceptance of life's passing, achieved with a soft, sustained final note.

Für Elise is to me Beethoven's picture, and promise, of a life of beauty, joy, troubles and passions conquered, and a final blessed release into the void of non-existence. The girl did not understand, probably wasn't ready for its message, and nor was I until recently.

Perhaps my brain has gone to mush and you think I am spouting drivel. That is fine. If I am deluded by that piece of music, I harm no one, and am the happier for it.

It is strange how we go through life experiencing all sorts of things but often not fully appreciating them. We don't see the gems amongst the pebbles at our feet until some external event opens our eyes to them.

My discovery of Beethoven's gem, *Für Elise*, has me giving even more credence to that old saying: *when the student is ready, the teacher will appear.*

May we all be endowed with an abundance of teachers, in all their many guises.

30. Taking the Offensive

The taking and giving of offence is a curious business. I've done both.

The *taking* of offense is far easier to admit to than the giving of it, the exception being when the offending is deliberate. The taking and the giving are distasteful events that can irreparably damage relationships, even the seemingly unassailable ones. We have all suffered on *both sides* of the experience. I invite you to look over my shoulder as I quest to unravel the mysterious processes behind offending. Together we may discover strategies for prevention, salves for lessening the hurt, and perhaps even ways of reversing the damage done.

Maybe this exploration should be considered another aspect of the "art of giving" of which I have puzzled over in other essays. We give not just words and objects, but also the emotions, trains of thought, meanings and implications that are attached to them, all of which can be misconstrued by those on the receiving end. Unlike Mr. Spock, *Star Trek's* Vulcan, we can't clarify or confirm the validity of our received messages by doing a "mindmeld". We are restricted to the words said, or unsaid, and the sender's and receiver's non-verbal cues, which generally carry more weight than the words exchanged. Verbal or non-verbal, either medium has traps for the unskilled, which is most of us, and hence rarely can we be assured that an accurate rendition of any message was sent or received.

Enough of intent: let us start by examining an innocuous example. In the near future I face the possibility of attending a wedding. It is an event that should be replete with happiness. It is also one in which my wife and I would like to contribute to in a positive way but our attending, or not, could lead to offence to either side.

So far, the invitations haven't gone out thus my wife and I are bracing ourselves for either joy or disappointment. If not invited, does that mean our relationship with the groom has been delusional all these years, or perhaps it's simply that their budget constrains them to the bare essentials, parents and *absolute* best friends? If invited, is it because the couple regards us highly, or are we invited out of grudging societal expectations? Or perhaps we will be invited just to bulk up the numbers in order to enhance the public impact of their event, thus gaining the couple kudos, such as an impressive number of hits on a webpage, or a mountain of *likes* posted on a Facebook account.

Then there is the business of wedding gifts – the price of attending. These days the dilemma of choosing such gifts has been mitigated by today's couples publishing a wish-list of what they want, and possibly even need. A gift we must adhere to once we have communicated the item selected. Gone are the days of the surprise marvel, or the ten toasters, or the utterly tasteless or grotesque offerings. It's a well-organised business now, but I can't help wondering if something isn't lost in all that efficiency. To me, this new approach turns the gift giving from a process of finding, after much consideration, a physical manifestation of our affection and best wishes into a form of tax collection. In all this I exaggerate, but …

The wedding gift business also highlights another blindness in our society: our cultural fascination with accumulating stuff, to tout, as well as to use. And yet the stuff that is truly precious in our busy lives is time, especially that spent one-to-one and actually engaging with the other, not simply sharing close proximity but doing and/or talking about things of some importance. *Time together* is sadly an item left off most lists of must-have items.

Deliberately giving offense needs little discussion other than to say that it is thankfully rare amongst normal souls and that the reactions of the battered recipient can never be taken for granted. We humans are an unpredictable lot and often the stunned receiver, after recovering from the initial shock, will take the time to formulate a longer-term response. So, deliberate offenders beware, your act of bullying or humiliation may seem a triumph at first but your victim may, in time, find a way of gaining retribution that may prove very debilitating if not fatal.

Inadvertent offending is the type we most often encounter and will be the focus for us from here on.

The feelings attached to the offence will vary in strength and endurance depending upon the story it induces in our *narrative mind* [1]. Something unexpected happens and we are forced to make sense of it, usually by coming up with an explanation that fits in with our established view of the world.

For example: one Saturday morning, whilst walking down the street, we turn the corner and find ourselves on a collision course with a stranger. What do we do? Thousands of sensory readings are being automatically taken by our body, such as, how fast we are going and how long before impact, all of which demand responses. Do we stop, or go left, or right? And what of the other: are they friend or foe? We must decide in the seconds left [1].

Rarely can we stop and engage in a laborious conscious debate, so our unconscious decides for us. Automatically it collates millions of pieces of current sensory data with that of its vast collection of information on similar situations, gathered either directly or from trusted others and … we run like hell in the opposite direction, because the guy is big, unshaven, dressed in a black leather jacket and jeans similar to the bikies who just roared past on their Harleys. And worse, he's carrying a huge ring spanner in one hand and has a serious look on his face. All of this *tells us* that he's a thug spoiling for a fight.

The man of course laughs at our ridiculous antics because he's simply been to the hardware store to get a spanner big enough to adjust the big steering-head nut on his cheap-to-run 125 c.c. motorbike. It's an innocuous machine parked in the garage of his trendy townhouse around the corner, a place purchased courtesy of his success as an accountant.

That's how offence is taken. We sense, feel, recall information, decide and then make up a story to fit the feelings, erroneously in the example above, and conclude that the man is *a bikie with intent* and hence to be avoided at all costs.

Later, we rehearse the incident, by telling others of our lucky escape. Doing so reinforces the correctness of our decision in the unspoken hope of avoiding future trouble faster next time. But as they say in the computer world: G.I.G.O. – garbage in, garbage out. The same goes with *our* decision making.

Most of our troubles come from acting too hastily and from overreacting. We don't take the time to run it past our slower, conscious, rationalising and story making mind. Having limited conscious data processing capacity, we must automate most of our responses to the *ordinary*, to free up bandwidth to deal with the *extraordinary*, which is often associated with physical and/or social danger, or, if lucky, when delightful circumstances are sprung upon us.

Learning involves growing new connections between neurons in the brain, which requires effort, hence our preference for thoughts off-the-rack rather than going through the effort of making tailor-made ones, even though these would be more suitable for the unique specifics of the current situation.

Lazy thinking often works, but not always. When it doesn't, we get the wrong end of the stick and suffer unnecessarily from the fear, rejection and humiliation resultant from reading into the other's words and behaviours something that wasn't there.

If offended, first stop and think, do I have all the data? Do I really know what is going on in the other's head? Does their action, or non-action, match previous behaviours? Do I *really understand* what caused an apparently rude or uncaring anomaly?

But such questioning requires courage, adroitness and *time* to gather the clarifying facts, preferably direct from the offender. After which we must dispassionately weigh the additional data and calmly create a more accurate *story* to explain the *actual* event.

Such clarification needs to be done swiftly, whilst the issue is still "hot" and fresh in the memory. But being hot means emotions are high, making hasty and undiplomatic accusations easier to think and voice, usually resulting in damaging recriminations.

Letting the incident slide, leaves one person offended and the other oblivious to the hurt caused. The unintentional offender is then liable to repeat the same offending words or demeanours.

Eventually, the offender notices a strange unease has entered the relationship. Both suffer, inexplicitly and unnecessarily and if left unresolved the relationship may sour and eventually die.

Fear and loathing are the children of a lack of understanding and the difficulty that most have with accepting that we, and they, lack infinite powers of comprehension.

Also, an offending incident may pose *too much risk* to either side's *fragile worldview*. Self-preservation then forces them into saving themselves by active denial of the offence. Denial quickly turns into *anger* towards the person who *dared threaten their sacred views*. This is especially so the greater the validity of the other's "offending" stance.

None of us likes being proved wrong and so, rather than swallow the bitter pill of the truth, we seek the comfort of make-believe and in doing so risk the pain when our fantasy collides with brutal reality later on. Too many relationships collapse because one, or both, fail to admit and deal with annoyances when they happen. Instead, they paper over them with limp excuses and unconvincing or fictional explanations until a final offending incident, probably of no greater impact than previous ones, causes a volcanic eruption of emotion, after which no amount of truth or negotiation can bring them back together.

The business of being offended is further complicated by the differences of meaning we all attach to words and deeds, courtesy of our differing genetics and cultural upbringing. For example, in our house, my dear wife does the washing because she has concluded my abilities there are lacking. I do other things around the house, like gardening, house repairs and maintenance, during which I mostly wear overalls, which I often get pretty grubby. The guy across the road is very fastidious and extremely good at keeping his house and garden in immaculate shape but he seems to do so without getting dirty. My wife often playfully asks why I can't be as clean as him. Though playful, the implication lingers that I deliberately go out of my way to give her a hard time with the laundry. I always assure her that I don't deliberately get dirty, it just, kind of happens. She seemingly accepts my contriteness but I still fear some residual offence is being accumulated.

And that is the crux of getting offended, our inability to fully comprehend that *people are different*. We all see, or *not* see, things differently, hence we all act, or not, differently than others would, all of which annoys us to varying degrees until a stage is reached and offence is taken.

How to deal with it has been hinted at earlier, as has *the risks of broaching the issue* of specific offending words or actions. What is sorely needed is some practical help to get the clarification process underway. I offer some pointers, gathered from personal experience and that of others.

When feeling offended the principal emotion quickly morphs from hurt and disappointment to anger, and, *an angry mind is a stupid mind*. That anger must be physically discharged by tactics such as delay and non-violent physical activity. If escape is not possible, slowing our breaths before responding helps, and if forced into responding, do so first with a long silence, or simply admit to not knowing what to say.

If escape is possible, and won't make the situation worse, take a walk, especially a walk in a park or garden as natural scenes are considerably more calming than streetscapes. It is critical to take some of the emotional steam out of the situation. It will leave the mind in better shape to find constructive responses.

If we are being accused of being offensive, when no offense was deliberately intended, we will get our backs up, feel righteous indignation, then anger and be in the same stew as them and suffer the stupidity of an angry mind. The same strategies apply as outlined in the paragraphs above, with slowing the breathing as the starting point. The police are trained that, when being harangued, to calmly respond with the occasional, "I see", with appropriate body posture and head nodding to denote that they are still listening. Doing so gives them the time to hear the accusation and then develop a response. Their verbal tirade allows the accuser to deflate their anger and once they run out of steam, they will be more amenable to rationality.

But hopefully we will recognise that mostly they are beyond rational alternatives to their story. Thus, it's best not to force solutions onto an unwilling mind. Asking, "What do you want me to do, <u>specifically</u>?" may come up with solutions we hadn't considered and also denotes our willingness to be accommodating. Recognition of that willingness may prove sufficient to allow the parties to get down to specifics. Once an issue is broken into *bite sized pieces* it becomes very much easier to resolve.

In both giving and taking offence it is best not to expect miracles of immediate mutual agreement, especially if the offence has a long history. The starting point is in *both* parties recognising the *specifics* of the problem. Once some speck of agreement is achieved then further points of mutuality can be found, which then opens up the prospect of a resolution.

If we want happier relationships, then we need to take the offensive and wage a ceaseless campaign of awareness of the falsehoods and half-baked stories we tell ourselves about the behaviours of others.

But beware, we all harbour a limited capacity to deal with unpalatable truths [1]. Brutal honesty causes as much grief as living in *La La land*. Every day we walk the tightrope between truth and delusion. When delusion fails us and we fall, hopefully there are good friends in our life to act as our safety net. If not, one can seek solace from strangers, either professional counsellors, or the kind souls that luck brings our way.

The process of interacting with our fellows and dealing with those incidents that rub us, or them, the wrong way is an art not a science. When misunderstandings occur let us not be too hasty in our criticism of ourselves, or them. Our annoyance is the call to clarify things. We may be inept in our response but the desire to understand the truth of the matter is the first step to a mutually satisfying resolution. Even if the resolution is slow and fumbling to arrive at, doing nothing can be far worse because issues left to fester often end badly.

Feeling offended is a call to action, to re-examine things, mindfully and with generosity. Though a minority use offense as a weapon to bludgeon their victims into submission, very few of the vast majority of "normal" people *offend intentionally*.

Thankfully, those *unintended* moments of offence are infinitely easier to understand, live with, and better still, resolve.

¹ To learn how our minds work consult: *Thinking, Fast and Slow* by Daniel Kahneman.

31. Asperger's Syndrome?

At a small gathering, the word *Asperger's* was said disparagingly of a person who had declined their invitation by simply not turning up, a person we had all known for decades.

The person referred to was a man I liked and admired, though he induced a certain frustration in me, principally because of his perpetual, self-contained apparent happiness with his life and who he is.

In contrast, my mental state over the years has suffered wild fluctuations, from despair to elation, though thankfully with age, education and introspection it has of late mellowed to a more consistently happy phase. His steady happiness has been a recurring source of desirous fascination, tainted, I am ashamed to say, with hints of envy.

To be labelled, correctly or falsely, as potentially suffering from Asperger's syndrome is hardly a charitable accolade and, from my point of view, it was grossly unfair to attach it to him.

At the time I said nothing but, having a great abhorrence of injustice, my mind was unable to let the matter rest. Even now, almost three years on, the issue still rankles.

So why read any more of an event unlikely to impinge upon your world – except to waste your valuable and irreplaceable time?

The short answer is that we humans, at various times and situations, can suffer temporary lapses, of varying intensity, into our own unique version of that syndrome, which can then impair or even destroy relationships. It is an inadequacy I wish to better understand in order to ameliorate its effects within myself and, in doing so, it may prove instructive and possibly useful to my discerning readership.

There is a very large tome called *The Diagnostic and Statistical Manual of Mental Disorders* [1], or *DSM* for brevity, which can probably give you a very detailed description of Asperger's Syndrome. Google offers shorter versions.

My working understanding is that Asperger's sufferers [2], have a diminished capacity, and inclination, to read and consider the emotional states of those around them. They concentrate almost exclusively on what interests them and regard others only when their activities and attitudes adversely affect their own. When that happens their underdeveloped "emotional intelligence", for want of a better expression, can lead to misunderstandings and conflict.

For various reasons, I too was not enthusiastic about the setup, but people are less inclined to accuse us of Asperger's to our face. In not attending, he committed the sin of not being there to feed their need for recognition. His absence denied them the "mutual grooming" that their inner apes craved. His refusal to attend had them feeling offended because his non-attendance implied that he not only considered the event unworthy but also its supporters.

Their accusative labelling, I deemed evidence of their own unwitting brand of Asperger's because they had *failed to read and understand the emotional state* of their "victim", which allowed them to negate any possible acceptance of the validity of said victim's motivations for not attending.

The "accusers" were all snobs [3] of varying manifestations, people I define as those who live principally for praise from their selected peer group as well as the envy of lesser folk. They are thus in constant need of confirmation of their illusions of superiority in their chosen brand of snobbery, be it financial, social status, physical prowess, intellectualism or piousness.

Psychologists would label their actions a classic case of transference: despising others for what they secretly lack, in this case, sufficient ego strength to lessen their addictive need for the temporary comfort of fickle external praise. They secretly despise their "praise addiction" but being unable to admit to it, chose instead to cast their self-loathing onto those not addicted to external adulation.

The key word here is *addiction*. We all need *deserved praise* from others to encourage useful behaviours, which then helps keep our lives on track and heading towards a happy ending. We can't live a meaningful existence without it. But equally, we need specific and kindly worded feedback on our mistakes, to awaken us to alternative viewpoints and the possibility of improvement.

Biochemically, praise stimulates our brain's reward mechanism, making us feel good. It is the exact same system stimulated by most pleasure-giving drugs and hence praise is easy to become addicted to. This is doubly so because criticism, no matter how diplomatically given, stimulates brain areas involved with interpreting pain, which is why negative feedback is not something we readily embrace.

No pain, no gain is a rather gross simplification of things but if we are to remain reasonable, we need to understand the need for deserved praise *and* considered criticism, *both* from qualified and appropriate sources. And that's the difficulty because all those sources are human and humans are fallible, emotional, and have cognitive limitations [1]. Accepting those qualifications, it becomes apparent that we need to be humbler in our opinion of ourselves, and of the opinions of others, whether flattering or deflating. We also need to understand and control our addiction to praise to avoid going off the rails, into the megalomania of the autocrat, or the odiousness of advanced snobbery.

The event occurred at a house bordering bushland and, not long after that the unkind comment was voiced, a wombat distracted us by wandering across the host's lawn, and in doing so probably wiped the word Asperger's from the minds of the other attendees.

I too was forced to consider the meandering marsupial but did so along vastly different pathways to their expressed admiration of it. I instead saw the wombat as an animal manifestation of that disparaged man!

What is a wombat? It is a slow-moving creature, who lives close to the ground, is never reaching for the sky, let alone the stars, has no grand ambitions that risk grand disappointment and pain, and has a thick hide and fur to insulate it from the abrasions of the world— just like the man, a beast totally and annoyingly contented with everyday existence!

But I am being ungenerous. The fellow in question has a deep curiosity on an eclectic range of topics and hence is a fine one to talk with, and learn from. He is not overly interested in preaching his ideas and, if one can constrain our own urges in that direction, is a rewarding two-way conversationalist, where both points of view can be expressed and, to a greater extent than normal, heard.

That incident, and the other disastrous aspects that preceded it, later morphed from an amorphous disquiet to a growing acknowledgement of my own propensity to slip into a brand of low-grade Asperger's when interacting with my fellows. I read people wrong and my unwise responses upset them. It is an embarrassing fact that I must become more fully aware of if I am to have a chance to mitigate its negative effects.

It also highlighted the different solutions people come up with in regard to their place in the scheme of things and how best to create a satisfying life with the least disappointments.

But not all of us can have wombats as our totem. I seem to

have been born with a thin skin and hence I am overly sensitive to real and imagined slights. I also get upset over outside events that I have little power to change, which is why reading the newspaper is almost always distressing.

And, being tall and skinny, I cannot realistically choose the wombat as my role model.

Oscar Wilde once quipped: *Be yourself, everyone else is taken*! But who and what am I? After six decades I still lack a satisfactory answer. And even if I did have a definition of myself, how do I develop and maximise my potential and be happy with the end result?

Perhaps the who and what I am is not as important as finding a *generic* way to a better life. Overcoming my peculiar form of Asperger's now appears to be part of that path to said better life.

Looking back over my chosen incident, I knew things were going wrong the moment I walked through the door of the host's house, with the Asperger's comment only one of many moments of disquiet. Unfortunately, at the time, I lacked the skills to have the confidence to put my unhappiness to the front of my agenda, and then raise the issue in a manner that would not make things worse.

The main stumbling block, I now realise, was the group dynamics of the situation.

How many cop shows have you seen where they interview the witnesses, or suspects, *as a group*. Why do they bother? Almost never is much of any significance divulged because each person severely edits their responses in line with their judgement of the sensibilities of those present or does so to hide their guilt.

The truth only emerges when the suspects are interviewed individually and then only after much negotiation to overcome their reluctance to admit to wrong doings. They do so only if forced by weight of evidence, or if given sufficient genuine understanding and acknowledgement of the mitigating circumstances that pushed them to act as they did.

My mistake was not heeding my unease at the time and not being brave and rude enough to break the protocol of politeness and force the issues to the fore. I sometimes think it would have been better if we'd had a shouting match. So long as no physical harm was done, at least both sides of the issue would have been voiced, even if not heard. In doing so, the depth of the emotions expressed would have clearly signalled that something important was at stake, which, once calm was restored, could have instigated peace negotiations.

If the differences in the viewpoints shouted at each other had been so wildly divergent that compromise was clearly impossible, that too would have brought clarity and a resolution of sorts.

In my essay *Knowing When* I mulled over the wisdom of recognising when our ability to respond to a difficult situation in a constructive way has been reached, after which the best course of action is to keep quiet and/or move away, physically or by diverting attention onto calmer topics.

In this current exploration of being human, it seems the obverse also needs to be studied. Knowing when and how *to argue*.

This brings me back to my brand of Asperger's and learning to listen to my internal feelings when they are small and manageable. After which I must learn how to more accurately discern the causes of the various emotional states of those I am engaged with. Once achieved, I can then decide which plan is better: quiet retreat or active confrontation.

As to how best to argue our point of view with any chance of it being heard and genuinely considered. I am no expert, but recalling the few occasions in my married life when my wife and I had a falling out, over issues that neither of us can now recall, my response to them seemed to have worked.

The crucial first step was recognising that something was wrong, which is a lot easier with someone we live with, and of whom we have some deep understanding, the downside of which is that such persons are much more important to us and hence we don't wish to cause them unnecessary pain by making a mountain out of a molehill. Unfortunately, quite a few molehills hide mountains underneath. How to tell the difference?

If an apparently trivial remark, or action, causes a frostiness or stiffness in relations then internal alarm bells should be ringing. Like driving the car, a marriage needs constant and habitual monitoring, not just *our* internal emotions, but signs of displeasure in the significant other, if we want to avoid drifting off the smooth and into the rough. The same applies to any relationship of any value.

When I'm not happy and/or she's not happy, someone has to make the first move. Being male (less talk and more problem solving) and loath to be unhappy for prolonged periods, I was generally more willing to risk broaching the subject of my unhappiness or the perceived unhappiness in my dear wife, *and nothing else*. Keep it simple and tentative, the only fact we have is our unease. What we need is more facts to find its cause. It is best not to guess the cause too early as there may be more than one.

There is one other critical item required: bravery. A relationship that can't survive the light of *compassionate* scrutiny is a sad place to inhabit. If it can't be fixed, then it's better to end it than persevere and live a lie.

But before we talk of drastic cures, the malady needs to be defined.

Again, humility is the key. Being humble allows the facts to emerge in an organic way. I would start by confessing my unhappiness, and uncertainty as to its causes, and then make a few tentative suggestions, reiterating my puzzlement regarding both the causes and potential cures. I would admit my ignorance of what to say, or do, and then restate the high regard I had for our relationship, so high that I was determined to not go anywhere or do anything else until some understanding had been brought to light and an amicable resolution reached.

Announcing our ignorance and intense desire to hear the other side of the story, if genuine, will do one of two things: get the necessary discussion that leads either to a friendly resolution, or to the revelation of a horrible truth that needs to be accepted if both are to move on, either separately or as connected beings.

I have been lucky. Our marital altercations have been very few and I have been brave enough to admit my ignorance of, and remorse for, any hurt I unwittingly caused. I have always restated my one hundred per cent commitment, *with* one hundred per cent commitment. I have always been willing to lose everything. I have never desired sham intimacy. Semi-commitment has never been an option. I can't conceive of marriage as being anything but all or nothing. It is one of the few cases where my view of the world lacks hues.

But not all relationships are as wonderfully special as a marriage of true minds. I thus must consider more nuanced responses to other relational difficulties, which again requires me to understand my style of Asperger's, if I am to find fuller viewpoints and better solutions.

Returning to my specific Asperger's incident, I admit to having made many mistakes, as was to be expected of the person I was back then. Much bitterness has been swallowed, chewed and finally digested such that I can write these musings on the topic. I feel the slogan *anything that doesn't kill you makes you stronger* at work within me.

The painful bits in my life have always resulted in my big moments of mental progress. Hence, I should be thanking my antagonists at that event for the internal resolutions and increased awareness they caused to develop within me. It is a precious gift indeed.

The task ahead, when the opportunity arises, is to take my enhanced understanding of my human fallibility and test it, either on the antagonists of my chosen incident or on others that I shall undoubtedly encounter as life unfolds.

Time will tell if I can successfully use this newly acquired humility and sense of what is achievable. May I, and you, dear reader, also be up to the task.

Whether successful or not, something can be learned from every interaction.

---

[1] *Cracked* by James Davies was where I first learned of the existence of the DSM manual. The book itself was an eye-opening exposé on the incestuous relationship between psychiatry and the pharmaceutical industry.

[2] *Sufferer* is a word I find unsatisfactory in this situation because do such persons *suffer* life any more than regular folk? Perhaps, most of the time, *in their view*, everything is rosy or neutral.

[3] My essay *Snobbery* has a fuller exposition of my thoughts upon the condition.

32. Like the Sun

Quite a few years back Penguin produced a series of mini-books, one of which was by an Indian by the name of Kristinaa Gozales. It contained excerpts and short stories, including one entitled: *Like the Sun*.

That story acted like a mortar lobbed into my wife's and my brains, exploding with a burst of brilliantly espoused insight. It was a simple tale. Sekhar, a teacher, decides that for one full day he will only speak the truth. His day of truthfulness unfolds as a procession of good intentions leading to unintended dramas that for the world-wise were entirely predictable.

"Truth is like the Sun," is a phrase often spoken in our household but seldom understood if we utter it to others. Few see the allegory: plants need the sun but only in amounts dictated by their physiology, be they a cactus or a maidenhair fern, and probably none could take its full blast twenty-four-seven. Similarly, without sufficient understanding of the truth, we cannot survive for long, and yet too much brutal reality is equally deleterious. It is thus imperative that we understand as much of the many aspects of indifferent reality that our individual and fluctuating abilities can cope with.

I have the desire to cope better. Being past sixty I have gathered much knowledge, endured the truth's humbling spotlight, mulled over my dealings with others and seem to have made some progress in better managing life's most challenging aspects, which are mostly to do with my interactions with humanity. Age has made me a *little* more accepting of my physical and mental limitations as well as those of other people. It has given me marginally more strategies to use when faced with interpersonal difficulties, especially those causing anger, offence and disappointment.

And yet, as I write these lines, I find myself thinking of a person who stretches all of my claims to increases in wisdom. In their regard, I find myself temporarily immobilised. They are one of those mentioned in my essay *Asperger's Syndrome*, which explored the event that resulted in our currently damaged relations. It is a state I would like to see improved.

A number of unresolved issues currently prevent me from implementing some of the skills that I thought I had mastered.

The first conundrum is whether the person has the emotional and logical capacities to significantly hear my side of the dispute. And if I judge that they do, how best to deliver my view so it isn't too threatening to their ego and hence has a greater chance of being fully heard? Of one thing I am certain, doing so in writing is the worst method.

A curious fact of our rancour is that both of us feel like the victim! How is that possible? Who then was the perpetrator?

The answer of course is that we were both victims and perpetrators. I have confessed that fact, and have admitted to them how my behaviours were inadvertently hurtful and tried to explain the mitigating reasons for my ineptitude but the other side still refuses to admit that their "unreasonableness" also injured me. Progress can't be made until they too admit to the full scope of their actions and non-actions and the consequences of both.

We are like two alcoholics attending our first AA meeting. I have admitted my addiction to the bottle and desire to give it up, but they refuse to admit that they drink, that it is ruining their life, and are further displeased for my dragging them to the AA meeting in the first place. They are still convinced the collapse of our relationship was because I suddenly turned totally bad, whilst they remain perfection personified. Thus, I am no longer worthy of any regard, not even that normally granted to a complete stranger.

Another obstacle is that the person I have in mind is older than me, and also has years of experience as a relationship counsellor, which raises two hesitations to my making further efforts towards a reconciliation: a respect for those older than I, and amazement that *I* should be the one to suggest that they use their professional skills and their presumably superior emotional intelligence in our dispute and not restrict such abilities to strangers only.

The issues between us raised the broader consideration of: when is it our task to teach another of the folly of their ways, as judged from our approximation of the truth? Is it possible to teach wisdom? I think not.

Is it crueller to disabuse someone of a foolish delusion and in doing so shatter their lives, or let them suffer the inevitable sad end from maintaining that skewed view of reality? In deciding, we use *our* beliefs, knowing that all beliefs are prone to falsehoods. Can we realistically decide that they have the skills, willpower and resources to cobble together a new worldview and life, which in our eyes is far better than the one they currently have? I don't know.

And not knowing the answers to all these questions I have given up communicating in grudging acceptance of my chosen one's silence. But I am still staring at two inconvenient truths: my continuing unhappiness and my lack of courage to either accept the messy end to a long amicable relationship or to do something about it. I have the time, some new skills, and a certain amount of money to finance a face-to-face encounter but...

A story from a *Friendship Book* received many years back

comes to mind. A young fellow, strolling along the beach at low tide, sees hundreds of starfish stranded on the sand. He begins the impossible task of throwing them back into the sea. An older gent sees his actions and admonishes him for taking on such a pointless endeavour. The young man's reply, after looking at the starfish in his hand, is something like: "It may be pointless but it means a lot to this one!" before tossing the lucky creature back into the ocean.

I too have to make a decision to act, or not, in what appears to be a hopeless situation, whilst wondering how much good will come of it. I haven't decided because Sekhar's story is weighing on my mind.

At the end of *Like the Sun*, having endured a whole day of speaking the truth, he finds he has to deal with the unpleasant consequences. His wife is upset, and his headmaster also becomes displeased with him, so much so that he cancels the extra time to mark exam papers that he had granted Sekhar, meaning he will be working long into the night to finish them by morning.

Sekhar's failed experiment with truthfulness gives weight to my postponing further action. Hopefully, some *external* change* may bring better prospects of resolution. And one of those externalities is time. Sometimes doing nothing allows things to sort themselves out.

Time and unknowable externalities are real factors to consider. Problems are resolved not only by finding more and better facts but also by having the time to come to grips with such facts, especially if they are seemingly outrageous or ego-bruising. Broaching the truth thus involves knowing when and how to broach it.

I have seen and felt the consequences of too little and too much truth, as well as not being ready for it. Truth *is* like the sun; we need it, and we have to get used to it because what is the alternative? Active ignorance and delusion?

---

*That salvation or resolution often requires the intervention of external forces appears to be a recurring theme, one previously encountered in my essay *Enslavement*.

33. That's Just the Way It Is

Back in 1986, *Bruce Hornsby and the Range* had a hit song called *The Way It Is*. It impressed me then and ever since because of its theme, reiterated in the chorus lines: "That's just the way it is, some things will never change. That's just the way it is. Ah, <u>but don't you believe them!</u>".

Like the song's composers, Bruce Hornsby and Ricky Skaggs, I too don't believe them when they say: *that's just the way it is, some things will never change*. We would still be scratching a living as hunter-gatherers if a sizeable proportion of humanity hadn't rejected *the way it is* and sought better ways.

I give praise to our discontented ancestors' efforts because, for the most part, our modern lifestyles are immensely more comfortable and secure than those of hunter-gatherers, though of course a heavy price was paid in human misery and ecological damage.

Many people lose no sleep over the way things are because they are having it easy and don't care much if others aren't. If their lifestyle helps trash the planet and means others must suffer, that's just the way it is. It's what previous generations did, and anyway, what can one person do to change things? One person can't achieve much on a global scale, so why bother! Right?

Theirs is an attitude I envy because I *do* lose sleep when I read something in the newspaper that irks my sense of justice, or experience closeup, human stupidity, bloody-mindedness and cruelty. That's just the way it is with me. And I want to do something about it.

This essay is part of my response. It specifically addresses a flippant remark aired a while ago by a work colleague: *the poor will always be with us.* At the time, circumstances weren't conducive to rational debate. I hope to do so now.

Who are the poor? Why are they poor? And why should they always be a permanent fixture in society?

The way that statement was proclaimed implied the impossibility of change, with passive acceptance being the only credible response, thus negating any desire to try and alleviate the suffering of the poor.

Armed with such a self-serving slogan we can blissfully ignore homeless people, and argue against the idea of increasing the official minimum wage or welfare payments. In fact, we could easily condone slavery, as it too has always existed. So again, just live with it! Some could and do, but not I.

To counter my colleague's assertion, we need to understand who are the poor and why are they so.

Poverty is a relative state. There are official poverty lines that attempt to represent the barest wage necessary to house, feed and clothe ourselves and our dependents. The validity of the number of people at or below these official minimum incomes may be rubbery, but they still give some indication of the civility of a society.

The sufferings of those in poverty, however it is defined, will vary according to social expectations and attitudes to wealth and status. Here in Australia, we are bombarded by advertising inducing us to spend our way to happiness, with the implication that we are of little worth other than as consumers. No money, no worth.

In our capitalist and individualistic society, in which our destinies are supposedly entirely in *our* hands, being poor is not only hard financially but more so psychologically since it represents a brutal societal accusation of inadequacy. The heretical notion that poverty can be viewed as the failure of society to do its job of adequately supporting *all* its members, is given little airtime or endorsement. To divert our attention away from considering this heresy, our media, politicians and unthinking members of the populace continue to blame our economic and social ills on external forces, and at home, on "dole bludgers", welfare recipients and other people with little influence over the rules governing society. All these factors make being poor in Australia a very heavy burden.

That burden was easier in our past when income inequality was less severe and the cult of consumerism and loose credit not so entrenched. When I was growing up in the sixties and seventies, in a working-class suburb, in a one-wage household supporting eight people, I rarely thought of myself as being poor because the vast majority of my peers weren't much better off. But now I am bombarded by other people's apparent success through unescapable advertising, and everyday events such as seeing a neighbour's new car (but not the debt used to buy it) or the lifestyles flouted in the media which subtly, and not so subtly, implore me to *keep up with the Kardashians*.

One's experience of poverty is highly subjective. I recall in *Man's Search for Meaning* by Nazi death-camp survivor Victor Frankel, that those who survived with some manner of dignity and mental resilience, did so largely because of their ability to find some personal meaning in their terrible ordeal, which usually involved helping others. In the concentration camp, a person is at the most extreme level of poverty; they have no money, no rights, and definitely no future.

What Victor Frankel points to in regard to our poor is the idea that *poverty of mind* is as much a part of their suffering as insufficient income and lowly prospects.

I know of refugees from the war-torn Balkans or war-ravaged

parts of Africa who, uprooted from home and family, find themselves over here surviving on welfare in a land where they can't speak the language. They have joined the poor, and yet, within several years, most usually have found jobs, established households and have joined the better off. Curiously, many Aussies in the same queue in Centrelink, continue to languish in poverty, despite having the same access to services *and* possessing the advantages of speaking the language and understanding the culture.

There are many reasons for the disparity but I suggest the main one is poverty of mind. Possibly they have a greater acceptance *of the way it is* for them and hence struggle less to change things. The successful refugees see the barriers to success but also see the opportunities for progress. Those who stay poor appear overwhelmed by those barriers. They rail against the injustice of their position instead of diverting their energies into fully exploring the opportunities seen and used by those refugees. Perhaps they simply cannot imagine a better way, one that is worth their effort. I don't know what is going on, I can only note the differences in outcome from similar starting positions.

Another huge deficiency in our social chatter about poverty is the general lack of discussion and deep recognition of *the role of luck* in all our lives. The fact that I managed to retire a few years early, have some money put away for tomorrow, am debt-free, educated and healthy, is mostly due to good luck.

My life, and yours, dear reader, has been shaped by thousands of *random* events and yet few of us like to admit to it because doing so steals our self-worth by discounting *our* contribution to *our* life.

We usually only invoke the presence of luck if things go wrong. Like managers, coaches and politicians, when things go against us, we blame external forces. When things go well it's due to *our* brilliance, not luck! Reality is a far more humbling prospect to own up to and hence few are willing to accept it in its entirety.

Poor or rich, it is mostly due to luck, *but not totally*.

The system we are embedded in can severely constrain our lifestyle options and influence our thinking when we make our choices. That system is created by our culture and its endorsed laws, which are designed mostly *to keep things the way they are*.

In the relatively unchanging existence of hunter-gatherers, maintaining the status quo probably worked well enough. But, in our fast-evolving civilisation, the legal and cultural outlook is largely determined by and serves the ruling elites, who, if wise, grant just enough slack on the chains of subjugation to stop the hard-done-by from rebelling.

And if you start to question the status quo, be warned by these words from Hélder Pessoa Câmara, the Catholic Archbishop of Brazil from 1964 to 1985: "When I feed the poor they call me a saint, when I ask why they are poor they call me a Communist!"

And that's the rub: any questioning of our capitalist ideology immediately has us branded a "leftie", if our temerity is mild, or a raving Communist if we suggest more sweeping changes. Our cultural indoctrination means either label reduces or destroys credibility and loses audiences, irrespective of any merit in the arguments.

If you are now thinking I'm turning red or leaning heretically left, then for reassurance read my essay *The Man on the Beach* and hopefully the rest of this one.

Anyway: what to do if a consideration of other ways is our bent?

Two notions are worth reflecting upon: *knowledge is power*, and, *an idea whose time has come is an irresistible force*. Thus, if we want to change the world, hopefully to the betterment of all, human and non-human, for today and tomorrow, then the first step is gaining a broader knowledge of the realities of the physical world, as well as how the people and organisations in it operate. We need to become knowledgeable to the point of knowing *what can realistically be done, when, why, and how.*

If that sounds a bit daunting, don't panic. Change is actually quite easy – all we have to do is *lead by good example*! Be ethical, humble and long-term in our behaviours and learn from that experience. Other people will pick up on it, see the benefits and do likewise.

But be wary of any organisation, or person – ourselves included – claiming to have *the* solution to poverty or any other cause we feel strongly about. There is *never only one solution*, for all time, in all circumstances, especially if we don't really understand the question to be answered.

As far as poverty goes, we are not powerless. Within our meagre abilities, we can make some difference. There are at least three ways an individual can change the world:

1. Money.

    Though our choices regarding paid employment can be very restricted on occasions, the average wage-slave, salary-man or even highly renumerated CEO generally has some choice. If we do find ourselves working for a repulsive and morally repugnant employer, we still have at least two options, to endure it, or actively seek better alternatives. And irrespective of how we fund our lives, we have the power to influence matters for the better by spending our hard-won cash in ways that support more ethical attitudes. Thoughtfully dispensing our money does shape the behaviours of the vendors of goods and services. Consumer buying pattern have created pasture-raised, free-range, and organic eggs when such humane choices were previously unavailable. We now have the choice of sustainably harvested timber, and fair-trade coffee and chocolate. If customers stop buying, businesses, to survive, *must* change their behaviour. One aspect to be aware of when choosing which businesses to support is how much tax they pay. Generally, it is better to support small and medium local businesses because they usually employ locals and are less likely to have massively effective tax evasion schemes with which to syphon large sums out of the local economy into off-shore tax havens.

2. Our words and deeds.

   What we say and do affects others. *We* choose the words and actions we set in motion. Why not do so in a way that benefits those around us and society's overall direction. It will be an ongoing and fallible process but each of our actions contributes to the culture of our household, workplace and in some measure to that of the wider community. Even the most minor positive behaviour, such as dressing with dignity and respect, wearing a kindly expression, or just returning the hello of passing strangers will make our culture a kindlier one. There are innumerable ways our little kindnesses and considerations can turn the collective consciousness towards more compassionate attitudes and behaviours.

3. How we vote.

   Sadly, our democracy has mostly been hijacked by the media, lobby groups and their public relations and advertising agencies, all of whom prostitute themselves to sell flawed ideas to the voting public. Hence, we, the populace, are fed a diet of falsities, half-truths and silences, especially on notions not benefitting the elites. They say *democracy is the least worst system of government*, and as voters we are often restricted to selecting the least worst candidate and political party. We can possibly have greater influence by actually trying to understand the issues at stake and what each party and candidate claims to stand for. It is an unenviable task. The easier task is to become knowledgeable about the issues we consider most important such that we can engage in fruitful dialogues with the people in our lives. Hopefully, in doing so we will find the weaknesses in our logic and delivery, as well as have the other party realise that their opinions are not totally valid in all circumstances. Possibly those chats will move them and ourselves towards a better choice on Election Day and contribute to a subtle but positive change in the minds of our elites, whose existence ultimately rests upon our votes and our continued functionality as workers and consumers.

But perhaps the most effective method to promote societal change is for us to *spread a new proverb, a new piece of folk wisdom*! Let me explain with an example.

I am fuzzy on the actual details, but after the Second World War the Americans enacted a piece of social legislation called the G.I. Bill, the thrust of which was to reduce the cost of tertiary education to returning soldiers. The rationale, *the folk wisdom*, was that a well-educated population is good for the *whole country*. Though restricted to veterans, it was a step in the right direction.

Later on, capitalist ideologues, such as Milton Friedman, convinced political leaders that the legislation was *benefiting the individuals, not the nation* and it was consequently watered down. That small distortion in the *legislated folk wisdom* then put higher education increasingly out of reach for greater numbers of "normal" people, which naturally benefitted the already wealthy through reducing the competition for better-paid careers, almost all of which require tertiary qualifications. It was a piece of class control brilliantly done!

If massaging our folk wisdom can work in a regressive way, then it can also work in a positive and sustainable manner. Therein lies hope.

From all the above, it is clear that we *do* have some ability to do something about the way it is. Applying those abilities on a daily basis is how we slowly change the status quo to a better one.

I find it interesting that no one says, with a dismissive shrug: *the rich will always be with us*. Why? Is it because most of us want to join them and thus gloss over the poverty of others as being an acceptable price for the wealth of the few?

The poor wanting to be better off is a natural desire, as is the wish of the rich to remain so. In that contest, the poor have the numbers but the elites have the know-how, finances and legislative influence to stay on the winner's podium. We may be the smartest species on the planet, with access to vast quantities of facts, but we seem unable to comprehend first, the precarious nature of our evolution, second, the all too regular rise and collapse of civilisations [1], and third, that a robust and healthy ecosystem is essential for our continued existence [1].

Both our rich and poor need a better understanding of this bigger picture and, most important of all, the *ultimate purpose* of society if our particular culture is to become sustainable in the long term, as measured in centuries and millennia, not decades or election cycles.

I find biology offers an instructive analogy of society and its purpose.

Our bodies are composed of millions of tiny cells which, in living, reproducing and dying, work together to the benefit of the enduring entity, us. Those cells are combined into tissues and organs, each of which perform specialised tasks. And overall, is the division between the mind and the body, with our mind equivalent to our ruling elites. But if our mind neglects the needs of our body, its poverty of health will eventually punish our mind's hubris. Likewise, listening too much to our body's whims will have us overindulge in food, booze and other short-term sensation-seeking behaviours, again to a bad end. Our long-term physical health, and mental happiness, require the mind and body to work together to the benefit of both.

If society is to be sustainable, then the thought patterns that enable the elites to abuse the "body politic" need to be modified if we are to restore the societal body to robust health.

We now return to the task of finding a new self-evident slogan to disseminate, as an antidote to the debilitating acceptance of: *that's just the way it is, some things will never change*, which serves so well the short-term wants of the ruling classes and their proxies.

I can't think of anything really profound at the moment. But perhaps: *There is <u>always</u> a better, kinder, more sustainable way*.

Finding those better ways and then implementing them requires an overarching credo, one that is relatively simple to grasp and hence easy to apply. I find the questioning ways of Socrates provides a starting point.

Perhaps our guiding credo could be: <u>Humbly</u> *question everything*. Asking awkward questions will force us to see the flaws in the status quo. Those questions will then point to better and more sustainable views and solutions – solutions that will clarify: why we are doing what we do; for whose benefit and for how long?

Ricky Skaggs and Bruce Hornsby wrote: "That's just the way it is, some things will never change. That's just the way it is. Ah, but <u>don't you believe them!</u>"

I believe Ricky and Bruce, not the voice of inertia. I intend to *mindfully and humbly* ask the awkward questions. I shall then do what I can to improve the way it is, which principally consists of leading by good example.

Will you join me?

---

[1] *Collapse* by Jared Diamond discusses this topic in detail.

34. Messiness

My dear wife and I live in a working-class suburb at the end of a cul-de-sac. All the houses are similar: single-storey, brick-and-tile modest affairs that are mostly well-presented, except for three. Those three homes are unkempt and messy but each in its unique and insightful way.

The first, diagonally opposite, has been rented out to a mesmerizingly lazy bunch who thankfully are quiet. Even after close on a year of occupancy their domestic arrangements have proved extremely difficult to determine from afar. Who actually sleeps there on any regular basis is not clear, not that it should be any concern of ours but, being human, we find the task of comprehending their lifestyle has become a compulsion.

Those three houses provide us with a continuous stream of discussion topics. It is as if we have been summoned to undertake an in-depth study of a strange and hitherto unknown tribe of humans, a task that has proved intriguing, and, dare I say it, entertaining. It has become a type of reality show that blends a David Attenborough wildlife documentary with a Miss Marple murder mystery, though minus the dead bodies.

That first house is particularly fascinating because they appear to represent three aspects of the human condition: sloth, lack of awareness, and untidiness, all of which I reluctantly admit to possessing to varying degrees, in spite of social imprinting's best efforts to rid me of them. Seeing others not so burdened by my concept of the ideal is both liberating and annoying – annoying, because they implore me to renegotiate my attitudes.

In accepting my own propensity towards slothfulness, I recognise that I cope by portioning my limited energies towards priority pursuits. I have reduced my garden to a minimum; no lawn, lots of concrete paths with garden beds populated by fruit trees or screening bushes. It is very low maintenance but not no maintenance. I am thus envious of the people across the road for getting their garden maintenance efforts several orders of magnitude lower than mine.

During the winter their "lawn" grew green and luxuriant with the rains. All that effort soon shrivelled with the heat and diminished moisture of an early summer. At that point, we were rewarded by the spectacle of one of the young men associated with the house making the one and, so far, only attempt to tidy up the now dying "lawn".

He had borrowed a mower, which he duly unloaded from his small car and, after much-unhurried prevarication, started it up, pointed it at the prostrate vegetation and, to our amazement, proceeded to lazily push the machine distractedly around in a completely random fashion. In my experience, most tasks can be achieved more efficiently with a little forward planning but his undirected efforts implied that such a minimum of forethought involved too great an expenditure of energy. Perhaps he was one of those persons who fully embraced the idea of *living in the moment*! Again, I feel envy. This time for his *spontaneity*. I yearn for his disregard of the future and his apparent disdain of societal pressure to be efficient, to be productive, to not waste time.

At seemingly unplanned intervals, he stopped to deposit the clippings randomly in piles of varying heights. When most of the grass and weeds had been subdued, he, in a surprising fit of enthusiasm, then decided to trim the only tree the house possessed.

It took pride of place in the middle of the front yard, a short, bushy bottlebrush still recovering from a near-fatal pruning by the previous tenants. This wretched plant was then hacked at, again without any apparent rationale, with the severed branches tossed indiscriminately into a rough pile on the verge beside their driveway. And that was that.

For the next two months, we watched the grass slowly being tanned by the relentless sunshine and drought and the pile of branches slowly being desiccated, with their leaves changing from olive green, to a dull red and finally to a jaundiced brown. The pile then developed a strange form of magnetism, attracting all manner of detritus, such as newspapers, brochures, drink cans and bottles, transforming it into a sort of crazed artistic installation.

It eventually got too much for my desire for order and I rang the Council's Litter Buster's service to "de-install" their creation, which could have been entitled *Lethargy's Legacy*.

The pile then had one last surprise to give. Its departure revealed a round patch of flattened dead grass haloed by a ring of green weeds. Revealed, was a uniquely Australian form of "crop circle", a phenomenon said to be evidence of visitation by shy and enigmatic aliens, which are normally restricted to European or American wheat fields. At last, Australia was on the map of visitation by such shy alien tourists!

The lethargy of the people across the road wasn't restricted to gardening but also extended to other dimensions, such as the astonishing way they moved. The older lady that sometimes visited, when exiting the car and waddling to and from the house, moved with such tiredness that merely observing her progress seemed to suck the energy from me. That she was old and overweight made her slow, arduous movements understandable, but the real amazement was to see the younger visitors and/or occupants move with the same world weariness!

I should find solace in their slow amblings as it makes my

slight slowing down at age sixty-three appear a major achievement by comparison. But I don't. Instead, I wonder how that way of moving reflects upon their mental disposition and their view of existence. Are they worn out before their time from living a hard life, or were they born tired? Do they have nothing exciting to look forward to, nothing to perk up their mental state and hence their bodily movements?

When I drag my heels, I do so because I'm depressed or suffering a physical injury, and yet these people don't look depressed or injured so what was going on in their brains? They highlight an alien way of being that piques my curiosity.

This otherworldliness is also revealed at their letterbox, where they extract the occasional letter then leave the advertising brochures and local newspapers to fall out and accumulate at their feet without the least sign that they are aware of the mounting pile of rubbish they unconsciously step over.

I religiously take out our bins for collection on Monday mornings; they do so as haphazardly as they attend to their lawn. If they place the wrong bins out, or miss the pick-up, I am certain they suffer not the slightest twinge of disquiet. I envy them for that marvellous and, for me, seemingly unattainable ability.

Their garden is a stubbled wasteland. Their garbage bins are left open or lie fallen in the weeds for weeks. Their papers and rubbish lie abandoned around their post box and yet, rather than being annoyed or upset, I find the scene they create and their odd behaviours strangely instructive in ways I have yet to fully comprehend. They give me something extra to live for: what will they do next; how will their story develop; how will it end? Like a "who dun it", they keep me guessing.

Perhaps in the grand design of things, they are there to remind me of humanity's vast capacity to think and act differently to me. They exemplify the often-mystifying value systems each individual develops to guide and justify their consequent behaviours. Not being divine, who am I to tell them the folly of their ways, especially knowing that all of us do what we judge is best, no matter how odd or self-defeating it appears to outsiders. They undoubtedly would consider my way of life equally peculiar and foolish.

Moving three houses further up, we arrive at the second of our collection of messy abodes. For many years it has been occupied by a fellow we call "Jumbuk", after the brand of car that once occupied his carport. The house itself, like our practitioners of indolence, is not in obvious disrepair but the front garden is. It sports a similarly abandoned lawn-wasteland but one of greater maturity. The dry straw of wild oats forms a tall, shaggy and moth-eaten beard around the edges of the house, as well as along the driveway and the roadside kerbing. Its anaemic yellow strands are broken up with a scattering of deep green, low-growing, broad-leafed weeds.

The occupant is an older gent, overweight, mid-fifties, and a worker, as indicated by the crumpled fluoro yellow shirts he wore on the few occasions we have spotted him, which has always been when he was getting in or out of his car. In our thirty years of residence, he has never been seen actually setting foot on his front garden.

He is possibly a F.I.F.O. underground miner, or a submariner, because he is very pale of skin. Either way, his car remains unmoved, gathering dust and cobwebs for weeks and more often, months on end. He is almost certainly single, as no other human visitation has been noted whilst subject to our scientific observation. If his garden was a measure of his joy of living then he is probably not overly happy. Perhaps his brand of garden neglect is brought about by weariness from a life restricted to working and sleeping – sadly, a lifestyle shared by too many others these days.

I sympathise with his plight and thus find it easier to forgive the feral state of his garden. He warns me of a way of life I wish to avoid and strengthens my resolve to control my existence and not be pushed around too much by circumstances.

The thought that he will eventually retire has me wondering whether the supposed relaxation and extra time that retirement is deemed to offer will brighten his outlook enough to produce some improvement in the aesthetics of his front garden. For his benefit, and mine, I hope it will prove so. Time will tell.

The final house on our list is towards the start of our cul-de-sac and on our side. The youngish couple who moved there six months or so ago have at least one small child of around two years old. The man, about thirty, is a worker, again as indicated by fluoro work shirts. His spouse was probably of a similar age but looks older, is thin and deeply tanned from spending so much time in her front garden and presumably the back. She displays an intense and almost furtive look during the times I have glanced her way whilst driving past, which suggests an uneasy mental disposition.

Her mess – she is definitely the creator of it – is on display in the front garden to the fascination of all. There is a massed collection of pots of multiple sizes and shapes that are planted indiscriminately with flowers of various types, though their floral output has been haphazard at best. That is the ordered, or, more correctly, the semi-ordered part, the rest of the space is cluttered with an indescribable collection of rubbish, from broken chairs and cupboards, old pallets, stacks of bricks and tiles, broken toys to an assortment of plastic containers. It is as though a general waste garbage truck had dumped its contents onto their front yard, which the lady then had rummaged through and moved the minimum amount to reveal a patch of lawn, shaggy but well-watered, and space on the driveway just sufficient to park their rather battered car.

She seems to enjoy spray painting. She first painted her brick post-box dark brown with patches of black blush, and then a stone lion that was proudly placed on top of it. The lion had a similar colour scheme and was rather resplendent in its deep chocolate brown tan embellished with gold sparkle.

Her constant though somewhat bizarre efforts to beautify her garden evidence a nervously energetic and semi-chaotic artistry that only she understands. To my mind, she reveals shades of Vincent van Gogh, whose frenzied output was little understood or appreciated during his lifetime but in hindsight is now considered the work of a troubled genius. I am being overly generous in my analogy but in reminding me of Van Gogh she keeps the genius and tragedy of his life in the forefront of my mind. It acts to inspire both a renewed appreciation for the meaning that art, and literature, can evoke, as well as a renewed warning of the dangers that can transpire from uncontrolled passions.

I find her style of messiness, hinting of designed purpose within the accumulated rubbish, also induces thoughts of what it would have been like, at the beginning of time, to have witnessed God's first moves in stirring the infinite chaotic nothingness to bring forth the ordered cosmos we inhabit. The girl's efforts, in her shambling and modest way, also remind me of my own godlike abilities, puny may they be, to fashion an orderly relationship with my experienced patch of reality, inanimate and human, and so carve out a satisfying life.

Like Van Gogh, my skill in using my understanding and appreciation of reality improve with application and practice, which feeds that commodity so essential for living: hope.

The sloth, despondency or confused creativity I observe in those three houses and their occupants can only be understood in the light of their opposite: excessive orderliness, of which our street also provides examples. Two in particular.

Both homes and grounds are fastidiously maintained and boast manicured lawns and symmetrically arranged flowers and shrubbery. I look upon these paragons of order and also see aspects I find unappealing, specifically, the cost in time and money to create and maintain them. As I see it, their owners are slaves to compulsive tidiness and order.

Obsessively messy, or tidy, in my view is not conducive to a happy life because of the opportunity costs of both. I have many desires and must allocate time for each; some things have to give space for others. Thus, our place is a little dusty, the hedge a little shaggy, there is painting to be done, but because of that neglect my dear wife and I have time to read, to write, to walk on the beach, to nap, to visit friends, to take a day off and go for a drive in the country, to do all the things that matter more to us.

Messy leads to minor unpleasantness from being unable to find things and then wasting time and mental energy in the frustrating search for those lost items. Or one can suffer the consequences of disorganisation leading to missed appointments, be they personal or business, which can give affront to friends, or diminish employment prospects if a job interview is missed. Disorganisation can result in fines from organisations for late payment of bills. Messiness, of the human kind, depresses the spirit because there is little pleasure for the soul from gazing constantly upon a rubbish tip.

But being ridiculously ordered and organised also wears thin. Like a straightjacket, it stifles creativity and spontaneity, such that we can never fully relax, and it gets boring – though the obsessively tidy may disagree with my assessment.

Perhaps my views have been too influenced by living in Australia and having spent much time walking and driving around this wide and ancient land. Views of the tamed and ordered landscapes of Europe, though beautiful in their way, seem not to inspire me as much as a eucalypt woodland because the vegetation here possesses an admirable individuality in its messy and disordered arrangement.

The mosaic of vegetation, and associated fauna, varies with an intriguing fickleness, which with more knowledge is probably the result of differing responses to subtle changes in environmental parameters, and the effects of random events, such as fires. The vegetation's incredible resilience also inspires me.

If trees get hollowed out by termites, burnt, or are struck by lightning, in their tortured decrepitude some spark of life often remains and is given form in a single twisted branch battling towards the life-giving sun. In the Aussie bush, chaos and order fight it out. Life there seems to accept the need for both. In fact, many plants require the death and destruction of bushfires, droughts and floods to set seed and restart the cycle of life.

Why do I prefer the Australian landscape to the ordered fields of Europe or elsewhere? Why do my feelings about the houses in my street vary so?

The answers seem to be connected to the interplay of the forces of construction and destruction. The chaotic individualism of the Aussie bush is more soothing because the chaos there is natural. It may be messy and hard to understand but that's because I don't know the reasons behind its nature and distribution. It is soothing to my mind because I *know* that there *is* a rationale behind it, whether it be the work of geological, historical and other evolutionary forces, or evidence of the creative output of the inscrutable mind of God.

Human messiness I find more troublesome and less endearing because we all have some power to understand and transform our physical and mental environments. Perhaps my annoyance is fuelled by my disappointment with my own limited capacities to create beautiful things and relationships, as well as to see more fully the beauty in others, or in the streetscapes and landscapes I am exposed to.

Perhaps the conflict between excessive messiness and orderliness that I experience in my street is really my struggle to come to terms with the eternal balancing act between ugliness and beauty, and the costs associated with both.

The people across the road thus irk me because they are mostly young but lack the concept of aesthetics as I see it. They appear to squander their transformative powers to make their patch of the planet a place I would call nourishing to the eye and soul.

Maybe we could label them existentialists because of their apparent belief in existing only, rather than what I would call actively living towards a purpose. I am being too harsh because I know nothing of their backgrounds, anxieties and hopes. If I did, I would undoubtedly have a kinder disposition towards their gardening efforts.

This rambling discourse has now revealed a surprising conclusion. Until this moment I hadn't realised what my overriding measure of worth is. It now has a name: "beauty".

If one needs a reason for being, and I seem to be so constructed, this cogitation upon the people and houses in my street has given me a "Prime Directive", to pinch a concept from *Star Trek*.

Perhaps my mission in life is to become more knowledgeable of how the living and inanimate world functions, and then use that understanding to create a better concept of beauty. Whether it be beautiful things, such as a garden, a sofa, a work of literature, or a tasty and healthy meal. But the greater challenge for me is the nurturing of *beautiful relationships*, not only with my wife, friends and family but also with those I encounter in the wider community.

My opinions of the mental states of the people in my street are undoubtedly grossly erroneous but in constructing those opinions I have found a wonderful clarity of purpose: *to create more beauty*.

One example of that clarity is enacted each morning when I make our bed. The task now elicits the affirming glow from having created beauty from messiness.

That positive start also reminds me of the balanced duality of the forces that rule the universe. Beauty comes from the bland and ugly, one can't be defined without the other. Knowing this, the messy and chaotic become less troublesome. To paraphrase Nobel laureate Marie Curie: nothing is to be reviled, only understood.

35. S'wonderful

Quite a few years back I was in an Op shop and found a Diana Krall CD from 2001 titled *The Look of Love*. It's a beautifully produced and sung collection of standard love songs from the 1930s to the 1960s, which upon closer examination of the album cover and sleeve notes revealed a puzzle. In all the photos Diana looks an alluring twenty-five but, being born in 1964, was in reality a fabulous thirty-seven when that CD was made. Not sure whose idea it was, but she is dressed, in most shots, in a knee length strappy dress with a plunging neckline and wearing equally strappy high heels. What I call standard sexy, though her facial expressions hint of things other than sexy, which to my mind was most probably annoyance. Cover design issues aside, being a romantic I enjoyed listening to it.

Yesterday morning in a fit of said romance, whilst my dear wife was preparing breakfast, I was overcome with the desire to serenade her with a song that Diana sings on that album. *S'wonderful* had the chorus line which was to be my chosen message to my wife: "S'wonderful, marvellous, that you, should care, for me."

Being unsure of all the lyrics I Googled the song on our smart phone and, having never seen Diana sing it, pressed the button, and there she was, 2014, live in Rio, sitting at the piano sharing a stage crowded with a full orchestra. Now fifty years old but looking a glamourous late thirties, she was singing that song, but…

The whole spectacle reminded me of a maudlin tune sung by Gerry Lee Lewis called *Change Places with Me*, in which he laments his desire to be the entertained rather than the entertainer, who has to "sing the songs with feeling, when all the feeling's gone" … who has to smile when inside he's crying.

Diana, and the musos backing her, looked all *so* serious. To me, they gave the impression akin to open plan office workers suffering under the eye of a tyrannical supervisor prowling amongst them. She at the piano was straight-faced, with no inkling of that "look of love" when singing that chorus line: "S'wonderful, marvellous, that you, should care, for me."

Her foot was tapping the beat but the rest of her posture was subdued. I wonder if the cameras capturing her tinkling the ivories were off-putting, likewise the close proximity of the orchestra players, in particular the older guy on the drums behind her, who, like her, was slack-faced as if terrified of fluffing a note.

My dear wife endures my croaking, off-key renditions of the love songs I feel compelled to sing to her, because, what they lack in finesse I like to think they compensate with my depth of feeling.

Two aspects emerged from my viewing of that YouTube performance, both of which are faces of the same coin: the desire for fame and success, and the fear of obscurity and insignificance.

We humans are social animals. We don't survive long in total isolation even if all our physical needs are met. Imagine being stranded on Mars as the sole human on the planet, living in the newly built, but not yet staffed Mars Hilton. Though fully stocked with food and water you find you are unable to communicate with humanity back on Earth and that they have no plans to ever return to Mars to rescue you. You have the means to sustain your body but with no human company or entertainment, no books, no TV, no phone, you would eventually go mad.

We need human interactions, especially those that deliver regular praise and/or affection, physical or verbal. Those interactions, if sufficiently positive in number, make our lives worth the hassle of keeping our physical body in working order.

Like Diana, I also want the pleasure brought from social success, however we measure it, whether in curtain calls, cash or cuddles. I have admitted to my disquiet regarding my ultimate insignificance in a previous essay and found a way around that depressing thought – by reducing my focus to the minimum, in people and time frames – but the fear of being of no consequence, whether for good or bad, remains always *a spur to action*.

What Diana and Jerry Lee Lewis highlight is the need to understand the price we pay for our solutions to those two motivations, desire for praise and fear of insignificance.

I do not wish to end up like a Jerry Lee Lewis and find I have arranged my life so that I have no other choices than to "sing the songs with feeling, when all the feeling's gone".

I hope Diana has not reached that state. I think not, because in other film clips, she appears to be enjoying herself. But like driving a car and keeping it on the road and heading in the right direction, life requires the constant gathering of information with which to make corrections to ensure a pleasant journey, despite knowing our ultimate destination is not inspiring (death and our fading from the collective consciousness).

Diana and Jerry Lee remind me that every moment of disquiet is an opportunity to reassess my thinking, my way of looking at the present situation, and my solutions to life's problems. It is an opportunity to ask myself: is there a better, kinder, and more sustainable path?

36. COVID-19

A few weeks back* when the viral tsunami of COVID-19 was at its peak, my wife and I got up early to make the most of the senior's-only shopping hour – from seven to eight – at Coles supermarket.

There were "guards" on the doors of the mall to keep out the younger folk, with a trickle of wrinkled and silver-haired people going in and out. A fellow on the way out gave us the cheery news that there was plenty of toilet paper, then pushed on with his trolley of loot, crowned by *a* packet of the precious paper – they were being strictly rationed.

It was good news because, though not desperate, our stocks of those unsung makers of civilised living were dwindling to nervous lows. But once through the automatic doors into the mall, it was like entering a dreary science-fiction dystopia.

Coles, our destination, was one of the few shops open and was attracting a steady trickle of oldsters. The mall was eerily subdued, devoid of muzak to rattle our ears, and little other sound but the occasional murmurs from the scattering of other shoppers, who appeared to share our desire to get in and out with a minimum of delay and unnecessary conversation. People for the most part obeyed instructions and kept their distance. I flinched every time accidents of close proximity occurred and puzzled over the odd mix of fully stacked shelves interspersed with large sections depressingly empty of a curious range of items.

We were happy to have obtained our one packet allocation of toilet paper and began the fruitless search for sanitising hand wipes, liquid hand soap, Vitamin C capsules, low G.I. brown rice and gluten-free pasta, amongst other things. None were available, all their allocated spaces brutally bare.

The young man on the checkout was none too happy to be handling my tainted dollar bills, as was I upon receiving his equally tainted change. We pushed off and weaved our way with a maximum of distance from the shoppers heading in.

Back in the car with our limited purchases in the boot, I removed my disposable vinyl gloves, took a breath and drove us home.

I had glimpsed a future and was depressed by it.

Since then, I have been reading a book about the past, *The Fatal Shore* by Robert Hughes. It tells the tale of the British settlement of Australia, as a dumping ground for convicts, for the unneeded poor and desperate, a class created by the capitalist transformation of Britain during the Industrial Revolution that displaced rural workers to become the factory fodder of the burgeoning cities.

The callous cruelty of the genteel Georgian ruling classes created a hell I thankfully could not have imagined and hopefully will never experience. But COVID-19 has given me a glimpse of what unfettered capitalism feels like. Walking through that mall, suspicious that every person I met was going to do me in, not financially or politically but by spreading viral laden air upon me, or smearing me with virus riddled sweat on the products I picked up, or on the trolley handles touched by the soiled hands of strangers.

The feeling that every other person was a threat to our well-being, here due to viral infection, is surely the same distrust engendered when everyone is driven by the invisible hand of the market forces, when everyone is a competitor for the necessities of life: employment, money and status.

When accumulating money in a "free" market, one free of legislative or societal restraint, is deemed the ultimate and *only* way for humanity to thrive, how can anyone have any regard for their fellows, except as either a mark to take advantage of, or an enemy to be thwarted? All relationships will be temporary affairs designed to trick the other for our benefit.

The Fatal Shore gave numerous documented examples of what eventuates when greed and self-interest are the ultimate arbiters of personal ambitions.

The strange thing is that the vision of über-capitalist societies, past and present, is indistinguishable from the totalitarian hells created by the *Communist* dictatorships as practised in the USSR, parts of Eastern Europe and Maoist China.

All were societies where trust between all but one's intimates was almost absent. Such societies were doomed to implode, but oh, the cost in human misery!

My dilemma is what to do with thoughts such as these?

These observations on the current course of our Capitalist vision are the probable reasons behind the lack of science-fiction writing that describes a future other than dystopian. It thus seems my gloomy outlook is shared by other thinkers.

But what I want are remedies – paths to a more humane and sustainable societal ethos – new ways that I cannot see existing without similar attitudes towards the ecosystems that underpin all life on our beautiful jewel of a planet.

The only resolution that occurs at present is to be as decent in my dealings with others, voice my concerns as best I can, and, when society palls, regain my mental balance from the solace I find in those remnants of nature that are still accessible to me.

---

* This essay was written in early May 2020.

37. Social Evolution

One of the many impacts of the current COVID-19 pandemic is a greater questioning of the societal status quo, in all manner of directions.

One of the recurring themes the virus has highlighted is the eternal battle between faith and reason, at both the personal and public scale. Leaders such as Boris Johnson in Britain, Donald Trump in the U.S. and Jair Bolsonaro in Brazil amongst others have denied, downplayed then delayed responding to the science behind the virulence and infectivity of the virus – attitudes that encouraged anti-reason in many of those they led.

But viruses are indifferent to opinions or attitudes. They mindlessly carry out their evolved purpose of blind reproduction. COVID-19 spread exponentially until the unpleasant reality of skyrocketing illnesses and deaths became too huge for most leaders to ignore. In denial of reality lies suffering. Worldwide, nations suffered in accordance with luck and the management strategies devised by their leadership. Here we had a bit of both: luck and grudging acceptance of reality by our Prime Minister.

America is ruled by the cult of the individual, a mercenary legal class, and apparently by the religious right. I learnt today (mid-May 2020) that quite a few Pentecostal and other literalist churches have filed lawsuits against the minimal social distance regulations reluctantly enacted by some state governors. They claim such containment measures prevent proper worship and hence are contrary to freedom of expression and freedom of movement. Thus, many church goers defied these distancing restrictions with consequent spikes in COVID-19 infections and deaths in their ranks. Naturally, such outcomes were seen as not God acting strangely but the result of dastardly scheming by evil scientists and their acolytes.

Their attitude shows the difficulty that reasoned debate and plausible facts have in overcoming blind faith. In the face of a mountain of evidence to the contrary, the faithful, whether to religious, economic or any other dogma, have cast-iron blinkers that enable them to *not see* the mountain but only the grain of evidence apparently against, with that mote justifying their view, in this case, in the lucky survivors. It is the same argument that smokers will give: "my grandad smoked five packets a day and lived to be ninety", which may undoubtedly be true and yet, get a bigger sample size of smokers and the odds of it being a wise lifestyle choice soon disappear. But such rationality now invokes the strident accusation of the data being *fake news* – the battle cry of the new ignorant, whose role model is none other than the President of the United States, Mr Donald Trump.

Perhaps the main reason for the reluctance of leaders to respond appropriately to the pandemic was the financial cost. The measures required have caused, and will continue to cause, massive economic dislocation. Leaders face the same choices that we all do if caught up in an epidemic, a war, an unsafe workplace or a violent marriage: our money supply, (the nation's economy), or our life (literally and figuratively). Money versus life. One or the other. Sadly, few seem to have the imagination to dream of both.

From a purely neoliberal, free market point of view, governments shouldn't be wasting their time worrying about the health of their population so long as the ruling elites, the "brains" of the "body economic", are relatively unaffected – which will be the case since their wealth grants them access to better health care, and security – in the event of social unrest resulting from their callousness.

In fact, with money as the measure of all things, with the invisible hand of personal gain as the central guide to our behaviour, a virus killing off a whole bunch of retirees would lessen government expenditure in subsidising aged care. In a way, Trump's plan to rescind the Obama Care legislation, with its health benefits to the average man, is a step in that direction, since skimping on public health should bring the "benefit" of killing off early, unproductive members of society such as the aged and unemployed. Again, cost savings would be generated that could be passed on to society's productive citizens and of course corporations.

It's hard to believe our "captains of industry" haven't proudly aired these sentiments in public. Most elected officials won't, if re-election is desired, but may do so if corporate boardrooms beckon. I am being harsh but the disregard by power and privilege for the less fortunate is a recurring theme.

As stated at the beginning, the only possible benefit of the pandemic may be a serious questioning of our society's current guiding values and decision-making processes. Perhaps healthcare and science and evidence-based decisions will be given greater priority. Perhaps longer time frames will be considered.

Pandemics are nothing new. Think of the Spanish Flu or the Black Death. That deaths from the current one are not yet as numerous as in those two events is largely due to our greater scientific prowess in medicine, not from increased belief in God's mercy.

Perhaps COVID-19 will have us rely less for guidance on the power of self-serving market forces to solve *all* social and economic problems. Perhaps the dramas caused by disruptions to global supply lines will encourage a move to greater national self-sufficiency in materials and technology. This may flow on to businesses and households in the form of a desire for lower levels of debt and higher savings, and lead to a greater ability for the populace to weather hard times when they inevitably arrive, generally when least expected.

One amazing reversal of the market fundamentalism that rules almost all political and economic thinking has been government cash grants to *individuals*, not just businesses. It was an amazing, if belated, recognition that a functioning economy requires people to have money to spend, money not restricted to the wealthiest one per cent. Not since the 2008 global financial crisis has that notion been dusted off and acted upon, though back then it was mostly directed at fixing the gambling debts of a financial system disconnected from society and the real economy.

In our individual and societal ponderings over these questions, I hope a better social and economic philosophy emerges because the report card on the existing one, for developed nations mesmerised by the destructive dogma of me, money and mine, is already in, and being ignored as only humans can.

Its name: *national birth-rates*. For the vast majority of OECD countries such as Australia, it is below or well below replacement levels and has been for several decades.

Our "societal genetics" have developed mutant attitudes that will lead to "societal extinction" unless "westernised" women, *as a population*, take the risk of having and raising a family.

We have reached the point where "western" women, as a group, see having babies as either socially unworthy, beyond their capacity financially and too onerous a task because of insufficient social support. They are also discouraged from parenthood because of uncertain incomes due to insecure employment and have serious doubts over the strength and longevity of their marriages, as well as insufficient faith in the direction society is heading.

This underreported, unconsidered and inconvenient fall in birth rates and faith in the future should be a blaring wake-up call to governments and social leaders, to use the rethink hopefully induced by COVID-19 to also address the reasons why too many younger folk *fear bringing children into this world* – a world that our elites engineered. It is a world they and the rest of society must reconfigure.

38. In Our Image

For a long time, I have been puzzled, and amused, by that line in The Bible, in Genesis, which states we were made in God's image.

It is a notion I like to call upon whenever my dear wife enters the bathroom of a morning to find me naked and admiring my ruggedly handsome face in the mirror. In actuality, she is witnessing my cringing cataloguing of time's unremitting assault upon my face and body.

Her interruption stimulates my justification reflex. With a flourish, I announce that she sees before her confirmation of the Bible's truth, that I am indeed created in God's likeness. Then, with God-like benevolence, I remind her of how lucky she is to be married to such a marvellous assemblage of muscle, skin and bone, with the emphasis in my case on skin and bone.

Strangely, she rarely displays the appropriate display of gratitude. This lack of praise and thankfulness has puzzled me, until recently, when the Bible's pronouncement of my glorious origins appeared in a book by Stephanie Dowrick [1] that I had received as a gift. Stephanie quoted the Bible's King James Version: "And God said, 'Let us make *man* in *our* image, after *our* likeness'."

As far as celebrity endorsements go, it doesn't get much better than that! But note: it's all about *man* – woman being a mere afterthought, apparently cobbled together from an unnecessary embellishment to the male anatomy: the legendary thirteenth rib. God removed it and decided to make a new version of man, perhaps to correct a lack of symmetry in having constructed only one variety of human.

Doing so he/she/it made humanity consistent with the dualistic theme that pervades the rest of his/her/its creation (Weak nuclear forces/strong nuclear forces, chaos/order, light/dark, positive/negative, space/time et cetera).

Some of Adam's male descendants would argue that God forgot the recipe for the production of perfect women after building Eve, because all subsequent versions seem, in varying ways, to not meet the divine standards of the first!

Armed with such a backstory, is it any wonder that females find prideful males less than appealing?

If you have read this far let me confess a general ignorance of things religious and beg forgiveness for the errors I make. But one thing all religions do is discuss topics other than the weather or the weekend sporting results. It is that broader viewpoint that I wish to consider in this essay.

Stephanie Dowrick's book induced a contemplative mood – its undoubted purpose – which had me honing in on the oft-overlooked aspect of that bold statement from Genesis: in *our* image. "Our" being the puzzling bit.

I am certain students of religion will correct me by announcing that the "our" refers to the Holy Trinity: The Father, The Son and The Holy Ghost. But, being more a biologist than a monk, I see the term "our" a little differently.

The first thing to recognise is that The Trinity is at least two-thirds male, being father and son with a Holy Ghost of unspecified gender. It is further indication of a Biblical male bias, which is unlikely to find favour with any of a feminist persuasion.

The second point of divergence is that I think the concepts of God and the *literal* "word of God" as supposedly recorded in

The Bible are misguided, because any conversation or communication between us and God, who, being omniscient, all-knowing and ageless, would be equivalent to a sixty-year-old professor of theology, mathematics, physics, chemistry, biology and every other aspect of knowledge, trying to explain in words and equations the wonders and usefulness of quantum mechanics to a two-year-old. To get any effective communication happening, the divine he/she/it would have to speak or write in words and concepts that a toddler could understand.

Because of the difficulty of dumbing-down God-sized knowledge into something mere humans can comprehend, I reckon the Bible's wisdom is couched in *allegorical* terms, including the *stories* in Genesis.

Once we abandon the literalist, fundamentalist view, then useable lessons and strategies for navigating through life can more easily be drawn.

In view of the immensity of existence, I conclude the multiplicity implied in the words: "our image", implies numbers very much greater than three.

Perhaps to gain a better understanding of God we need to understand his/her/it as being similar to looking upon a colour photograph which, when examined close up, consists of millions of pixels – tiny coloured dots – with the picture only fully emerging once we move back far enough to see the bigger patterns created by all those pixels.

God's image consists of pixels that consist of every human, alive and dead, every creature, similarly alive or not, as well as every speck of inanimate object ever created since the dawn of time. It is an inconceivably immense canvas. Thus, we can never fully understand the divine because we cannot "step back" far enough to see the complete picture. And attempting to do so would be pointless because we don't have the sensory and mental capacities to fully see or comprehend the immensity of that picture. All we can do is use our limited capacities to get to know our tiny patch of that infinite canvas and try and make sense of it.

The most troublesome aspect of that process is learning how best to interact with our fellow humans. And the closer they are to us, the more we must learn about and from them. That last thought was inspired by another line from Stephanie's book, buried at the end of a conversation with a lady called Katy, (page 259 of the 2010 edition): "... what a wonderful teacher an intimate relationship can be."

Which brings me back to the naked man in the bathroom and why both he and his wife are smiling. They have seen each other naked, shared their physical selves and more importantly shared and came to understand their emotional and philosophic selves.

Most importantly for us, is that we admit, often grudgingly, our imperfections. We, consciously and unconsciously, see a bigger picture of us than most others see and so we more fully understand our mutual suitability and the tangible and intangible benefits that our union delivers. And, in owning our histories, our motivations, and the reasons behind them, we can afford to be generous to the other because we are more fully aware of *our own shortcomings*. This body of knowledge, and the attitudes it generates, allow for the most precious gift of all: our ability to laugh at ourselves.

The development of such a wonderful state requires reciprocal courage. People need courage to be vulnerable, to expose their sensitivities and their shameful or painful hidden truths. It takes courage to trust and in doing so risk hurt and/or exploitation. *Trust begets trust.* Such trust will allow us to see and be comfortable with the whole of the other person, not merely their public outer shell. Once achieved, the shared depth of understanding and generosity then enables the easy humour that crowns many a happy marriage.

Perhaps the most important payoff from learning to put our tiny patch of God's creation into perspective is that it allows for more nuanced responses to all those human issues that hurt or niggle. That bigger view allows us to recognise when pride has become overblown, or when "just being practical" morphs into an insensitive and slavish pursuit of efficiency.

As a first step, one needs to recognise when things get beyond a joke. The next is summoning the courage to do something constructive about the issue, to turn viewpoints around to allow humour to return. Overblown pride then has a chance to be seen as ridiculous enough to be made into something playful and irreverent. Being overly task-oriented can similarly be mellowed to more livable proportions.

To laugh *with* someone requires the ability to laugh *at* oneself, and that takes a well-developed humility, which again comes from learning to appreciate the bigger picture, that tiny but expanded part of God's creation that we are capable of comprehending. It is the only way to put our abilities, wants and troubles into proper perspective.

As a rule, we are not as good, clever, or correct as we think we are. And the other person is generally not as good or bad, right or wrong as we think they are. Once that more humble truth is accepted, then suddenly life becomes looser and easier to bear.

Stepping back allows us to see *our image* in greater clarity. We more fully comprehend the limits of our abilities, the shortness of our lifespan, the restricted extent of our personal knowledge when compared to the immensity of reality and eternity.

Do that and we may find it easier to endure life's tragedies. That bigger perspective may make many of life's troubles jokingly small, so small and ridiculous that we can shake them off and then get on with living as best we can and with more joy in our hearts.

In accepting the truth of our limitations, our subsequent kinder attitudes will make us a whole lot more fun to live with, and make us wiser in assessing the true nature and worthiness of others. It will be easier to distinguish the good from the bad and from there find better alternatives.

The happiness made possible by an expanded understanding of reality seems to mirror the two ways of considering the Bible's content. The narrow, literalist, fundamentalist way that precludes humour and encourages disdain and punishment of broader views, as opposed to the allegorical view, which is open to interpretation and debate. This second view encourages multiple responses that reflect one's starting point and present circumstances.

My wife and I choose the multiple viewpoints and multiple solutions of the allegoric, rather than the monolithic interpretations and unquestionable "only" solutions of the literalist.

I certainly know which interpretation of "our image" I use when at the mirror. My smiling upon my proclamation of being made in God's image is me laughing *at myself*, and unseen, is a God, however imagined, undoubtedly laughing along *with* me.

Allegoric or literalist? Which do *you* choose, and for what reasons?

---

[1] *Forgiveness & Other Acts of Love* by **Stephanie Dowrick**

39. Statues of Stalin

The other morning (in May 2020), whilst I was preparing breakfast at the sink, my dear wife at the dining table read to me the latest developments in the "Trump Show", which is how we consider "news" from America – though it's more akin to following a bizarre and frightful reality show. She informed me that black people, incensed by the brutal killing of Mr George Floyd, were trying to, or had, cajoled authorities into removing a boulder upon which, or near which, African slaves had been auctioned off.

As you can see, my recollections of the details are sketchy, but the nub of their demands is what concerns me here. Their achievement was similar to the tearing down and removal of statues of tyrants like Saddam Hussein and Joseph Stalin, or imperialists like Cecil Rhodes, all in an attempt to … accomplish what exactly?

Does removing the symbols of oppression remove oppression? In some small way possibly, but I think such acts need further consideration if they are to have a greater, more positive and long-lasting effect.

In Germany, the concentration camps at Auschwitz and elsewhere are mostly preserved, or remain and are allowed to fall into ruin. Again, I am unsure of details but I worked with a chap who, whilst a tour bus driver in Europe, visited the deathcamp at Auschwitz and said it was an experience he'd never forget. Despite its terrible message, he was glad to have gone there because it made the Holocaust more *real* to him.

The Germans have preserved those horrid places and open them for inspection to keep them ever-present in their consciousness, as a reminder to them, as a nation and as individuals, of the evil they were capable of – an evil all of us are capable of, if pushed by extreme circumstances.

Auschwitz, statues of tyrants, and stones tainted by slavery are physical symbols of the dark sides of our nature. Without their physical presence, even if only as a photograph, it is very much easier to excuse and then forget past atrocities. Forgetting the mistakes of the past is generally the best way to repeat them.

These physical symbols, for those affected directly or indirectly through family history or other connections, would be too hard to bear on a constant basis – imagine being Jewish and forced by circumstances to live in a flat overlooking Auschwitz, or similarly, being an African American with a balcony view of that slave auction stone. Such circumstances would severely try the strongest of psyches.

What to do? And something has to be done by those who suffer by such symbols of oppression, but what?

Each person, and/or community of those affected, would need to customise their responses. The hurt would need to be *made manageable, but not forgotten.*

I am not Jewish or of black African descent, in fact, I am a white African, and I am thus …?

But I am firstly a human. One who also has suffered, to a degree, episodes of emotional pain induced by other humans, which gives me some small appreciation of this topic. All lives involve suffering to a greater or lesser degree, and so we all have some expertise in this field.

Perhaps a useful first step towards finding ways to cut those symbols of oppression and evil, *symbolically* down to size is to consider: scale and context. Auschwitz is not *all* of German history, and it does not represent all aspects of the German psyche. We only have to think of the music of J.S. Bach and Beethoven to be reminded of the many positive aspects of their collective and individual character.

Maybe those statutes of Stalin or Saddam could be placed in holes deep enough so that we must get reasonably close to the safety railing to peer down to look at them, standing in the mud and rubbish at the bottom, covered in dust and pigeon droppings. But still there, in their full but constrained ugliness. In such conditions they would help sharpen our vigilance of their possible successors, those who may lie dormant or, more worryingly, be masquerading amongst us.

On a personal level, I have a person with whom I have suffered a painful falling out. Their picture remains on display here in this office where I am typing. I keep it there because that person had many good aspects to them, which I do not want to forget. Their photo reminds me of their good sides as well as the bad, or more correctly, sadly foolish parts, both of which I wish to remember and learn from.

That photo is not the only picture of people in our house. There are many others, and quite a few of my dear wife and I together, all of which construct a physical representation of my life. That collage puts negative moments into a truer, fuller and hence more useable context.

It is my suggestion that statues and symbols of oppression need to be treated like the dangerous animals in the zoo; separated from us by glass barriers or surrounded by trenches, or put in cages or pits, all so that they may be viewed from safety.

Erecting such barriers around our statues of Stalin, and others of his ilk, will remind us that they – like large carnivores, tyrants of all persuasion, as well as oppressive ideologies – *are* dangerous, *are* real and *exist*, all of which must constantly be remembered. And in remembering, we will think and act the wiser for it.

40. Living on Scraps

Last night*, at a small gathering, I expressed an unkind summation of an ethnic group, naturally not my own, which I tried to justify using my limited personal experience of said group. Objections were raised.

Later in the discussion, disparaging judgements were voiced against people harbouring anti-science viewpoints and I, being a devotee of science and evidence-based decisions, made comments in agreeance. But one member of the gathering was brave enough to admit to the anti-science stance of not believing that people had landed on the moon. All those photos and supposed evidence were apparently propaganda created in a Hollywood studio for political purposes.

That brave dissenter reasoned that since they had never been to the moon to confirm our alleged visitation how could they honestly say it had taken place? To them, the theories negating the evidence of said landings were entirely consistent with their summation of human nature, especially in relation to politicians, who bankrolled the space program and hence were needful of it being perceived as a success.

More lively discussion ensued.

We started as friends and parted on the same terms. I certainly hoped so because *civilised* exchanges of divergent views need to be encouraged. They can possibly even lead us to question the foundations of our own views. Opposing views are an integral part of reality and ignoring such views, in my mind, is the same as driving through an intersection with our eyes shut.

Sometimes we may get away with it, but eventually, bad things will happen.

Contrary ideas, no matter how apparently dubious, need consideration because they give a fuller understanding of the reality beyond our own senses. They theoretically give us access to the thoughts of the seven or so billion people currently on this planet, as well as the recorded opinions of some of the multitude no longer with us. That extra information presented in disputed "facts" and the novel thought processes that validated them, *may* make it easier for us to navigate the troublesome waters of today's reality.

It is a laborious task sifting the rare nuggets of usable truth from the ocean of irrelevancies, lies, half-truths and misdirecting silences, and yet those nuggets of truth are worth the hunt because they provide the broader context needed for a more sustainable assessment of reality, from which better attitudes and better decisions can be made.

The argument that nothing is real unless we have experienced it firsthand is a powerful one, especially in light of the propensity of all humans to lie as well as to believe whatever they find expedient to uphold their self-image.

Unfortunately, it is extremely difficult for anyone to articulate a watertight argument to justify their opinions because all such opinions will ultimately rest upon facts and evidence that are deemed valid by both the giver and the receiver.

It is the nature of these facts and evidence that is up for debate.

If we attempt to bolster our opinion by calling upon experts to validate them then the same counterargument stands because no matter how learned, experts are human and hence their assessments of truth and relevance are also prone to self-serving exaggerations, dismissals and/or misinterpretations.

Have humans visited the moon? I haven't been there. My

knowledge of it is second-hand, so why do *I* believe that we have set foot on it?

How do we decide the validity of anything? What is the process behind accepting or rejecting the weatherman's forecast of a sunny day ahead, or *believing* the science behind the medications we take, or our attitude towards our spouse's explanation for coming home late, and a million other decisions continually foisted upon us?

It is a process of filtration. We filter our responses through our scrappy collection of personal experiences, and the "gossip", otherwise known as opinions, of our chosen authority figures. It is hardly a rigorous or accurate process and so we must approach our own decisions with the same caution that we apply to those of others.

And no matter how long or varied a life, we never have all the facts, however one defines the term. Thus, like jury members, we must decide *on the balance of probabilities*. We assess the evidence presented and then make a decision, bearing in mind the *probable consequences* of that decision. And that last part is the one we are apt to forget, deny or misjudge because it involves predicting future events – a near impossibility.

Physicists talk of action and reaction. Philosophers talk of Karma (that every deed has consequences). Both summations are implacable. Karma and the laws of physics and chemistry are indifferent to our opinions, beliefs or excuses.

If I ride my motorbike around a bend assuming the road surface continues the same as that experienced so far, and then encounter a patch of oil placed there by events unknown, Karma and physics are unconcerned. I simply suffer the consequences of my actions. If lucky, I live and learn from the experience. I adjust my future behaviour and become more cautious in bends in which I cannot see the road surface sufficiently ahead, and having learnt my lesson, consequently live to ride again.

We live and learn. If we don't learn we can still survive, but that survival depends upon the nature of the things we refuse to believe in and are then unluckily enough to encounter.

What are the odds that not believing in the truth of the Luna landings will have much impact on the quality and length of our lives? The same goes for my unkind opinion on my selected ethnic group with whom I currently have zero interactions. The answer is: not much. Hence, on those issues we can get away with being infected by any number of false or misguided beliefs without significant harm.

But some bits of reality *are* important to our well-being, both physically and psychologically. I *believe* the trick to a happier existence lies in learning better ways to assess the significance and veracity of the information I am daily bombarded with.

Some parts of reality may be too psychologically distasteful to broach with the level of skills and courage that we currently possess. But shelving a problem doesn't always make it go away. In my experience, it generally makes a livable solution harder to find and more traumatic to eventually put into practice.

Perhaps it is useful to develop our skills at discerning fact from fantasy by practising upon issues or subjects with low emotive value and preferably something peripheral to our daily life, such as moon landings, or the nature of groups of people we have little contact with. There are many such topics, the news bulletins are filled with them, with almost all having little direct impact on the average person's life.

With diligence and practice, the possibility then arises that one may eventually feel confident enough to apply said truth-determining skills to the deeply personal issues we have been avoiding, and in doing so break free of them.

Using the evidence of my own efforts in this regard, I believe it to be a worthwhile endeavour. Life becomes less complicated and I can then divert my limited energies towards *achievable goals* and away from chasing delusions. Admitting to the truth of my limited capacities means I have more realistic expectations of myself and of other people. This greater alignment with the truth then diminishes the suffering induced when unrealistic expectations are not met.

That amicable discussion last night reminded me to apply my rationality filters to *my* expressed opinion, which subsequently proved to be both under-considered and unkind. The result of that reassessment was the realisation that my disparaging view was founded upon a very small sample size of firsthand, and secondhand, knowledge, all gathered over a very limited timeframe and assessed using my current value system, a system that has evolved markedly over the years.

If we can admit to not being all-knowing, then we must face the truth that our decisions rest upon the *scraps of information* that come our way.

Scraps of information? Surely, I jest, when the internet gives instant access to oceans of the stuff.

For example: how dangerous is the COVID-19 virus? We can spend a lifetime surfing the net for the facts and stats and will still be as confused as at the start because of masses of contradictory evidence: many infected have mild symptoms and yet 110,000 dead Americans, and counting, suggest otherwise. If we are young, we can argue the virus kills mostly the old. True, but plenty of younger people died too. Thus, it boils down to how *lucky* we feel, or to our making a decision using the few general facts that continually surface from that wind-tossed sea of data and opinion.

The wise decide *on the balance of probabilities*. For COVID-19, we practise social distancing, use facemasks, spend less time in enclosed spaces with other people, become knowledgeable about how the virus is spread (droplet inhalation or ingestion through touching infected surfaces) and practise greater hygiene.

The same argument applies to finding a healthy diet we can live with, and many other conundrums.

We are awash with "facts". The difficulty lies in assessing which to give credence to and when to do so.

I choose which of those scraps I give weight to. I also choose the method for assessing their merit. I *can* choose to *own the consequences* of the decisions made from those choices, which will be easier to do when beneficial; less so when not! And I can try and choose wisely and truthfully if my desire is a less troublesome life.

This task of filtering the evidence, mine, and that of others, in as truthful a manner as I am physically and mentally capable of, I consider a worthy challenge.

I can only thank those present at last night's discussion for nudging the interconnections of my grey cells into a more effective configuration that hopefully will aid me in the decisional challenges of the future.

*This essay was written at the end of the second week of June 2020 (during COVID-19 restrictions when we all had to maintain strict social distancing and hygiene).

41. War and Eden

Starship Troopers by Robert A. Heinlein tells the story of a young man who joins the mobile infantry, in a future society where voting rights are only given to those who have seen active duty in the military. In my first attempt, over four decades ago, I never got past the first chapter – put off by its gung-ho ethos and testosterone fuelled certainty.

Recently I received a copy as a gift and, out of regard for the giver and a growing desire to expose my mind to contrary ideas, I gave it another chance. This time I found it compelling reading, though whenever I put it down, I became reluctant to pick it up again. But when I did, I was hooked anew. What was going on?

It took a few days of contemplation to figure things out. Put simply, it was the story's ideology *and* the way it was told that invoked both my desire to read it to the end and my disquiet of it.

Apart from a scientific treatise, or an instruction manual, all other forms of written communication seek firstly to get the recipient's attention, and once gained, maintain it long enough to get the message across.

For instance, having read this far, unless I give you something more interesting you will stop reading. It must be interesting enough to entice but not so much as to satiate, because I need you to follow my trail of crumbs to the planned conclusion.

Here is the first crumb. Have you ever suffered because your first impressions of a person, or a situation, proved horribly wrong? For example, a friend, or a job, that initially appealed but over time proved a disappointment or disaster. What did you learn from that experience? And how long was it before you got stung again?

Still reading and now getting annoyed from my attempt to be openly manipulative? Well, that's how I felt after reading Heinlein's book, but, instead of getting annoyed, I wanted to know how he had messed with my head. How did he get me to read to the end and then, have me favourably considering his ideology? Unfortunately for him, the more I thought the less I liked his method or his stance. But perhaps that was his purpose! In which case he succeeded – the sneaky devil.

Before any communication can succeed, we must have some understanding of our target audience since few messages of any length can appeal to all. The only exception that springs to mind is a fire alarm and even there many of us will be reluctant to respond, dismissing it as just another fire drill or a false alarm.

Heinlein's book is science-fiction and the main character is a young man. The audience selects itself: mostly men and those interested in sci-fi.

If male, even the dedication grabs us before turning a page of the story itself: "…to all sergeants anywhere who have laboured to *make men out of boys*".

Male interest is piqued because we males want to be men, not boys. We read on. Score one point to Heinlein.

Guys like action. The first chapter we get straight into it as we follow the protagonist into battle. Another point to the author.

The next point is *less* easy to see or concede. Heinlein wins it by choosing to write the narrative *in the first person*, from the eyes and mind of our avatar, Johnny Rico. Doing so makes it more personal and hence we find it easier to understand Johnny's motivations, and thus *agree* with them. If we are into positive thinking and reciting mantras to keep up our motivation, we do so by constructing our affirmations in the *first* person and in the *active* voice. Thus: "I am wise" is a much more effective affirmation (if one can believe it) than "I am not silly."

Authors are like salespersons; they must engage and convince. To do so they are advised to "sell the sizzle not the sausage", to create a hormonal response, to appeal to the emotions more than the intellect. When an author writes a story, he or she is wise to heed Winston Churchill's views on women's skirts, and make the story long enough to cover the salient features but short enough to remain interesting!

Heinlein is good, he sprinkles the philosophy in with the action in just the right amounts. He keeps the story flowing slow enough to grasp the ideologies and fast enough so you don't have time to think too critically about them. Hence, I give him ten points for his delivery.

The notion Heinlein is selling?

That military training and the experience of fighting and risking their lives for their country provides veterans with the decision-making skills, and crucially, the regard for their society that makes them the best persons to be given the right to vote and to hold political office. He delivers this argument with many examples – clear and simple examples.

For instance: a trooper, Dillinger, after a few weeks in boot camp, decides the army is not for him and deserts. Nothing is done because the army knows they are better off without him. Soldiers want their commanders and fellow soldiers to be committed to the cause. When the going gets tough and their lives are on the line, they need to be sure of the full support of *all* members of their squad.

I agreed.

Dillinger, whilst on the run, kidnaps a child, demands a ransom and the child dies. He is tried and convicted in a civil court but they realise he is an undischarged soldier so hand him back to the military. He is not sent to jail but hanged for his crime. Again, I concurred – initially.

I, like the vast majority, consider the deliberate killing or harming of a child the most heinous crime and deserving of capital punishment *if* we are *absolutely* certain of the facts. Heinlein knows this, which is why he included that *black and white* example in his book. But life is *rarely* black and white.

For example, an Aussie soldier on patrol in Afghanistan comes under sniper fire, retaliates by lobbing a grenade into the building containing the shooter and kills him. In "neutralising" the sniper our soldier gets a medal for bravery under fire. But what if the sniper's wife and kiddies were in the building and are also killed? Are those extra deaths real or dehumanised and dismissed as "collateral damage"? Is our soldier a hero, or a Dillinger and deserving of the death penalty?

The aircrew who dropped the atomic bombs on those cities in Japan and fried to death millions of women and children, are they heroes, or villains most foul? And what of the leaders who ordered their actions?

Similarly, if our country, in supporting economic sanctions against another country whose policies we disagree with, produces the conditions in which children of the poor die from malnutrition or lack of access to medicines. Those children we killed just as surely as if we had used bombs, or stuck *a knife in their chest**. Probably more so because their suffering would have lasted longer. Is it as easy to apportion morality and criminality as Heinlein suggests?

He is acting like a salesman. Like them, he simplifies. Salesmen highlight the *obvious* good points. They understand a customer's motivations and use them to *their* advantage.

A man wanders into a car yard looking for a car. The salesman reads his audience: twenties, in fluoro work shirt, and steers him towards a V8 four-wheel-drive. He tells him about its *power*, because men want to be powerful, then spruiks the car's go-anywhere abilities to appeal to the dream of many men to be *completely free* to do as they want. A desire most lack at work and, if married, at home as well. The salesman will probably try and highlight the features of the car that will give the customer something to brag about, to appeal to male competitiveness and love of touting their successes and cleverness. Not discussed is the steep purchase price, the high running costs or that the car will spend most of its time in suburbia. The salesman, like a magician, distracts the customer's logic by pandering to his audience's emotional wants.

Heinlein does the same. He uses simple scenarios with easy-to-understand solutions. The enemy is an insect-like race, split into rigid castes, with *unthinking obedience* to the queen. They are declared analogous to the horrors of a Communist dictatorship. Interestingly, we are blinded to *obedience* of our hero to his orders.

The alien race is given no other name but "bugs". A deliberate ploy by the author to dehumanise any of their attributes thus making them easier to revile. A standard approach. Hate your boss? Label him "an asshole" or any other derogatory term that denies his being fully human, it will make him easier to hate and easier for us to justify our subsequent negative responses to him.

Heinlein understands how humans make sense of the world. Reality is awash with information that we must sort through and then find satisfying responses to. Consequently, our brains are designed to filter information in order to get the gist of things.

The stronger the emotional response, the more confidence we will have in our views and subsequent actions. *Sell the sizzle*. The more sizzle the easier the selling. Good authors use clear, easy-to-understand situations and carefully selected words to create that emotional response, the sizzle. Likewise do speech writers and P.R. people.

In stirring the emotions, they make the world seductively simple. It isn't.

Returning to Heinlein's ideology that veterans, with their apparent demonstration of a heightened regard for their society, should be the ones to rule the rest. On the surface, it may seem a clear and reasonable proposition. But *only* them, and in *all* situations?

Do veterans maintain that apparent regard for their society over time? For *all* of that society or just a subset? Who specifically would they consider members of the society they risked their lives to defend? Who would be excluded and why? And will those two subsets of humanity change over time? Would being elected to a high office corrupt them less, or take longer, than nonveterans? Are the opinions of veterans any less easy to manipulate? And how do we create "blooded" veterans in times of peace? Their numbers need to be large enough so that voting rests upon views sufficiently diverse to reflect the needs of wider society and there has to be sufficient numbers to effectively run a government. Lastly, is participating in the risks of combat the best method of determining a person's long-term commitment to the populace?

History, and the present day, have plenty of examples of military leaders who permanently took control of their nations, with few of them creating conditions the bulk of the population would consider heavenly.

Sad experience suggests generals and soldiering are appropriate in wartime but why was war the option selected in the first place? War, as defined by the military theorist Carl von Clausewitz is "the continuation of politics by other means." Perhaps we need to put greater effort into finding and using means *other than* war because the death and destruction of wars seem a heavy price to pay to prove a political point. Under what restricted circumstances is the simple solution of violence and coercive force the best response?

Thinking of drastic responses brings to *my* mind a fresco by Masaccio that I first encountered in Alain De Botton's book *The Consolations of Philosophy*. The painting vividly captures the anguish suffered by Adam and Eve when expelled from Eden – that representation of paradise on Earth. A bizarre thought association?

Not to me because that painting seems to encapsulate the dilemma stimulated by Heinlein and is one that we battle on a daily basis: our desire to live in a *fairy-tale land of certainties*. To be like a soldier and have *blind faith* in military procedures and the wisdom encoded in commands received from those above us. To dream of the cosy unthinking domesticity of Eden with its easy obedience to a benevolent God. To have childlike faith in a simplistic world instead of coping with the much less pleasant, more demanding, contradictory and vacillating world of reality.

Masaccio's painting depicts our anguish. But was God cruel to expel us?

Why did God create *the tree of knowledge* and the serpent, who later enticed our progenitors into eating its forbidden fruit? What were God's motives in apparently setting up our happy ancestors to be tempted and then let them succumb? Why did God design us to be limited in our ability to resist temptation?

Were Adam and Eve equivalent to a pair of twenty-somethings who, having been educated and gaining paid employment, still linger in the easy comfort of the family home? Perhaps it was God's plan that we learn to deal with temptation, that we learn to eat of the tree of knowledge, to digest its fruit, and then to become independent minor gods existing on our own terms in the immensity of the reality that is God's creation.

Perhaps God, tired of waiting, whispered to the serpent to give us a nudge. We fell for it, which provided the excuse needed to justify our eviction. God was being cruel to be kind. After getting over our grizzling, we should be glad of that impetus to shed our childishness and become adults. Adults get to enjoy the rewards of gathered wisdom but also the punishments for hubris, ignorance and bad luck. God probably wanted us to understand both our mortality and the randomness he/she/it wove into the fabric of the cosmos.

Parents play God. They create the child. They provide the Eden – a home life that sustains the child until, God-like, they push it crying into the world outside and expose it to wider reality. Growing up is the laborious, frustrating and often painful process of engaging with our slice of that reality, a reality that is often brutal.

We are forced to craft an understanding of it to avoid its worst aspects and find the best bits. Being incapable of seeing and understanding *all* of creation, and *all* our interaction with it, we have to make do with approximations. We can do nothing else. Getting the best approximation is our path to an easier more satisfying life.

It is hard work and often painful, so arduous at times that we crave respite from it. It is then we fall prey to ideas that fit easily in with our established views. A trail of agreeable ideas can, with skill, lead us to viewpoints that arrived at suddenly would dismay us. Heinlein does this in his story. The car salesman does too.

Vote for an ex-general, or a strongman type who promises easy solutions to our poverty by beating up on people other than ourselves– usually those even worse off, such as the homeless or illegal immigrants. Do we really believe such leaders have our best interests at heart? Is scapegoating of the most vulnerable the best solution to our woes?

If Heinlein's fondness for the military mind is such a good thing on the national scale, how does it translate to the personal? Were his domestic arrangements one of him being the general giving commands to his wife, to honour and obey *without argument*? In the workplace, does management have an absolute understanding of the practicalities and psychology of the business they run to *always* make perfect decisions? Perfect decisions for whom and over what timescale?

Absolute trust in any human must be modified by constantly comparing their actions with their words. The only long-term escapes from reality are delusion, death or madness.

If still reading, and not incarcerated in an asylum, then you grudgingly have taken on the task of living in some semblance of the real world. Welcome to the club.

Our task appears to be to make the most of the "Reality Club's" facilities, the most useful being our intellect, especially when used with a good understanding of the human mind's limitations and desires. Our intellect has two prime concerns: for the body to survive and reproduce. Though the second is less important in a social animal such as Homo sapiens because, childless, we can still participate in the game of species survival through assisting the children of others of our species.

Metaphorically, we can't go back to being clueless and coddled in Eden. We can't physically go back to being children. Boys are meant to become men. To live as adults, we must develop our abilities to understand the true state of the world, human and otherwise, no matter how arduous and humbling it may be.

We need to get real! Deal with it, understand it and use as much of it as possible. It will make us flexible and strong. I am sounding like an advert for a protein supplement! But is there a better alternative? Reality is the only one I've found useable.

This contemplation upon Heinlein's book was initially for selfish reasons, to clarify the cause of my unease with his premise, but the exercise has developed into something that I hope can be of aid to others when they encounter seductively easy-to-grasp simple and seemingly "sensible" ideas. Hopefully, we all may be more wary of letting things slip *unexamined* into our minds because they may bite in unexpected ways later on.

We need to inoculate ourselves from being conned, from being hoodwinked by the simple. That fresco by Masaccio is the image that reminds me that God was right to give us the ability to digest knowledge and then force us to do so. We should not complain of God's seeming cruelty. Like a good sergeant, God's action was designed to make "men", in its most complete sense, from boys.

Masaccio reminds me I have the choice to either lament, or accept the challenge to deal with the world as it really is, to seek the knowledge required for more fully considered opinions, to question those who claim superior knowledge *without losing the ability to trust*.

It is quite a challenge but it appears we were built for it.

---

*This description is highly emotive and deliberately so. It is given as an example of an attempt to bypass your logic and have you thinking with your emotions. Did you notice? If you did, are such emotive strategies to be condemned, praised, or learned from?

42. Why I Don't Like Sex

Don't like sex?

I'm a man, so you know I'm lying. And even if female I would still be lying because women are capable of enjoying the act, even more so than men because, in the right circumstances, they can experience multiple orgasms. So, I start with a lie, or do I?

This essay was stirred by an episode of the hit TV cop show *Death in Paradise*. One of the suspects is found to have had an affair with the murdered woman but dismisses the significance of the connection with the line: "It was just sex." And yet we later learn that the meaningless encounter had taken place several months before in Thailand and was so meaningless that the young man had followed the girl to the other side of the world, to the Caribbean, presumably in the hope of more of that trivial behaviour!

It's never "just sex". Sexual intercourse between humans has so much more meaning and consequences attached to it. The notion of "just sex" is vastly inaccurate, as well as an insult to our intelligence for a number of reasons.

To start with, the use of the single word, sex, to cover such a significant behaviour appears a sad indictment of our obsession with cold, humourless efficiency, an efficiency that treats humans as battery hens, all productivity and no recognition of their emotional and psychological dimensions. This minimalist and callous view is reflected in the latest reduction of this complicated situation to just two letters, sx, when texting.

"Sex" is a statement of biological disposition, for the most part male or female, and thus it is inaccurate to also use it to describe the intricate behaviours, emotions and biological changes that are at play when humans engage in sexual activities. It certainly does not suggest the context of the act, the preliminaries, the aftermath and the meanings we attach to them. The brevity of the word trivialises the importance of all that context.

Perhaps I am being over sensitive but the word "sex" when spoken even has a clinical and harsh sound to it. If the process it describes must be condensed into a singularity, then at least one more pleasant on the ear could be found. My preferred option is "bonking". Spoken, it has a much softer, rounder and kinder sound and is the one I shall use when required.

Having stated my semantic objections, my next is that "just sex" in print, on the screen and especially if uttered in a face-to-face conversation, devalues the positive aspects of bonking and consequently leads to a corrosion of attitudes towards the act by the gullible and unthinking, which sadly is most of us.

The reasons behind this second objection require us to step back a pace and cast our eyes over the evolutionary imperatives that have led to the amorous couple gazing, with intent, into each other's eyes. Knowing why they do it may make their actions and attitudes more understandable. Comprehending human behaviours requires context.

If the world, physically and biologically, were static, there would be no need for organisms to exchange and reshuffle their genetic material, which is the basic evolutionary rationale behind sexual relations. But our planet is a restless entity. The heat of its birth powers the creation, shaping, disappearance and renewal of continents and oceans. These geologic changes alter the nature of habitats and climates and force living organisms to constantly adapt to those changes as well as to their co-evolving biological environment, especially their competitors and parasites.

Humans are similar to termites in being puny, fragile creatures who only survive in societies of co-operating individuals working, ultimately, for the greater good. It is a task that termites do considerably better than we do because they act mostly from instinct and are very closely related, all being the progeny of their queen.

We think, and argue, and are from multiple lineages, which makes our co-operating a much trickier endeavour because it often involves improving the reproductive success of others, who are rivals for resources and mating opportunities.

Our children take many years to reach physical maturity and many more to mature mentally and hence a group effort is required to raise them [1]. Thus, the ties that bind us need to be strong and persistent. At some stage in our transformation from ape-man to caveman, then subsistence farmer and finally to city dweller, lust mutated into love, and I became we. It was an incomplete and situation-based transformation.

And it is essential that the transformation be incomplete. Can there be a lasting marriage, in the relational sense, without the chemistry, without a strong physical attraction between the pair, without a certain lusting for the other? It seems to me that lust needs to be there if friendly regard is to transform into something that has the strength to create a commitment that can overcome the myriad problems generated when two different beings live together. And the physicality needs to be such that the bonds formed can compensate for time's cruel effects upon the body, when the intimacy mellows from bonking every spare moment to the less demanding kissing and cuddling, handholding, or the simple joy of being in each other's company.

Such bonds will be difficult to develop in a self-obsessed person, whether born that way or made so by societal values.

Unhappiness similarly befalls a person who, by inclination or social pressure, subverts too much of their individuality to the needs of others. To flourish we need to develop both our unique natures and still have regard for our impact upon others, now and into the unknowable future.

Which brings us back to "just sex" or, "hooking up" in current parlance. Such descriptions reinforce, normalise and condone the idea of loveless bonking, of physical intimacy without any lasting psychological regard. Such a utilitarian attitude, one that reduces "lovemaking" down to an act of "scratching an itch" seems to me a dangerous one because it quietly corrodes mutual regard, the magic behind our success as a species.

Interpersonal relationships are not merely another type of service to be used and binned at the first sign of dissatisfaction, or when a newer, though not necessarily more satisfying model becomes available.

If intimate physicality has so little meaning as to be labelled "just sex" why are most of us, in most societies, shy to bonk in public? If bonking is so devoid of ramifications why is not bonking such a big deal? Few people would consider a marriage real if it was never consummated. How do we view men who remain virgins and why with age does that fact attach a stigma that downgrades the fellow to "loser" status?

If it's "just sex" why do most people get extremely upset – often to the point of homicidal thoughts, if not deeds – when they discover their regular sexual partner bonking someone else?

And if sexual intercourse is practised merely to scratch an itch, to satiate an immediate sexual urge then surely this whim is more efficiently satisfied through self-stimulation. It would save time, cost nothing, and carries no risk of venereal diseases or awkward social approbation, if done in private. Despite that logic, admission of engaging in such a solution carries the highest disapproval ratings possible. People would easier admit to murder than masturbation.

Satisfying our sexual desires is one of the most complicated dilemmas facing human adults. Solving some aspects of that dilemma can be found if we examine the evolutionary purposes of lovemaking.

As mentioned earlier, apart from making babies, its key role lies in reinforcing relational bonds between the couple such that they stay together long enough to raise any children created, which also explains why the act in humans evolved to be pleasurable, ideally, though not always, for both participants.

So, forget this talk of "sex". People, for their own mental harmony and that of society at large, need to "make love" and talk and write about "lovemaking" because doing so reinforces in our subconscious the concept of mutual regard. Without that mutuality, sexual intercourse devolves into a form of physical assault.

When we talk of "sex" we focus on the moment of release, the climax of the act and dismiss or devalue the before and after, and in doing so turn humans into mere rutting beasts. At the point of ecstasy, we may well be so, but before and after we are humans, sharing an experience, one that hopefully both wish to treasure or at least walk away from mentally unscathed.

If one has difficulty seeing the significant differences between lovemaking and sex then perhaps writers of songs can help. Love is the topic most sung about, and even if sexual desire is a large part of it, it is rarely the crux of the song. If still unconvinced try singing a selection of songs, where the word "love" is prominent, but replace it with "sex" and see if you can't feel the difference.

Romance writers sell millions of love stories and even when the bonking is a large part of their appeal, the central message is always that love, not sex, conquers all obstacles. They are not deemed "sex stories". Sex stories are pornography, which is all about the act, not about any long-term or even short-term commitment or regard for the other, except as an organic machine for stimulating and satisfying a biological urge.

Sexual intercourse is not like defecating: the tension builds, you go to the loo, enjoy the relief, do the paperwork and leave to think no more of it. Lovemaking should not be reduced to its equivalent! The thing we are physically engaging with is not a piece of meat, a blow-up doll, or a dildo. They are another thinking and feeling human like us.

So let us be human, and humane, and write, read, watch, talk of, and engage in, "lovemaking". Love, and lovemaking, even if the glow doesn't last, associating the relationship with the notion of love, reinforces the creed of mutual regard, of treating others as we would wish to be treated. Doing so subtly and yet powerfully trains our subconscious with an understanding that promotes kinder and more sustainable relationships, which may then positively influence society, and even spill over into a greater regard for the planet and the ecosystem that sustains us.

The words we speak and think in are immensely powerful. We glow and grow when kind words are said about us in public, but if insulted or denigrated, we fume or cringe.

Words can build or destroy reputations and lives. They can have nations co-operating, or at war.

And if there is a word upon which a better world can be built, I reckon its "love", not "sex".

---

[1] N.B. Solo parents are rarely raising kids *totally* unaided, they are embedded in a society and hence receive varying amounts of help from relatives, friends, day-care facilities, as well as financial and other aid from the unseen taxpayer.

43. Water Under the Bridge

My first memory of an older male relative came in my tenth year. It occurred in the dining room of our family home when he was sitting next to the old HMV radiogram twisting the dials on the radio, all AM in those days, searching for music to his taste.

The latest song from the Rolling Stones, *Paint it Black*, started up. It was a hot track, rocketing up the charts, no doubt fuelled by its driving drum beat that stirred the blood. He cranked up the volume and I slipped closer to share the aural high. All too soon it was over. But he turned the dial and immediately hooked it again. I edged closer still and again tagged along for the ride. Song over, once more he tried his luck and again *Paint it Black* ruled the airwaves. He repeated the process for I don't know how many times, with its ending of little consequence, because riding that extended wave of musical appreciation had branded two marks on my soul: music and that older male relative.

Those seemingly endless minutes of shared excitement had placed him into the "good guy" category. He's still there fifty years on, though no longer the towering figure of that ten-year old's imagination and in a box whose selection criteria has evolved with time.

We shared a brief reprise of that bonding, again brought on by music shared and appreciated, when, in my fiftieth year, I rode my motorbike from the west coast to the east to spend a few days in his company.

He'd bought a new four-wheel-drive and was keen to show

me its charms. We headed out of town for a cruise around the backroads, through forests, hills and incised valleys. He selected the music, the most memorable of which was Bob Dylan with the Paul Butterfield Blues Band playing really souped versions of some of my favourite Dylan tracks from circa *Highway 61*. It was another shared musical high.

Eleven years later came the last breaking of barriers via music, this time at his new house a couple of hours out of Sydney. The weekend proved disastrous on most fronts but I did manage to convince him to join me in listening to some of my favourite music CDs played through his fantastic Hi-Fi system. It really showed up the technical limitations of Santana's live rendition of my all-time number one track: *Europa*, as was to be expected from a concert recording in the early seventies. The highlight was discovering the sensational aural crispness of the studio recording of Gary Moore playing *As the Years Go Passing By*. A revelation I shall always treasure.

Sadly, those precious few shared moments and others from our past have been overshadowed by the corroding of bonds caused by decades of physical separation and the smothering fallout from my last, mostly disastrous, visitation.

I have struggled to understand the process of that relational disaster. I have clung to unrealistic expectations of the nature of human relationships, emotions, and ways of thinking, and thus have suffered for being unable to "give it up". Even after two or so years I continue to struggle to comprehend the souring of our previously amicable relationship, though now with less fervour and a greater acceptance of things I cannot comprehend or change.

These struggles have resulted in letters (some sent, others not) and essays (again some sent and others left for my eyes only), all in the hope of improving my understanding of past events in the hope of finding better strategies for dealing with future difficulties.

One of my newly developed strategies is to send the occasional handwritten letter with attached printed essays in the hope that, if communication from east to west appears too unrewarding, communication from west to east, as the mood finds me, may get my views on various topics aired so that he gains some idea of the changes in the other. One way communication seemed better than none.

Some opening of discourse has resulted from this new policy. And for me those acts of essay writing helped clarify, and make more manageable, the issues that have held my mind captive for too long, issues now reduced from catastrophes to irritating disappointments.

One of those recently reciprocated communications was a long phone conversation with him. Being excitable and desirous of clearly stating my viewpoints I talked too much, tried to cover too many issues and probably wasted my time and his. If nothing else was communicated, I hope that my having called, and then talked of things other than the weather, held some significance in his mind.

Such conversations are frustrating experiences, for both. The barrage of words, emotions and ideas are too much, go too fast and are not repeated enough for any idea to be remembered. How much of a two-hour conversation can anyone remember?

Being human, I remembered little of it. On several previous occasions, he had stated the benefit of letting go of the past, extolled the virtues to be had in concentrating on living in the present and then considering the future. Forget the past; "it's water under the bridge" was mentioned.

Call it Taurean stubbornness, but I am uncomfortable with the advice to forget the slights of the past. How does one forget an emotion enhanced event? I can understand the desire to do so, especially if the event was truly traumatic, but can it be done?

It seems to me that the only way such unpleasant memories can be tamed is if the issues they represent can be discussed and understood by both sides – after which, either a reconciliation occurs, or both are satisfied that they have been heard and can then accept the irreconcilable nature of their differences.

My memories of him *are* who he is to me. He *is* the water running under my bridge, a stream of remembered experiences that have waxed and now, sadly, are waning. Is it desirable to forget *all* our past interactions, both the good (the vast majority from my viewpoint, he may disagree) and the less good and hurtful (fewer in number, but the negative are always felt deeper than the positive). Can he only exist during the act of speaking with him? When the conversation stops, does he magically disappear from my memory? That idea takes the concept of "out of sight, out of mind" to its ultimate expression. It is a trick I am incapable of.

How do I keep him alive in my mind if only the pleasant memories are to be kept? Is that half-man truly him? I don't think so. He is *all* my scrappy assortment of recollections of our times together. What I want is to refresh my fading concept of him by adding in new shared experiences to my stored stream of consciousness. I want to grow and sharpen his picture.

Time will tell if new shared experiences can revitalise the canvas or whether it will suffer the fate of all neglected things: to slowly shrivel and crumble into dust.

§

Time has passed since the above was written. In the near future my wife and I will drive to Geraldton for a week and then spend the first week of September in Carnarvon before heading back to Perth.

The thought of visiting Carnarvon has reminded me of

another "water under the bridge" scenario.

The Gascoigne River at Carnarvon is over a hundred metres wide as it passes to the north of the town. The bridge over it is consequently exceedingly long, but for over ninety percent of its time that bridge has no water to cross. It spans a "river" of rusty coloured sand.

Is this the bridge eulogised by that oft quoted saying: All the water that has gone under that bridge, all the old memories are buried and rarely do new memories flow past to annoy us into repeating the forgetting process?

But look closer at the situation. Under the dry sand and gravel that marks the river's course is a hidden river, an aquifer that is tapped into by the clever farmers who line its shores. They use its life-giving liquid to grow bountiful harvests of fruit and veggies for the clambering millions in Perth nine hundred kilometres to the south. The underground river is carefully and constantly monitored for quality and quantity so that they and their many customers all benefit. They understand the necessity to carefully manage its vital legacy.

For me, the Gascoigne River is an analogy of the good that can be done with *mindfully husbanded memories*. My memories, good and bad, are needed to provide the context with which to judge the present and from there guide me into the future.

In fact, who I am, who anyone is, is a mosaic of memories of past interactions with a parade of people that are painted onto the canvas of our recollections. The portrait of us that emerges into the foreground of that mental canvas is made of points of colour left behind by those interactions, with the important ones adding more points than the trivial.

Thus, the stream of human interactions flowing under my bridge, the remembered and the mostly forgotten, has shaped the person I am today and is the stuff I use, consciously and unconsciously, to guide my thoughts and create my future.

The better I understand the nature of the process of memory accumulation, distortion and diminishment, then the better will be my attitudes and subsequent actions. Hopefully, a more accepting and happier portrait of myself and those important to me will emerge.

44. Celebrations

Perhaps with Christmas* coming up it was only natural that my writing group settled upon celebrations as the theme for our January homework. I was the only one not enthused by the topic because of my confused and hence unresolved attitude towards celebrations, large or small.

This confusion is a relatively new phenomenon, perhaps the result of having reached a tipping point of accumulated knowledge gleaned from books and a wealth of life experiences.

After several weeks of cogitations, I found inconvenient questions arose, to which I had no satisfactory answers. For instance:

1. Why do I feel the need to celebrate certain events?

2. How do I decide what is worthy of celebrating?

3. Having decided the occasion is special enough, by what reasoning do I choose the appropriate manner of that celebration?

4. And when the party is over, how do I judge its success?

Apart from these four questions, my examination of the issue had me reassessing the cost/benefit ratio of past celebrations and, to a lesser extent, those yet to come.

Celebrations are scattered throughout most of our lives and I've participated in my fair share, be it a send-off for a departing colleague, birthdays – mine or other people's – Christmas gatherings, weddings, and funerals – if one considers them celebrations of the life of the dearly departed.

I am hoping the answers to my four questions will emerge after a brief examination of some examples, three from my life and a number of imagined scenarios.

My first memorable celebration was the end of high school party, an all-night session held in a corrugated iron hall in a hamlet close to the country town I lived in. It had the mandatory booze, loud music, a certain amount of dancing. It resulted in my first experience of kissing a girl on the lips, of getting drunk and surviving my first "morning after".

My twenty-first had some similarities. The differences were the location (my sister's house in Sydney). Those gathered were family and a selection of my acquaintances, and the food was better. The similarities were plenty of booze, loud music and dancing, though this time with no smooching. It again resulted in my eventual inebriation.

My thirtieth was the same locale, a different crowd as befitting my changed circumstances. Again, it was another evening/night/early morning of music, food, dancing and booze but with a few kiddies' games added that generated a welcome level of uproarious laughter. This was the celebration I remember the most vividly and fondly – firstly, for the fun factor, and secondly because photos were taken that have consequently kept key moments well embedded in my memory.

These three offer some insights but a few more permutations need to be considered before fuller illumination is possible.

After happily working for an organisation for quite a few years you decide it's time to move on. How do you feel if:
  a) no send-off celebration is organised, or
  b) a very half-hearted, grudging, minimalist one is arranged?
If you organise a big bash to mark a significant personal

milestone, invite a bunch of significant people, friends, family, colleagues et cetera and

a) no one turns up, or

b) only a few turn up, or

c) those who attend do so without the expected friendly good humour, instead are unhappy and leave early?

How do you feel in each scenario?

How do you feel if a big event in your peer group is planned and you are not invited?

Is it possible to celebrate an achievement by oneself and still have it generate some significant measure of lasting satisfaction?

And on the other side of the coin, what non-verbal messages do you send if

a) you decline an invitation to participate in a ceremony without giving convincing reasons, or

b) attend when unhappy with either the event's style and/or those attending, and consequently dampen the other people's enjoyment.

Having mulled over all of the above, two broad aspects emerge: the desire to remember, and the desire for social recognition, with both desires interconnected.

Thus, the solitary celebration is probably better than being poked in the eye with a burnt stick but that burnt stick would be considerably more memorable.

All the celebrations I have experienced, directly or indirectly, had some hope of being memorable, especially for the person whose achievement was being eulogised. This is where biology comes into the equation, specifically, the biology of how we remember.

For a memory to be stored in the brain the data from our senses must have strength and endurance. It needs to be stronger than background "noise" (the stronger the better) and last long enough (the longer the better) to grow the new neuronal interconnections that are our memory.

Unfortunately, or fortunately, depending on one's timeframe and values, we evolved to be more sensitive to negative events, thus the fearful and threatening are more memorable than the pleasurable, and very much more than the neutral. This bias underlies post-traumatic stress disorder, depression and energy sapping pessimism.

Being fearful saved our ancestors from being eaten but unmitigated negativity and fear also threatened our survival. Hence evolution also favoured a mechanism that rewarded constructive behaviours. It did this via a range of hormones that we can call the "happy" hormones, the principal ones being, serotonin, dopamine, oxytocin and vasopressin. All have multiple effects in our body and on our mood. Dopamine from the brain is particularly crucial because it not only generates feelings of joy, but heightens situational awareness (to better remember details) and stimulates the growth of neuronal connections (to hardwire those details into memory). Oxytocin in women and its male equivalent, vasopressin, are important in regard to celebrating because of their enhancement of interpersonal bonding.

An endocrinologist, in understanding the hormonal influences affecting the brain's storage or rejection of information, would find it easy to explain why I found my thirtieth birthday particularly memorable. There was good food (hence increased serotonin from the visceral nervous system), booze (alcohol, like many drugs stimulates dopamine production as one of its effects). Dopamine and other happy hormones are also stimulated by music, if pleasant, and moderate physical activity, such as dancing, as well as laughter. Dopamine and the bonding hormones are elevated by the presence of friends. The photos of that event then enhanced the time available for those happy memories to be rehearsed and refreshed.

To counterbalance our innate and heightened sensitivity to the negative is why it is wise to remember the good things as well. Doing so achieves two things. It gives us a more realistic view of the world from which more realistic and hopefully constructive decisions can arise. And, in cementing the memory of our achievements into our psyche, our self-esteem is also strengthened, which gives us the hope and confidence needed to move forward, to try new things, and to survive mistakes and periods of bad luck.

Solo celebrations, or being excluded from celebrations, or celebrations where the attendees fail to be jovial and convivial, are unappealing, if not tragic, because they fail to provide the most treasured of human wants: social recognition.

Humans are social animals. We did not survive our evolutionary ordeal on the predator-friendly savannahs of Africa by being rugged individualists, we lived or perished according to our ability to work together for the common good, rather than mere self-preservation.

And getting on with our fellows still remains our greatest biological asset. This is reflected in our obsession with other people's opinions of us and the hurt we feel if ignored, disparaged, criticised in public, passed over for promotions and the numerous other ways our need for social inclusion and regard can be thwarted.

We celebrate to remember the good bits and to have those bits and ourselves recognised and remembered by others. This requirement for social recognition explains the types of events deemed worthy of celebrating as well as the appropriateness of the selected manner of such celebrations. Both are determined by social upbringing and societal norms interacting with our genetic predispositions, which also create the expectations we have of such events.

But how do we judge their success, the cost/benefit ratio of a celebration?

When we are young, everything is new and hence a big deal, because there is little context against which to judge things. Everything is more noticeable the first time around, maybe the second time, but the millionth? Thus, my most memorable celebrations were all in the first half of my life, when the world was new. These days, I still see the party and the dancing, but also the hangover and the financial burden.

For example, my dear wife and I were honoured with an invite to a gala wedding a while back. It produced much joy but, from my older perspective, the outlandish expense incurred could have been used to better effect, either in the bank as a financial buffer against the vagaries of employment, or allocated to the couple's sizeable debts.

Here in my home office hangs a photo of my retirement do. I had worked there for over fourteen years and my colleagues and I are all looking happy, me especially. That memento reinforces fond memories of colleagues and the work I did, but it also reminds me of the disappointments encountered at that workplace and previous ones.

The gala wedding and my retirement do are celebrations remembered. But how long will those memories last?

Even the fondness for my thirtieth is tempered by the knowledge that most of the friends invited are no longer in my life, or linger in a faded or diminished capacity. So, how much of a success was it? The answer seems to be less than I thought at the time. And yet my memories of it are not totally extinguished and, though the glow has lessened, it still does glow within me.

Big, expensive and/or showy celebrations probably have their place, and yet my longest-lasting interpersonal connections seem to have depended on regularly engaging in simple activities, shared with a minimum of people. That said, the desire to celebrate, to commemorate a joyous occasion, to mark an achievement in a memorable way, to find a means to remember the good times, still beats in my heart. What to do?

The answer appears to be that I am already doing it.

Over recent years I have instinctively cultivated a habit of actively acknowledging the many good things in my life, past and present, as a way to take the sting from unexpected bouts of depressive thoughts. It is a behaviour I currently call upon in regard to events like COVID-19 and the pre-election antics and ravings of Trump and his like.

As mentioned in earlier essays, our house abounds with pictures of either happy events or scenes that instil gratitude and thanks. When tapping on my keyboard, if I delay too long, the screensaver inspires me by scrolling through pictures of get-togethers and photos from our numerous forays into the countryside.

My wife and I reaffirm our wedding vows, not with the occasional flashy affirmation ceremony presided over by a celebrant, but in the many conscious and unconscious acts of kindness and appreciation done throughout the day.

The benefit of this habitual *micro-celebrating*, which also includes regular acknowledgement of our happy circumstances, is not that we remember each moment of kindness or appreciation, but from its ability to rebalance our thinking. My wife has always been more sensible than I, and so had less distance to travel in this regard, but my practising of micro-celebrating has increased my progress towards her level of contentment. These days I rejoice more than I lament!

This newfound appreciation for the many good things in my life, and the greater understanding and hence increased acceptance of the negative bits, recently found form when I reacquainted myself with the song *How can I keep from singing*, sung by the Irish singer Enya.

Though the lyrics are a response to political issues, their hopeful theme resonates strongly in my soul.

In my daily practise of appreciating and understanding, how can I not join her – like her, how can I keep from singing!

* This essay was written in December 2020.
Lyrics to *How Can I Keep from Singing* as sung by Enya can be found on the internet.

45. Opinions

I can't remember in which *Dirty Harry* movie it was that tough guy cop, Harry Callahan, played by Clint Eastwood, uttered this immortal line, but it hit me in the seventies when I first heard it and resonates still: "Opinions are xxxx xxxxxxxx, xxxxxxxxx'x xxx xxx!" ([1] To prevent misdirecting negativity please read this essay first. The full quote is at the end of it.)

It was said as a jibe at an authority figure's pronouncement. I was both shocked and envious because I would never have dreamed of saying such a line or have been capable of getting away with it, which, presumably, is why it lodged in my brain – lodged but never seriously examined until recently.

I now find myself motivated to explore the issue because I am obliged, in my writing group, to give feedback on other members' work as well as receive judgement on my own. Their literary creations are as precious to them as mine are to me and hence praise is especially desired and criticism found hard to swallow. The process is equivalent to the public assessment of one's children.

Dirty Harry's one-liner is an example of the principal barrier to reasoned debate: "confirmation bias" [2]. This is caused when our strong belief in the correctness of our view clashes with the opinion of others, resulting in an equally strong dismissal of any contrary to ours. For Harry, it is: *I'm right, you and everyone else are wrong*. No further conversation is required or possible.

We all suffer from confirmation bias because throughout our

evolution our survival increasingly depended upon our ability to solve increasingly more complex problems created by social interdependence, which constantly threatened to overwhelm our brain's limited processing and storage capacity. New data requires energy to grow new neuronal interconnections (memories) and we only have so much energy and so many neurons. One of the brain's responses is to act like a triage nurse. It sorts data into what needs immediate attention, based upon past experience, and what can be left for later or completely ignored. Ignored will be anything too far from established norms or contradictory to them. This logic results in the strengthening of preconceived ideas (confirmation bias).

One consequence of this is that the older one gets the harder it is to countenance new viewpoints. Age thus gives us hardening of the arteries along with *hardening of the attitudes*! If we need proof, we only need to try dissuading anyone of a long-held belief. For proof, attempt to convince a committed atheist of God's existence, or persuade a true believer of the falsity of their faith and see how far you get.

In keeping with the apparent dual nature of reality, evolution has also created brain circuitry that can dampen expression of reinforced opinions, when they threaten our physical and/or social existence. This mechanism appears to be rather underdeveloped in many people and hence is not to be relied upon too heavily in discussions with those not sharing large chunks of our viewpoint.

Thus, the brain's methodology for dealing with data needs to be considered if an exchange of ideas is desired. This is not always the case. Many conversations consist of people talking *at* each other, with little interest in the opinion of the other. They consist of telling, not talking.

And sometimes spoken or written opinions are used as weapons to cudgel the "opposition" into submission. Issuing effective invectives is a skill much prized by politicians and others, with cricket players apparently in that number because it seems that, to be successful, they must learn how to bat, bowl, field and *sledge*.

Back to the more civil arena of my writers' group.

The feedback sessions involve two tasks: giving feedback in a manner that is both not so threatening to be instantly dismissed and specific enough to be useable to the recipient, and, when on the receiving end, learning to control our confirmation bias, which, being sure of our brilliance, is loath to hear anything to the contrary.

If you are a person lacking the pretentions of being a writer you may find my problem hardly worth considering but similar challenges abound in most people's daily interactions. Many situations arise where our pride is subject to social assessment, to our joy or humiliation. If you need examples, experiment with voicing an opinion that upsets your spouse, boss, dear friend or colleague. Doing so will induce considerable negative consequences because the recipients will get indignant, possibly offended, which may then transform into anger and possible retribution. Thus, the emotions produced by our utterances need to be well understood and controlled if good outcomes are to be crafted.

The consequences of airing an opinion are dependent upon many things:

1. *The power relationship between giver and receiver and whether the giver seeks to give or take power from the other and whether the receiver is willing to put up with that arrangement.*

A viewpoint expressed will induce thoughts of rejection or acceptance, such as: "What gives *you* the right to comment!" or, "If *she* thinks that, then I really must be getting better and do have a talent worth developing." or, "I'd better not say too much or my spot on the team and possibly my whole career will go down the tubes." or, if making a weaponised pronouncement from an unassailable position of power, "What a load of crap that was, get out of here and don't come back until you have something vastly better."

2. *Who is witness to the comment?*

Being a social animal, group dynamics play a crucial role in determining our thoughts and subsequent behaviours. Hence, negative opinions will be much easier to handle if only the giver and the receiver are party to it. Any damage done will be easier to contain and later bury or build upon. The damage done will of course be multiplied by the power difference between sender and receiver and whether any realistic possibilities of reversing that difference exist. The classic situation is the emotions engendered during a job interview or a performance review. Oh, what fun they are!

Add an audience of more than one and the hurt of negative comments is multiplied in proportion to the number looking on as well as the nature of that audience. Being disparaged in front of a group of our peers and/or people we wish to impress is far worse than being reviled before a gathering of our enemies.

If we find ourselves in a round table discussion where opinions are called upon, the first person asked has to stick their neck out and hope not to offend too many of the others, especially the most powerful. The second and subsequent members have an easier task as they can use the reactions to the first speaker to modify their responses. If last on the list and holder of an opinion contrary to the majority the urge to hold our tongue or repeat the popular view can be overwhelming, particularly given the knowledge of the fate of most "whistle-blowers".

The power of a group to coerce consensus, to encourage groupthink, can be tragically real. The choking to death in May 2020 of George Floyd by the arresting policeman, watched on by his fellow officers who, in not intervening, gave mute confirmation of the arresting officer's non-verbal opinion: that black lives don't matter as much as their brand of in-group loyalty.

Thankfully, a similarly drastic outcome is unlikely to occur in my writers' group feedback sessions. Even so, I would be lying if I didn't admit to feeling some "heat" when asked to give truthful and useable opinions, and similarly suffering when waiting to receive the verdicts on my own work.

3. *The manner of an opinion's delivery and frequency.*

"It was good" is a comment that will elicit a pleasant glow in the recipient, but is not something that offers much information in regard to which specific bits were amazing versus those that were only moderately good. If that comment were to be said of all of one's works, it drifts towards meaningless and risks becoming suggestive of sarcasm rather than praise.

A global criticism such as: "That was complete rubbish" is especially hurtful because it is all-encompassing. It was not ninety per cent or fifty per cent rubbish but one hundred per cent garbage. Such a comment offers no scope for saving face and gives little reason to want to improve upon the offending creation. A list of specific rubbishy bits hurts less through its implication that there were better bits upon which to build our hopes.

It should be noted that our limited ability to remember a long list of items restricts the effectiveness of giving too many specific comments, especially if given verbally. I don't know about you but I'm pushed to keep more than three items in my short-term memory long enough to make it into my long-term memory.

4. *One's assessment of the recipient's state of mind.*

How will they handle my praise? How will they cope with my criticism? Are they really interested in my opinion? At what "level of development" are they? What values do they use to judge my words and the way I say them? What "facts" do we agree on? What are our areas of disagreement? What are their "buttons", those hidden sensitivities that can trigger a disastrous reaction? What points will they become fixated upon so that all subsequent aspects fail to register?

In trying to answer the above questions it becomes clear that issuing an opinion is considerably more dangerous than receiving one because we never fully understand our audience. Thus, the words chosen and their manner of presentation require careful consideration if the messages sent, explicit and implicit, are going to be received with any accuracy.

So far in this study, I have concentrated on negative comments and yet praise also has its complications.

Most of us, myself included, are happy to receive without debate any confirmation of our abilities and achievements, and yet the four points above still influence. Surely the nature of the giver, the audience and the manner of delivery must heighten or diminish the value of such praise?

The compliments of a person held in high esteem must surely be worth more than those of an ignoramus? And more so if publicised. But how do we allocate such esteem? By what values do we judge one person's positive feedback as being more truthful and worthy than another's? And how do we judge the sincerity of a compliment when there is such a thin line between genuine praise and flattery?

Harry Callahan was spot on, everyone does have an opinion. I have one, he has one and millions of other people have them on a billion different topics and situations. The thing is, in dismissing out-of-hand all but his own, Harry assumes he knows everything and has a brain huge enough to comprehend the meaning, the consequences, in the short and long-term of that enormity of information.

Harry also assumes his opinions are his own, but are they? Are my views my own? Nietzsche made the assertion that: *all the things we believe in* (our opinions), *at any given time, reflect not the truth but someone else's power over us.* I am inclined to agree with him.

Like Harry, none of us choose our genetic predispositions. We do not choose how our caregivers, when a child, adolescent or young person, engage with us. Interactions that were critical to the development of our views on how things work and the values we use to assess the information life's random circumstances continually pushed our way.

If chance had allocated us a father who solved disagreements with persons having contrary viewpoints by thumping them into tacit agreement, whether us, our mother or any other person, those experiences would have involuntarily trained our values to be either fearfulness before tyrants, or into fighting fire with fire and approving violent countermeasures against perceived bullying.

We all cling to our opinions as being ours but, like a housetrained dog, much of those cherished viewpoints, values and justified behaviours are not ours but the forgotten and internalised influence of others upon us. It is a humbling concept to consider.

Perhaps, in the movie, Harry does have all the relevant facts, possesses an unassailable value system with which to judge them and the imagination to come up with the correct course of action to rightly dismiss all other views. But Harry is a fictional character in a fictional world, it is *my opinion* that reality is different and closer to Nietzsche's world.

Mark Twain shone light on that difference when he remarked that *ignorance and confidence are all one needs to succeed in business*, leaving unsaid the other vital ingredient: plenty of good luck. Only the fully foolish think they have a cast-iron grasp of the way the world works.

Unfortunately, reality is too enormous in scope for any one person to fully understand it. There are too many interacting variables and too much randomness. Hence the ability to pass or hold an opinion with anything approaching one hundred per cent truthfulness appears to be proportional to one's level of ignorance of the immensity of factors involved in producing such a "true" viewpoint, especially in regard to our biologically constrained capacity to understand the full breadth of physical reality.

Perhaps with advances in computing, artificial intelligence and human-to-computer interfaces, my current view will become unsustainable. Until that happens, I am stuck with the conclusion reached in my essay, *Living on Scraps*, that I formulate "my" opinions automatically, upon the rubbery hope that the "facts" I possess are sufficient in number and validity as well as sufficiently understood. All this is assessed by a value system moulded by my unacknowledged physical and social history, and easily swayed by the brain's peculiar way of doing things, which makes it prone to confirmation bias and other perceptive and computational shortcomings.

Thus, all opinions, especially my own, whether shared or not, need to be taken with "a grain of salt". If an opinion is to be believed and acted upon, we also need to be well aware of the consequences of doing so, which is why I try to enact this piece of simple wisdom: *praise in public and chastise in private*, with any chastising done with compassion and restricted to the few most salient points.

I am loath to end on a down note but feel compelled to admit to one failing of this investigation: it has not significantly lessened my desire to mindfully share my opinions. It seems I shall remain that "opinionated old guy with the beard" for a while longer yet.

[1] Harry declared "Opinions are like assholes, everybody's got one!" Whilst I recognise the truth of his words and their implications, I think there is much more to the topic than Harry's brief summation and arrogant delivery.

[2] Confirmation bias is one of many that hamper our thinking, all of which are discussed in detail in *Thinking, Fast and Slow* by Daniel Kahneman.

46. Doing It for Money

Way back in my teenage years, I was struck by a curiously unreasonable societal attitude. It was to do with a specific aspect of the fee-for-service economic model: prostitution. I was puzzled then, as now, of our societal inconsistency of attitude towards prostitution.

For instance, why do we demonise the prostitute but not the client? Is it because they are almost always female? I have never heard of a gigolo suffering the same indignities before the law, or receive society's condemnation in a manner equivalent to that metered out to a female prostitute. But surely, if the transaction is immoral, illegal and socially destructive, then both the prostitute *and* their clients deserve the same sanctions? But that hardly ever seems to happen.

Why?

And why am I raising an issue that the majority of us have little first-hand experience of, whether as a prostitute or a client, and possibly little inclination to gain any? The short answer for me is that I am considering the act of "prostituting" myself in the near future, and wish to clarify my attitudes towards that possible act.

I am not contemplating selling myself for sexual services but am considering whether to get my just-completed novel published, and sold, for money!

Have I lost the plot? Bear with me; I shall explain.

If we have had the experience of being an employee, whether

cleaner, clerk or C.E.O., then we should have a practical understanding of the process of selling our body's physical strength and skills, if a manual worker, or our body's brain power if a knowledge worker. If we *lease* our bodies, our minds, and possibly our souls, for a wage or salary, are we any different, philosophically, from that prostitute soliciting underneath the lamppost?

The difficulty most have in equating their paid employment to her situation is that their work seems to be vastly different from the squalid truths attached to the word "prostitution" in its usual usage. We, respectable citizens, take offence at the absurd notion that our behaviours are in any way connected to the immoral values and lude actions of that woman in the impossibly short dress and overdone makeup. And yet the connection can be made. The difference is merely one of degree and manner. Most employees are simply more conventionally dressed and work in better circumstances and, some would claim, for more noble reasons.

Of course, "doing it for money" carries vastly different moral and emotional meanings depending upon what the "it" is, and the circumstances behind the monetary reward being offered. If "it" is mowing the lawn, and the mower man and customer agree to the arrangement without any form of coercion, then all is fine. A win-win situation and both are happy.

It is the *happiness* aspect that is the central thrust of this essay.

That novel I wrote had a lot of me in it. It dominated my life for the better part of a year, rewarding me with an immense dose of one of the thirteen types of happiness for which the Sanskrit language has a name, *krtarthata*, the happiness of achievement.

What I fear is, that in pursuing the next logical step – getting it published for sale – all that wonderful *krtarthata* will be diminished or possibly entirely lost, firstly, by the arduous process of either convincing a publisher to publish and then promote it, or self-publish and incur the cost in time and effort of getting the manuscript up to a publishable quality, get a cover design and a back cover blurb organised, and finally locate a printer to produce copies at a reasonable cost.

Any monetary rewards from either path will require me to expend time and effort in promoting the book (less so if the publisher takes on the task, though at the cost of a lesser slice of the profits) and then taking on the unpaid task of keeping track of income and expenses for the benefit of the taxman and social security.

All of this sounds like too much work for the probable meagre rewards. It induces too much of that feeling of me returning to being an employee, a feeling I had hoped to have left permanently behind after I retired from *work*. I wonder if Sanskrit also has a word for the brand of happiness and welcome relief that comes from our joyous exit from the rulebound and coercive world of employment? Even though my working life was less onerous than most, such a word and its attached feelings of release from servitude, would be a welcome extension of my vocabulary and would receive regular usage in our household.

As far as I can see any novel, short story, or memoir is ultimately written for it to be read. But is it enough if the only reader is the author? Surely society suffers when brilliant ideas and talent remain silent just as much as when dangerous and destructive notions are unwisely released and promoted. I naturally include my output into the brilliant and talented category!

Alain de Botton, in his book *Status Anxiety*, describes an idea as being like a colourless, odourless gas that when released permeates through society, via word of mouth or any of the multitude of other methods for dispersing ideas, such as television and the internet. In time, the idea eventually becomes part of the *unchallenged* understanding of "the way things are", rather than the more aware state of: "the way things are *now*". We are like fish, in being blind to gradual changes in the ideological waters in which we swim.

Do I have something worth dispensing into society's waters and at what cost, in its broadest sense, to myself and society, or more correctly, that small portion of it who is my possible readership? I suspect the answer depends upon how resilient I consider myself and society to be.

From what I can determine, the things I had to say in my novel have been said many times before, and possibly in more succinct and entertaining ways, so I see little harm in putting mine before a wider audience. In fact, some of the notions I explored in that novel need more "air-time" as a counter to excessive uncritical acceptance of the way things are.

This leaves my decision to pursue publication concerned mostly with the costs to myself of doing so.

Wanting to display our achievements is a common enough desire but what exactly do we hope to gain from doing so? This is a topic mulled over in other essays with my overall answer being: the *innate need for social recognition*. But from *whom* and in what manner? How much recognition is enough? And how will I benefit if the feedback, whether in the form of cash or opinions, is insufficient or unflattering? How much ego strength do I invest in those possible disparate outcomes?

My current thinking is swayed by two breezes: firstly, the sentiments expressed in the book *Your Money or Your Life* by Joe Dominguez and Vicki Robin, whose central idea was that the money we earn comes at the cost of our irreplaceable "life's energy" and our irreplaceable time – time and energy which could have been spent on other things. The question Joe and Vicki put to their readers is: Is the work and time allocated to getting the cash, worth the "fulfilment value" gained from the goods and services bought with it, and is that notion of fulfilment value uniquely ours to determine?

The second influence was found in an anecdote from a book, whose title escapes me, which made mention of a group of charity volunteers doing door-to-door soliciting for donations. The charity, being kind-hearted, decided to take pity on their volunteers and compensate them for the travails suffered whilst "beating the streets" and decided to pay them a small stipend. The result was *unexpected discontent* amongst the volunteers and a significant drop in donations collected. Why? Because doing the collecting for free gave the volunteers the immeasurable pleasure of feeling that they were giving their time and effort selflessly for the benefit of the less well-off. When they were paid, they no longer saw themselves as being magnanimous but turned into poorly paid collection agents.

Something done for the love of it has a very different ambience than the same activity done for money. That dynamic also underpins the happily married. If we marry because we love, and really like our spouse, life is very different than when the primary reason is financial security the other can provide and/or the desirable social status they impart.

My current financial situation is one in which working for others has become an option, not a necessity.

In putting my writing "up for sale", whether any sales are made or not, how does that enhance or detract from the amount of fulfilment value I will get from my creative effort? Does doing so return me to being an indentured servant of a fickle public and a money-obsessed publisher?

One thing is certain: writing for the money will make it much harder for me to maintain any illusory sense of moral superiority regarding the behaviour of prostitutes.

Money, sadly, is the *opinion* most listened to in our society and hence any desire for recognition as a writer is only unequivocally found in massive sales of one's literary output. Some may deride huge book sales as pandering to populism, of such works being mere "pulp fiction" for the plebeians and not to be considered "real literature". But I suspect fat royalty cheques would have a way of taking the sting from any such criticism. Dismal sales on the other hand require far greater mental energy and ego strength to come to terms with.

Unfortunately, making pots of money from writing "literature", or any other branch of written expression, appears to carry worse odds than of winning a lottery jackpot. This brings me back to the questions: how much praise for one's novel is enough and how to measure the value of such praise.

How many endorsements from friends, family and fellow writers are equivalent to that of a single stranger parting with fifteen or more dollars of their hard-earned cash for a copy of one's creation?

Why is the financial recognition of this stranger seemingly more valuable than the cash-free views of family, friends and peers? Is it a brutal case of money speaking louder than words? Or perhaps it represents this author's lack of appropriate gratitude for the immeasurable value of the encouragement and feedback freely and generously given by his friends and others? Feedback that enabled him to develop the skills to produce a work that generated all that intoxicating *krtarthata* and also made real the possibility of financial and societal recognition that substantive sales can offer.

What happens if our friends and peers love it but publishers reject it, or, if a publisher does like it enough to publish, only to find it a commercial failure and have both publisher and author suffer the ignominy of the public's rejection?

And how does each of these scenarios affect our relationships with publishers, the public, our friends and, ourselves?

If the blaming kind, who do we demonise for our lack of commercial success? Do we curse our "misguided" friends for encouraging us, and likewise our publisher? Or do we blame our own ineptitude and hubris? Most, myself included if I am honest, find taking on blame a distasteful business and hence prefer to redirect it rather than accept too much of it. Money and blame appear to be opposites. We can never get too much money, and never accept anything but the most inescapably small quantity of blame.

And how much of the credit for any success, financial or otherwise, can any of us credit to being of our making when we are all enmeshed in a society that, mostly unrecognised and unacknowledged, made any such success a possibility, mostly when accompanied by a generous dose of good luck. The same applies to the blame for apparent failure. Success or failure, it's not all ours.

And few want to recognise the burden in time and energy of staying successful, or the unenviable task of coping with the fading or abrupt end of that success. "He's off his game" or any number of similar comments may not be compensated by the enlarged bank balance, though my very practical wife would probably disagree!

I'm sure many employees, and possibly some prostitutes, work under terms they set, with conditions so benevolent that they enjoy their toil and find sufficient compensation for their time in the fulfilment value they obtain when they spend their cash.

As a writer what are the conditions under which I can join them and set my own terms, so that I write for pleasure first and financial reward second?

The specifics of those conditions are beyond my imagination at present but one thing is for certain: money is a powerful and often corrupting force that I am determined will serve me and not I it.

47. Silence

I recently read* *The Silent Patient* by Alex Michaelides, a psychological thriller that had received the praise of a cousin-in-law. Liking the lad, I read the book in the hope of finding out more about him using the logic that we are not only what we do but what we read.

The book was well written, a page turner, but for me too stark, too grim, with too little to lighten the soul. There was an excess of unhappy and twisted people and only one minor character that I found to be of a kind and generous nature to counterbalance the others. I *survived* the book, rather than rejoiced for having read it.

But it wasn't a total loss. There was one sentence in it that struck a chord: "Silence is a mirror.". I wasn't sure at the time whether it was a profound statement or not, but in these next few pages I intend to find out.

The book wasn't the only sign that silence needed thinking about. The universe soon provided two more aspects to goad me into action, one tragic and one hopeful.

The tragic was learning of the suicide of a person known to my wife since his birth. He hanged himself after enduring months of a debilitating disease whilst waiting for an operation that, with medication, would have made a normal life possible though not offering a cure – a man on the cusp of retirement after a long career in an occupation in which he had a good reputation – a man who enjoyed a home life with a "one and only" wife. He was a father with adult children, all doing well and some on the verge of marriage and a hoped-for next generation.

He had a lot to live for. Thus, his suicide was shockingly unexpected. But the worst thing for his immediate family and his siblings was that he left no note. He left them to writhe in the grief wracked silence he bequeathed them.

The opposite of that terrible silence came a week later in the shape of an out-of-the-blue phone call from a chap I had called friend. He had once been like an older brother but had not contacted me for several decades, in spite of my initial attempts to remain in contact once I'd moved interstate. Eventually, I had written him off as an active part of my life, though his photo remains in my collage of male friends and relations that occupy a picture frame on prominent display in my shed, there to remind me of their existence whilst I work or laze about.

His call felt as though I'd accidently barged into a séance and was suddenly hearing the voice of one who has passed over to the other side. I had grieved in my way for his diminished role in my life and now had to find a response to his chatting as though our last phone conversation was a few days back, not decades. I learned of a few recent developments in his life and I told him a few of mine and, at his suggestion, emailed a few of my stories and essays as a means for him to further understand the changes in my thinking. I am now in the early stages of the silence of his yet to materialise response.

It seems any dose of "the silent treatment" is only bearable if the reasons for it are known and accepted by the recipient.

Both of the silences above carried implied messages of disregard, dismissal and possible disdain towards the receivers. Inaccurate messages need to be clarified. The real tragedy of the first case is that the needed clarification can never take place. His grief-stricken wife, children and siblings will always carry the pain of that silence, which may fester if they fill it with wrong meanings.

In high school science we were told that nature abhors a vacuum. It appears the maxim also applies to human interactions, specifically, the vacuum of human silences. If the relationship between the parties has some value to one, or both, then an empty response begs to be given reasons and meanings, which, in the absence of real evidence are fictions that either flatter or flagellate our egos. This same mental architecture was discussed in my essay on the giving and taking of offence (*Taking the Offensive*) and likewise the nature of our judgement upon a silence will depend upon evidence of the *intentions* behind it.

We are wise to be careful before attaching intentions to most non-verbal communications, and especially so with silences, where there are no gestures, postures or tones of voice to give guidance.

And some silences are accidental. A letter can be lost in the mail, an email can be overlooked or actively deleted before reading because it is mistaken for spam. A return call made may not have been received because of lack of signal, which could then result in the delayed response creating unnecessary ire in the receiver who attributes the delay to the sender's tardiness, instead of assigning it to the limits of microwaves as a means of carrying a message.

Many silences are active. They have a purposeful rationale behind them, but such rationales are many and so again it is best to collect reliable evidence before affixing any particular meaning to the puzzling and/or annoying "break in transmission".

Some people subscribe to the wisdom of *saying nothing if they have nothing good to say*. Few of us like criticism, hence such a policy has much merit unless the recipient notes the lack of comment and, rather than ask for clarification, decides upon the most insulting interpretation of that silence.

Not commenting can in fact be a powerful and effective response to a malicious slandering of our person or actions. Our silence suggests that the slander is so ridiculous as to be unworthy of rebuttal and also implies our overwhelming confidence in the falsity of the slander. Such a silence can act as a fire blanket, cutting off the oxygen needed to feed a verbal conflagration.

A similar silence is often used if we actively wish to discourage a relationship without being overtly rude. We give them the subtle hint of non-communication to put them off. We do so in the hope that they get the message without the pain of having to "spelt it out" to them. As a technique it is not always successful.

Taken to the extreme, discouraging with silence can be used as a means of political control, for better or worse. Donald Trump being blocked from spreading his "reality" on Twitter and other electronic platforms was such a case.

Censoring dissenting opinions can also be silenced by "noise". These days "truths" can be obliterated by being drowned in an ocean of manufactured falsities and distractions using Tweets, Facebook posts, fake news items and emotion grabbing conspiracies to divert attention from those inconveniently contrary observations or questionings. Curiously, trying to drown a dangerous lie with a barrage of facts is more difficult than the opposite, and it sometimes ends up being counterproductive, with the lie actually increasing in power and influence.

When under coercion, a deliberate silence can be seen as a test of character. Thus, the silence of a captured soldier, spy, or criminal, can be deemed, by some, as a heroic act of loyalty to their organisation and/or credo. Such a silence, in a man, becomes proof of their manhood, because real men don't cry and real men don't grass on their mates. Presumably the same applies to "real women".

Not all silences are whole. Some are relative, ones of volume rather than existence or not.

When young children are quiet for too long most wise caregivers will become concerned because those silences sometimes mean the child is up to mischief. The kid has fallen into the pool, or escaped from the yard and is wandering unsupervised along a busy roadside, or is in a place with hazards unknown to the child. My relative quietude raises warning bells in my wife and can result in her asking me if something is wrong. Often, she is right and I am brooding, usually upon some aspect of my stupidity or society's.

Another variety of relative silence could be described as partial silence. Like half-truths, they can be equally misleading and troublesome.

A partial silence occurs when portions of a message, generally the core meanings, are missed because they are silenced by a distraction, such as an emotive word or statement that the reader becomes captured by, so much so that the bulk of the message is lost. Such distractions are the equivalent of a mute button being suddenly switched on. When that happens, half-baked notions are set loose with insufficient context to pull them back into line. Hurt or unsupported happiness can result.

A recent example was my attempt to highlight the one good aspect of Communist ideology in a short story (*The Happy Communists*, later renamed *Kev Calls for a Celebration*). No matter how I tried to verbally sugar-coat the pill it remained a miserable failure, largely due to the deeply associated fear and loathing glued to Communism, as a word and concept. Fear, it seems, easily obliterates curiosity and generosity. This also helps explain the effectiveness of mudslinging and fear campaigns during elections.

Partial silences and the confusions they create can also occur when there is a disparity between the verbal and non-verbal messages, between what is said and how it is said, as well as the actions or inactions generated by it. The workplace is a good source of such confusions. For instance, when I worked as a driver assessor, the department's declaration of a commitment to road safety in mission statements, policy emails and from the mouths of my immediate bosses seemed to evaporate when I would question the suggested benefits of their policy changes. I, and others, were allowed to say our piece – we were "heard" and "consulted", but their subsequent actions suggested that the negative consequences for driver assessors and the safety of the driving public were *not* heard, or, if heard, not considered as being relevant.

Most silences irk the receiver, but not all.

There can be wonderfully companionable silences. The utter quiet when my wife and I are propped up in bed engrossed in our books, is, when I occasionally stop to hear and feel it, a rather precious phenomenon because it means both of us are really enjoying ourselves and are totally content. Such moments in life are rare and deserve to be savoured and remembered.

Likewise, one of the pleasures of going for a motorcycle ride with a group, so long as we stick to our own pace, level of skill and risk, is that we are *silently* enjoying time together. Those meditative silences make the chatting in the café later on all the more pleasurable.

Just as 'absence' is said to make the heart grow fonder, in the right measure, so too can well-crafted silences. They build up pleasant anticipation, which then makes the aural reward all the more powerful. The most satisfying of such gaps occurs when communication is non-verbal, specifically, when communicating via music.

In my restricted knowledge, the greatest exponent of the

heightened drama and pleasure that carefully placed musical pauses can bring, is to be found in the early works of Brazilian jazz composer and musician, Antonio Carlos Jobim. The vinyl record *Jobim Plays*, from 1963, has Claus Ogerman providing beautiful orchestration upon which Jobim overlays his themes on the piano in his famous one-finger style. His Latin melodies are given life with a minimum of notes and a maximum of anticipatory silences between them, resulting in a marvellous languid sensuality, especially on tracks like *O Morro*, *Insensatez* and *Meditation*.

There remains one final aspect of silence to be broached; that of being, or becoming deaf.

To be born deaf is a handicap but not one that precludes some semblance of a normal and satisfying life. But having our hearing abilities diminish over time, slowly or rapidly, is a very different challenge. It is similar to being born poor and staying poor, versus being born wealthy and then becoming irrevocably impoverished.

The creeping silence of going deaf is accompanied by constant misunderstandings by the sufferer, from only hearing partial messages, annoyance in others, from the sufferer constantly getting the wrong messages and incessantly asking for things to be repeated. And, in the eyes of many, to be hard of hearing apparently renders such people idiots or dullards. Declining hearing generally comes with age, which also makes it harder to learn coping mechanisms, such as lip reading or sign language.

As a music lover, losing my ability to enjoy music doesn't bear thinking about. A dramatic statement coming from a compulsive thinker.

I know of a person who has a sizable music collection and a fantastic Hi-Fi system but now suffers from severe tinnitus as a side-effect of pain medication, which, in dampening his nervous system's sensitivity, has resulted, upon cessation of the treatment, in his nerves overcompensating and becoming oversensitive. He can now only listen to music in very small, subdued doses. I feel for him and dread that it should ever happen to me. The only upside of his plight is that it has made me more appreciative of my hearing and, very wary of pain medications.

Silences can be accidental or intentional, and come in all shapes and sizes with a multitude of reasons and meanings attached to them. Silence, like any phenomenon, can be good, neutral or damaging, so it is best not to ascribe falsities or half-truths to them. That way you escape unnecessary errors in interpretation and the resultant stress to ourselves and others.

Alex Michaelides suggested that silences reflect reality like a mirror. But mirrors only show a small portion of the world. They lack a wider physical and temporal context, which greatly limits the validity of any conclusions drawn from them.

Mirrors can also have built-in biases: they can be flat, concave or convex, producing neutral, magnifying or minimising distortions to the reflected image.

Our view of a silence is also rarely without some emotive bias. Sometimes we are oversensitive and magnify any messages, real or imagined, or we may be habitually thick-skinned and/or myopic, and hence wrongly reduce or dismiss the true significance of a silence.

So, perhaps silence *is* a mirror, but *a magic mirror*, one that mostly reflects the will of the viewer than objective reality. The subjective reality of a silence is thus *ours* to create, for better or worse.

*The book was read in December 2020

48. Enlightenment

Five or more years back I started writing a sci-fi story with the working title: *The Glorious Enlightenment.* The human race was to meet an enlightened alien species, one of whose desires was to enlighten us, for their benefit and possibly ours.

I had big ambitions but a couple of chapters in it ran out of steam, stalled by the realisation that I hadn't sufficiently grasped its central theme: enlightenment.

How do we recognise enlightenment to the point of it being a useful concept and humanly achievable? Is its usefulness worth the effort? How do we judge its worth? And is it possible, or wise, to pursue enlightenment if our peer group remains unenlightened and possibly unimpressed by our newly enlightened attitudes, perhaps to the point of feeling threatened, resulting in rejection and/or retribution.

Seeking guidance, I put the question of enlightenment to my writing group. A lively discussion ensued. A few days later, I received emails from two members who had given the matter greater thought and between them managed to summarise the issue.

One consulted her dictionary. It stated the term is born of the Buddhist idea of "Bodhi", meaning *awakening* (a term equally tricky to define). Achieving enlightenment, or awakening, apparently occurs in seven stages:

1. Mindfulness – to develop a greater awareness of reality.
2. Investigation – to actively discover the nature of reality.

3. Energy – to power the mental and physical effort required.
4. Joy – presumably resultant from using one's new knowledge and skills.
5. Tranquillity of mind and body – from further mastery of the above skills.
6. Concentration – improves so that one can fully focus the mind.
7. Equanimity – the payoff: accepting reality without cravings or aversions, the seventh step being the Buddha's goal: the end of suffering for oneself, and better responses towards those we interact with. The suffering conquered being more to do with banishing mental disharmony than eliminating physical discomfort.

She then gave a more personal description of enlightenment as knowing our particular purpose in life and then pursuing it with joy and calmness. She considered Mahatma Gandhi, the current Dalai Lama, Mother Teresa and Fred Hollows as examples of the enlightened.

The other lady, having taken part in the debate and after reading the first's emailed response raised the conundrum of whether enlightenment was only possible by giving up everything to live as a monk or nun. She pondered if it is possible to be enlightened and exist in the "normal" world.

Her personal definition was "being honest with yourself about who you are, accepting who you are, and being happy with who you are. And accepting others for who they are."

She then raised the moot point of a serial killer reaching the Nirvana of nonsuffering through total acceptance of themselves and their evil ways. She asked: "Are they enlightened?", and "Can you be evil and still be enlightened?"

The first response highlighted the process. The second's

questionings brought into focus some of the less obvious aspects of freedom from aversions and cravings.

For me, both the process and the goal are problematical.

Our survival as a species relies upon our evolved ability to co-operate in ever larger groups. Our biological "Prime Directive" is learning to co-operate for the common good, most of the time, by most individuals.

It's a complicated business hampered by a large brain that is not large enough. Our problem-solving organ gets around this with coping mechanisms that favour remembering the gist of things not the details, and a preference for making problems fit its existing solutions rather than waste time and energy on the laborious task of starting from scratch. We are also lousy at understanding probabilities and randomness, amongst a host other limitations and biases that all undermine the accuracy of our decisions. (*New Scientist* magazine of 28 July 2018 has a concise summary of these limitations).

No amount of ability to calm the mind and then focus it, and no mountainous accumulation of "facts" can lead to any level of enlightenment, however one visualises such a fuzzy idea without a deep appreciation and acceptance of the restrictions our body and brain put upon our thinking.

Again, I found buried wisdom in one of the *Dirty Harry* movies of the 1970s, probably the same that inspired my essay *Opinions*, and again hidden in an insult. Tough guy detective, Harry Callahan, played so convincingly by Clint Eastwood, criticises what he deemed a weak response by an authority figure with this line: "I guess a man's got to know his limitations" or words to that effect.

Fully knowing the extent of our physical and mental limits is the first insulting and bitterly humbling medicine we must swallow if we seek enlightenment's promise of relief from our innate foolishness [1].

Buddhist practices for controlling our emotions to promote the state of calm necessary for wise consideration of life's problems has much merit. In a way, it is an extension of what parents and teachers do in guiding children to more adult behaviours. But biologically we can't stop emotions arising because they are spontaneously generated by the brain in response to sensory inputs. My disquiet is that in focusing too much on control, on suppressing emotions, we lose sight of their usefulness.

Aversion, fear and terror have their place as much as pleasantness, happiness and ecstasy. Prolonged meditative calm can be overdone to the point of losing usefulness and may even become inappropriate if urgent decisions are required. Imagine that an earthquake has the monastery roof collapsing upon us. How much more "navel gazing" is required before we decide which way to run? And excessive physical stillness is unhelpful if it leads to a lymphatic system that flows too sluggishly to do its work, or creates bedsores or bruised buttocks from being too long in one position.

The seven stages of the Buddhist path to enlightenment, as I understand it, seem ultimately unworkable because they appear to over-emphasise the head over the heart – they see our mind-body duality as a MIND-body one. They need to re-appreciate the concept of yin and yang that seems to rule us.

I suspect almost all Buddhists, at some level, acknowledge the utility of the interplay between yin (chaos) and yang (order). The symbol for it is a circle bisected by a curved line, one side white (order), the other black (chaos) but within each half is a dot representing the opposing force.

In the present discussion, we can label one side emotion, the other reason. My observation of the human world, present and past, for individuals and societies, is that an excess of reason, which seeks to completely control our chaotic emotions, will fail because our emotions are an essential part of us and require expression. Likewise, a person or nation ruled by the dictates of capricious emotion will lack the order and restraint required to function in the real world and so they also will fail.

Buddhists should firstly realise that their actions are powered by a *craving*, which could be labelled: the *desire* for enlightenment. They should also know that maximum enlightenment, and the contentment and happiness it presumably confers, lies in balancing both our thoughts *and* emotions if one is to stay in the "enlightened zone", their famous *middle way*. We, and they, should understand the need for both order and chaos. I cannot conceive of an enlightened life that is totally regimented and predictable, or one that is totally chaotic, both would be too stressful for me to handle.

Thus, the answer to the question of whether enlightenment is possible outside of the controlled confines of a monastery is that true enlightenment can *only* be found in the *real* world, in our everyday interactions with our fellows as well as with the non-human world. A monk in a monastery is like a ship in the safety of the harbour: it functions well enough there, but its true purpose is to transport people and parcels to and from that harbour and many others. How can we judge the worth of our thoughts and actions unless they occur in the hustle and bustle of normal existence?

Armed with a humbler view of our biological limitations and a recognition of the need to balance unconscious emotions against our brain's innate algorithms, and its unconscious and consciously reasoned solutions, the next aspect to be addressed is a greater understanding of enlightenment's purpose. What good do we hope will come from achieving a modicum of enlightenment for it to be worth the cost in time and effort?

The wording of that last question provides clues to its answer. As I see it, we seek enlightened thinking in the hope of doing "good", of making the world a better place, a place with less suffering in it. The biological source of that emotion-derived aim lies in our brain's reward mechanisms, which evolved to biochemically promote beneficial behaviours.

And good behaviours, from an evolutionary perspective, for a species that requires a high degree of group coherence to survive, are those that encourage the recognition and encouragement of behaviours that promote social cohesion, and, in keeping with the concept of yin and yang, encourage recognition and punishment of socially bad behaviours. Thus, valuations of goodness and badness are given according to the behaviour's ability to promote individual *and* societal survival. By this biological yardstick, the calm psychopath who kills or diminishes the success of others for their self-interest fails to be good or enlightened.

The need for better thinking has always been important. I would suggest it is even more important now that we are faced with increasingly complex situations resultant from our crowded cities, in an ever more interconnected world awash with ever-present and ever-changing technologies. The new problems we must respond to, individually, nationally, and globally include rampant under-restrained globalised finance, climate change, biodiversity degradation and a similar reduction in cultural and ideological diversity brought on by social media and the internet.

Such wiser thinking requires an enhanced commitment to gathering sufficient data, determining the veracity of it, and then finding the meaning in it to create sufficient wisdom to use it to the betterment of the individual, society and hopefully the non-human world in the short and long term. All this whilst still promoting immediate survival to allow enough time for longer-term strategies to be put in place.

This plethora of commendable activity will not always be appreciated by the uninformed, or even those claiming to be better informed. The latter may have greater data and rationalising abilities to concoct differing views whether from the same or a differing dataset as ours. Trying to impose our "enlightened" views and actions on others will result in our finding out firsthand the truth in Arthur Schopenhauer's summation of the three stages of the truth: *First it is ridiculed, then it is vehemently opposed and finally, deemed to be self-evident and hence requiring no further comment or consideration.*

That said, it is my belief, and that of many others, that enlightened thinking is the way to go, both from a personal standpoint and from society's.

I also consider the actions of people such as Fred Hollows to pass the benefit to society test. It should be noted that doing socially acceptable things purely for their ability to confer social approval and status is entirely different from expanding the meaning we give to our activities, such that in our pursuit of our life's purpose we benefit society and ourselves, in that order. I suggest Fred Hollow is the second category and deserves my praise. A socialite running a charity principally for the social kudos it brings as well as its augmentation of their personal finances, is in the first category and hence has more in common with the narcissistic sociopath than the enlightened.

En*lighten*ed thinking and actions, as the word implies, lighten our soul by giving something of ourselves to another, for their sake, not ours. That we feel good about it is secondary. The fake motives of the businessman who donates to win social approval are all about them, such motives have a heaviness about them, the heaviness of "The glory will be mine, mine, all mine" versus the lightness of, "You look all in. Take a seat, relax. I'll make you a nice cup of tea."

And the truly enlightened understand that the glow of doing the right thing needs some other measure to validate it. And even if it is confirmed by outside forces, to then take that endorsement with a grain of salt because those endorsements are constructs of fallible human minds and hence prey to the foolishness of our human biases.

The enlightened also understand that enlightened thinking and actions are not restricted to intellectuals, monastery abbots or great people such as Fred Hollows. They are within reach of every person when they ask the right questions and are unafraid to face viewpoints other than their unexamined defaults.

Children, in their unrestrained actions and awkward questions, inject lubricating chaos into the rusted-on immovable viewpoints of their adult carers. Their actions and questions may loosen adult opinions enough to consider new and possibly better opinions and behaviours. A child's question, "Why is the man sitting there on the ground with that hat with a few coins in it?" if not fobbed off, may prove most useful if the adult gives it greater thought. The encounter with the destitute man may nudge the parent into reconsidering their wasteful spending habits, it may induce a fear of poverty enough to spur them to improve their employability by doing extra study. It may even open up more worthwhile purposes for their life than yearning for a flashier car.

Enlightenment is a human concept. Its quality and quantity are measured in relation to its benefit to the individual, the society they are dependent upon, and ultimately the ecosystem that underpins both. Socially and environmentally unsustainable behaviours fail the enlightenment test on the grounds that they harm humanity in the long term.

Being human, and recognising that an enlightened moment is going to be subjective and hence difficult to define with precision, such moments will be similar to happiness, in being episodic and a response to specific pleasing thoughts and/or actions. Biochemically, feeling enlightened, blissful or blessed can't be maintained for prolonged periods. Though, strangely, anxiety and sadness seem easier to hold on to.

Being a construct of the brain, moments of enlightenment will be judged by this fallible, biased and capacity-constrained organ and, if we are brave enough to be honest with ourselves, will be valued as merely being the best response we could produce under the circumstances.

The enlightened will thus not be inclined to believe their own publicity, and so will more easily admit to errors of judgement. Consequently, they will be able to laugh at themselves, and unlikely to laugh *at* others. They will not experience *schadenfreude*, the finding of happiness in another's misfortune.

The enhanced awareness of reality in those with increased levels of enlightened thinking will develop a nuanced worldview that will induce a greater sense of compassion for human, beast and the planet as a whole.

As I see it, the basic purpose of treading the path to greater enlightenment is to improve the quality of our decision-making; to better understand the odds; to produce balanced solutions to life's problems, such that the greatest benefit flows to the greatest number of people over the greatest time – a balancing act that requires application of our moral dimensions.

Our biology encourages us to tread that middle path. It wants us to wise up, to learn from our experiences and those of others. The desire to find better solutions is the strategy evolution has reinforced within us as a way of immunising ourselves and our communities from the privations that result from ignorance and our innately biased way of thinking, all to better prepare us for coping with the shocks of random events.

Life is for learning. To be enlightened in any measure is to know that, despite accumulated knowledge and the greater wisdom derived from it, we are deeply influenced by our biology and the culture that supports us.

Enlightenment also acknowledges that we exist in a universe

where randomness can make the wise and the fool equals. The awakened mind is humbled by this and hence never takes any of its apparent successes too seriously.

[1] *Thinking, Fast and Slow* by Daniel Kahneman is great for understanding the unconscious foundations of our emotions, thinking processes and behaviours, with further dimensions explored in books such as: *The Ethical Brain* by Michael Gazzaniga and *The Science of Happiness* by Stefan Klein

49. A Chat with Solon the Wise

(A prose reworking of my essay on enlightenment)

'Hello, Sol. This *is* an unexpected surprise. Please, come in. Grab a seat.'

'Hope I'm not interrupting. Heard you were having another go at that story you'd started when we first met, all those years back. How's it going this time around?'

I delayed my reply, first, to allow Solon to settle in at the dining table but mostly to gather my thoughts.

No matter how much sci-fi one reads, and writes, it's always a shock when a philosophical giant from ancient Greece steps into your house, immaculate in a powder grey suit, though minus a tie, the open collar giving intriguing glimpses of a medallion weighing down a heavy gold chain. It was even more of a blow to see his magnificent white mane and equally impressive beard trimmed to a shadow of their former glory. But coping with the unexpected was one of the many things I wanted to do better. Perhaps his turning up out of the blue, with the radical new look, would give me another chance to learn how to deal with unplanned events that demand novel responses and it might even produce more answers than questions. It was possible, but I had plenty of reasons to doubt it.

By now he was seated and was expectantly splitting his attention between myself and the kitchen area. Sol was always fond of getting the basics right, like physical comfort, good food and drink. Reckoned a man did his best work on a happy stomach.

It had taken a few millennia but he was finally proved right by the award-winning behavioural economist Daniel Kahneman [1]. Economics had been founded on the assumption that people make decisions rationally. Kahneman decided to put that assumption of rationality to the test and in one experiment put the behaviour of judges under the microscope, in his case Israeli Parole Court judges, on the assumption their training, and experience, should make them exemplars of rationality. Sadly, he found their impartiality of judgement fluctuated in a pattern throughout the day. They grew progressively harsher in their decisions as they grew more hungry and tired.

That our physical state affects our mental attitudes was something most grandmothers and many other ordinary folks had long figured out. Kahneman had finally given such folk wisdom the authority of scientific backing.

But I'd been silent too long.

'Had your morning tea yet? I'm about to brew a cuppa.'

'Thought you'd never ask. And a snack wouldn't go astray.'

I busied myself in the kitchen.

'That story of yours ... was called *The Glorious Enlightenment*, wasn't it? You were planning to have an enlightened and technically superior alien race visit the solar system to enlighten us humans, apparently to serve their purposes and benefit us as well. That the gist of it?'

'Yep. For an old guy your memory is still pretty sharp.'

'Look who's talking. You're no spring chicken ... must be on the wrong side of sixty by now. And at that advanced age you should realise that getting the gist of things is all we humans are good at. Which explains why we do so many foolish things through ignoring the inconvenient truth of the devil being in the details.'

'Okay, you got me there. But shouldn't I be on the *right* side of sixty, if we're going to be talking about wisdom and enlightenment?'

Sol emitted a good-natured chortle that made his craggy features shine. It was one of the things I liked best about him; his generous and playful sense of humour.

'In theory, older people *should be* wiser, having had the time to gather plenty of information, extract its meaning and then put that knowledge to good use, to make and enact *enlightened* decisions, but …'

I interrupted as I placed the tray, with the tea and plates of nibblies consisting of cured meats, nuts, fruits and chocolates in the middle of the table and then continued for him, 'But you were about to say that it's not the quantity of time, or the amount of accumulated knowledge, it's the *quality* that counts. Right?'

Solon's wry grin returned but he chose not to reply, instead reached over and shovelled a slice of prosciutto into his mouth, followed by an olive and then a fig, after which he grabbed hold of his mug, gave it a sniff, appeared to decide it was too hot, put it down and finally leaned back to return his attention to me.

'I've eaten in your house three times over the last fifteen of your years, and each time the food and tea has been good. Perhaps that's why I keep popping in …' His eyebrows seemed to question his words, '…but I wouldn't wager too many drachmas on it. Not enough data. You claim to have read Taleb's book *Fooled by Randomness* and so should know that even if I'd had a million of your meals, I could never be entirely certain that the next would be up to scratch unless I understood *why* your food was good. Maybe I'd just been lucky? Similarly, if I'd popped in every hour of your, let's say sixty-five years, to see if you were still alive, those …'. He gave a magical wink, before continuing, '… five hundred and sixty-nine thousand, seven hundred and ninety observations would not be "proof" that you would live forever. One needs a better understanding of the why of things before wise, and possibly enlightened conclusions can be made.'

What could I say to that bald truth? I delayed by concentrating on blowing the steam from my tea. Solon filled in the pause with more sampling of the victuals and occasional glances in my direction, perhaps to make sure I was alive enough to add another worthless data point to his theory concerning my possible immortality.

To change tack, I asked, 'What's with the new image? You look like a super-relaxed CEO. And what's that medallion you're sporting? Wasn't there before.'

His response followed his first tentative sip of tea, which seemed to meet his approval.

'I'm glad you asked. They are the most important things I've learned in the last couple of millennia.'

He gave a start when I almost dropped my mug from surprise. Sol was an immortal, time-travelling philosopher who must have seen enough of humanity to agree with the Bible's conclusion that, as far as human behaviour goes, *there is nothing new under the sun*. I couldn't believe he'd actually disproved that apparent law.

'Don't look so surprised, all this ...' He put down his tea, then used both hands to jiggle his collar to emphasise his new image. '... is not a new idea. It's merely my greater application of knowledge I've long known but not fully appreciated until an embarrassingly short time ago. Let me explain.'

'Before you do, is this going to help get my story moving again? Is it going to improve my non-existent hold on the slippery concept of enlightenment that I was hoping to weave into that story?'

'Possibly.'

I groaned. That was the trouble with philosophising: you

never get any certainty.

Solon raised a placating index finger. 'Bear with me.'

I settled. He smiled, apparently enjoying my efforts to control my frustrations.

'My new look and your moment of emotion are part of the same thing, an understanding of which is the foundation of any measure of enlightened thinking, no matter how you define it.'

He paused, with eyes twinkling, perhaps from an understanding of what was going through my brain, which was filling with the angst one gets when about to hear a long joke with little hope the punchline being worth the wait.

Having savoured my disquiet, he continued, 'That first step is acceptance of our biological and hence mental limitations. I know what you have read.' He fixed me with a censorial stare to quell my incredulity. 'And don't ask me how, or how I got here, or whether I am real or just a construct of your fertile imagination. Listen first; judge later.'

I emitted an ambivalent grunt but nodded to confirm my willingness to listen.

'Perhaps the best way for you to understand is by answering this question: why do so few people make the effort to tread the Buddhist's sevenfold path to enlightenment, or any other path you could choose?'

I sat stupidly for a while making inane facial movements reminiscent of a fish blowing bubbles. But it didn't help to come up with anything convincing, so Solon answered for me.

'Because most people rarely see the need for enlightenment. They face problems and find solutions that seem to work well enough for them, most of the time. And whether common folk, managers, CEOs, politicians or generals, they all *believe in* their decisions. They feel good about taking the praise for the good outcomes, and rationalise away the bad with conspiracy theories that usually involve the interference by outside agencies such as luck, unscrupulous competitors or capricious deities. For most, the concept of enlightenment, like the promises of Telcos and politicians, is oversold and under-delivered, and hence any rewards are deemed not worth the apparent effort. This raises the question of what motives you and others of the minority, of which I am one, to make that unnecessary effort.'

Again, I lacked an adequate answer and again Solon carried on the conversation.

'Because you and I have read too much and too widely, cogitated too much, have examined the antics of our fellows, and ourselves too critically, and have concluded that *ignorance is not bliss*. We see the unhappy results of that ignorance, of the biased, skewed, half-baked ideas it generates and then the consequent actions, and reckon that, with a bit of directed mental application we can do better, for our benefit and for the good of those around us. Am I talking sense or gibberish?'

Reluctantly I admitted to the logic of his summation whilst also saddened by a growing awareness of the possible futility of my yearning for that better way of being.

'Don't look so downcast. You should understand that asking the right questions are what scientists and philosophers do, and that accurately worded questions often reveal the path to the answer. The first thing to ask is, why are our thoughtful conclusions and actions so often "underwhelming", shall we say?'

My blank stare again kept him talking.

'Because our big brain isn't big enough to deal with the complexities of social living and the vagaries of the natural world, which is much under the influence of randomness. Our biology developed coping strategies, one of which we mentioned earlier, our propensity to boil complex situations down to a nub of meaning small enough for our computing capacity to handle. You even saved page thirty-six from the *New Scientist* of 28 July

2018 because it gave a very concise summary of most of our brain's shortcuts and biases, almost all of which are done beyond our conscious control.'

'How did you know about that page?' I replied, feeling somewhat annoyed. And anyway, none of what he'd said was news to me. So where was he going with it?

'If I can travel through time, it's logical that I can do lots of other useful things. But let's not get distracted. You exhibit a bit of annoyance and impatience. That's good because it demonstrates what I'm trying to show.'

Like a conjurer, he snapped his fingers and that page from the magazine appeared in his hand. He passed it over to me and let me have a read to refresh my memory.

'Better thinking will not happen unless you understand the limitations of the thing you do that thinking with: your brain. Read this and be humbled. In it lies the beginning of wisdom, which is, the recognition of our ignorance and biases. Imagine you retire and decide to sail single-handed around Australia, perhaps in honour of Matthew Flinders. Before you start, it would be very wise to understand the size of the task, the capabilities of your boat, and most critical of all, your own physical and mental capacities if disappointment or tragedy are to be avoided. Humans are fragile and the universe abounds in randomness, which brings unexpected wonders as much as unseen disappointments and the possibility of an early demise.'

Didn't like his dire warnings regarding my retirement plans but I was getting the picture and, after a quick read of the proffered page, gave him my summary of my current understanding of how our brains function.

'The brain receives constant sensory inputs, which are automatically assessed, generating a stream of conclusions, which are influenced by our highly edited memories and our brain's desire to avoid work. Hence, we prefer ready-made solutions, even if they aren't the best. Almost all of this is done unconsciously because conscious thought is too slow. And the brain doesn't seek the best solutions, it seeks the quickest, easiest that will be good enough. So, yes, I am starting to see where you are leading me.'

'Good. But you need to focus more on the motivational aspect, on the brain's allocation of emotions to the body's changing biochemical state. We are emotional creatures first, rational ones a distant last. We must always bear that in mind. We need to better understand and control our emotions if we are to find better solutions than those automatically generated, all the while paying homage to those automatic responses because more often than not, they are all we need.'

'But how does this relate to the suit and haircut?'

'They show I understand the emotional states I *nonverbally generate in others*, emotions that I will use to manipulate them; for their benefit I assure you.' He smiled like a shark sizing up an abalone diver but one unsure of how hungry it was.

'So, you're saying you have to understand the rules and their purposes to successfully play the game?'

'You're finally getting it.'

'What about the medallion? Looks like the yin-yang symbol to me.'

'Enlightenment is just a fancy way of saying being clued up *and* compassionate.' He fished out the medallion and held it lovingly in his right hand. 'This I wear in recognition of *my* human propensity to forget. I have it to remind myself of the most useful principle to be found in the human universe: the eternal interplay between yin-chaos and yang-order.'

'I hope you're not overselling it?'

'Maybe. But every time that its presence aids my thinking, I'm in front. It reminds me to be wary of excesses in *my* thinking as much as that in others.'

His intense gaze had me squirming, until I realised that he was hoping I'd take up his intellectual baton and keep the debate running. A few breaths later I accepted.

'My dear wife – who strangely is never here when you are – is always saying that anything overdone is bad. Too much yang, too many rules and restrictions at home, or at work, leads to unhappy people motivated to find a resolution to their unpleasantness. Situations that can't be fixed peacefully may be resolved violently. Excess order then gets balanced by excess chaos.'

'Close enough. The symbol is such an elegant design. Riding the curved line that separates the black of chaos from the white of order is where our optimal state of being lies. The opposing-coloured dot in each side is the opposing force that lies in wait should one side threaten to overwhelm the other. That opposing force then hatches to restore the balance. It is such a beautiful and useful idea that finds equivalents in numerous other balanced dualities that populate reality. But for us it's about balancing chaotic emotions with reason's order.'

'Sol, that's so easy to say. But easy to do?'

'Didn't say it was easy, but few things worth doing are easy, which, in a way adds to their worthiness. But back to my new image. Assuming one has the audacity to consider our view on an issue superior to the general consensus, all the while remembering how wedded we are to our opinions, then the next hurdle is convincing others to consider the merits of our viewpoint. Again, we do battle with all the unconscious limitations of the others' brain. So, we soften them up by appealing to their emotions. We use our knowledge of the external factors we can display to help them see us, and our attached views, in a friendlier light. Thus, the suit. It puts the informed and uninformed in a more positive frame of mind. The influencing power of 'framing' was one of the many phenomena discussed by Kahneman [1]. Similarly, if I want to be taken seriously by current decision makers, then the hair also has to represent rational control, hence the trim. I am doing no more than a good advertising agency or PR firm does on a daily basis. Being a writer, you too manipulate with your emotive words and metaphors.'

He paused to let me contribute.

'More yin and yang?' I replied, 'We are manipulated, and in turn try our hand at manipulating those around us.'

'Exactly. And both sides of that process have consequences, good and bad depending upon whose viewpoint you take and over what timeframe.'

Progress had been made. Solon peered at me as if trying to either read my mind, or emplace some notion into it telepathically. A silence developed that we both filled with distracted snacking and sipping.

Solon was first to drain his cup.

'Can't stay forever enjoying your hospitality. Up next, I've got some of your influencers to influence with a few of my carefully emplaced questions. Any last remarks?'

I silently cogitated all the way to the front door. We shook hands. He turned to leave.

A parting confession slipped out, 'I still have the desire for enlightenment.'

'Yes?' he said. A single word, overripe with expectancy.

'But realise it arises from a *desire for order*. My task is to rethink how much order I think appropriate, and how much, and what manner of chaos is useful.'

'Good. Sounds like you've just remembered parts of Stefan Klein's book *The Survival of the Nicest*.

'Yes. How did you know?'

'Let's say it was an informed guess.'

'Specifically, I was thinking of his notion that healthy

societies need to have a certain low percentage of thieves, abusers and human parasites to immunise the rest from their strains of disruptive thinking. Those antisocial people force those societies to maintain their ability to detect and repel "infections" of bad behaviours. A level of chaos is needed to keep order in a healthy state and vice versa. In that vein, perhaps a small percentage of *humbly uncertain wiser people* is required to keep a society's thinking flexible enough to produce better responds to the problems of an everchanging reality.'

'Well, you seem to be on the right track. So, thanks again for the tea and nibblies. Until next time.'

He squeezed my hand, walked a few paces towards the road then dissolved into the late morning sunshine.

Back inside, doing the dishes, I saw my hoped-for greater confidence in having a better grip on the idea of enlightenment going down the plughole with the soapsuds. In its place a very yin-yang idea emerged.

That my desire for a more realistic understanding of the world by accumulating facts and then becoming aware of my brain's biases and lax algorithms hadn't produced much understanding I could actually use. Any wisdom I could label as such didn't seem easy to put into practice with any sense of certainty. And if I wasn't certain of my ideas then how could I successfully sell them to other people?

Having dried and put away the mugs and plates, I stood leaning against the sink with Sol's visit still reverberating in my mind.

His latest legacy was the idea that *realistic* confidence comes paradoxically from the *lack* of confidence that arises from acknowledging our ignorance. The humility this brings to our decisions gives us a good starting point from which to encourage the flexibility needed to respond better to an unknowable and evolving universe.

Better to be confident of our ignorance than trust the confidence that *unacknowledged* ignorance imparts.

It was my personal yin and yang moment. A precious taste of clarity I hoped would glue humility to any professed moments of enlightenment.

Glancing around our combined kitchen, dining and living room, I suddenly realised I had already made some progress in getting that balance between yin and yang optimised.

Our house has much yang, in that it is orderly, but not excessively so. My mind is relatively ordered, but not so rigid that it was derailed by the "chaos" of Sol's sudden appearance and his questioning, which pushed me towards novel viewpoints on and around the definition of enlightenment. Few people, apart from my dear wife, would have coped with, firstly, the impossibility of his existence and secondly, understand and accept the validity of his guidance.

Perhaps the greatest benefit Sol had highlighted was enlightenment's lack of appeal to the majority. My task, and that of others on the path to more enlightened thinking, was to find ways to reverse enlightenment's over-sold and under-delivered status because our overpopulated and hyper-connected world seems desperately short of the more nuanced long-term thinking needed to immunise global society against bad ideas that now can quickly gain too much sway.

For me, living humbly in the most enlightened way my limitations permit is the most valid way to be involved in that process. I vowed to set a good example, for my sake and society's.

[1] *Thinking, Fast and Slow* by Daniel Kahneman, *The Ethical Brain* by Michael Gazzaniga, *The Science of Happiness* and *Survival of the Nicest* by Stefan Klein, as well as science magazines such as *New Scientist* all contributed to the factual foundations of this alternative exploration of the vexing theme of enlightenment.

50. The Truth Issue

Early in May 2021 I visited a newsagency, in an aspirational suburb, and stumbled upon a magazine I'd never encountered before. Its strange name, and the issue's boldly stated theme, truth, had me delving inside. After reading most of the first article I was convinced it was worth the nineteen-dollar price tag and so bought a copy.

When I got home, I read it cover-to-cover, and, suffered the consequences. My days and nights became perturbed by frustrations and perhaps a new variety of despair.

The following "diatribe" is my endeavour to regain my mental composure. If the essay achieves this, I even harbour the desire to send a copy of it to the magazine's Editor* in the hope he would stoop to read it, and, dispassionately consider its contents. Proof I am not entirely lost to optimism.

Perhaps I should curse that first article for raising my hopes rather than the others for deflating them, but cursing, whilst enjoyable, is rarely productive. And my disappointment was not total, being mostly confined to the interviews section, with the final interview offering some degree of compensation.

That first article was the key to my nascent optimism because the fellow, a counsellor working with the wives of men gaoled for sexual crimes, uncovered the role that *deep denial* of their husband's offences had in blocking their progress towards a better life.

Denial of unpleasant truths is a recurring issue in all our lives, mine included. What continues to bother me is that so few clues are readily available as to how best to overcome our propensity to deny. That counsellor offered up one such clue when he described his *one* success. That success came because he managed to help his client to recognise how she had grown stronger and more independent whilst her husband had been in gaol. Acknowledging her *true* worth and abilities empowered her to the point where the costs of denying her husband's crimes were outweighed by the benefits of exercising her newfound and truer self-image. She finally accepted the truth of her husband's offences and was able to move her life forward.

That first article was a good introduction to the magazine's theme of truth – a word much used but apparently little understood. Part of that dearth of understanding comes from the language and words used to discuss it. But words can illuminate, obscure, or distract us from the many aspects of the truth. The first is the one that slips past most readers: the word "the".

There is no: "the" truth.

Only God can fully know and comprehend "the" truth in all its glory and horror. Humans don't physically have the brainpower, time, all the information, or the comprehension to attach the words "the truth" to an opinion. We mortals can only work with biased approximations of it – usually those that align best with our current views [1].

Luckily, we don't need to know everything to be able to function in our slice of reality; all we require is a sufficient grasp of it to get by. My task, and I hoped that of the magazine, is to accumulate facts of sufficient quantity, and *quality*, and then subject them to some considered thinking.

The lady who wrote the second article gave arguments for the need for more critical thinking. She observed that cults control their members by the degree to which they can stop their members from thinking. Non-thinking is not confined to restrictive religious sects, it pervades general society, especially now that our minds are almost permanently distracted by our addiction to smartphones and the internet. That constant stream of information neutralises the significance of any important facts hidden within it by not allowing our brains the time to see them as they rush past, or if glimpsed, to view them critically. We are akin to a person gorging on an endless feast but not absorbing any of the food's nutrients.

The third article concerned the inconvenient truths and swarms of lies attached to the issue of our ecosystem's dire status and prospects. The presenter, an environmental activist, gave a moot example of another barrier to getting a more realistic appreciation of the true state of the environment.

The presenter described an incident during question time at the end of one of his talks on the consequences of climate change. A man stood up to ask his question, but before he spoke, pointed to the window, which looked out across beautiful Sydney harbour, basking in the sun, and then asked how the presenter could suggest the world was really so badly off when outside all seemed as beautiful as ever.

That comment was a good example of the second half of the *peak-end rule* [1], in which we preferentially remember peak experiences and emotive facts, with the most recent given the greatest weight. It also highlighted humanity's bias to the short-term and our poor ability to comprehend risk and probabilities [1,2].

We were not told how the presenter responded but given time I would have suggested telling the guy that his optimism was equivalent to that of a man falling backwards from the balcony of a fifty-storey apartment block, perhaps on the shores of said harbour, and gazing up at the sky on the way down whilst enjoying the massaging pressure of the air beneath him, and concluding that the all that guff about death and dying from falling out of buildings was grossly overstated because, so far, his experience said otherwise.

The fourth article was a little lost on me, I guess because of too many woolly words, such as "discernment", "intelligence", and the concept of a "post-truth world".

Then followed the first interview: of a lady whose specialty was Jungian analysis. I found it hard going, and was particularly disappointed by the unchallenged use of psychological jargon like "individuation". On the plus side, I did respond to her mentioning of Jung's declaration that "all isms are dangerous" because words like sexism, existentialism, racism, capitalism, to name but a few, are mostly used as if we have a real sense of what they actually mean.

Next up was an interview with a man with a long career in journalism, who was now turning his writing skills towards social issues, such as misogyny, ecological degradation, and the power of the internet and social media to spread lies and conspiracies.

By this time, I was becoming sensitised to the way words and concepts were mentioned without much thought given to clarification, let alone critiquing. Thus, when he was asked to expound upon his view of the role of the patriarchy in producing many of the world's current miseries, he began by declaring his love and regard for all the females in his life, friends, colleagues, his mother, sister and his daughters before moving on to discuss his awakening to the plight of women in society.

Frustratingly, the interviewer never asked the questions that his declaration immediately invoked in my mind: "What about your wife, the person you loved long enough to produce daughters with? What of your love for her? Why did it start and then end, and what part did you play in its ending? What did you *learn* from the experience that you can *share* with the reader to help them live in greater harmony with their spouses?"

Later on, conspiracy theories and their promulgators had him ask the question: "How do you talk to those people?" His disdain for those with radically different opinions was highlighted two pages further on when describing his reaction to finding out that an American relation he'd picked up at the airport had voted for Trump; the shock of which almost had him chucking them out of his car. He didn't, but …

His inability to deal with those of a radically different worldview led him a page later to admit that *we* need to increase our desire to want to understand those we disagree with. But it seemed suspiciously as though he was using the royal "we", meaning that other people, not himself, have to make the effort to understand those we disagree with. It would have been instructive if the interviewer had prompted him to suggest the causes of their contrary opinions, from which ways to bridge the ideological divide might have been revealed.

I moved on to the next interview with sinking hopes. Those hopes reached their nadir because that interview proved the most frustrating and disappointing of all.

The Editor had interviewed an indigenous lady, with an Anglo-Celtic name, whose current quest was the teaching of the Aboriginal's side of history, primarily to Aboriginals.

As a man of Danish and English descent, I shudder at the words I am about to type because I am going to voice criticism of the opinions of a person who identifies as Aboriginal. In doing so, will I automatically, and eternally, be labelled a racist? If designated so, do I join Trump supporters, conspiracy advocates and anti-vaxxers? Am I really a foreigner to the truth, your truth, the majority's truth? Do we sanctimoniously ignore each other, or be brave and listen to the other? If brave, read on.

I did Modern History in high school. It skimmed over the history of British and European peoples and related events. Trying to add the Aboriginal side to that extremely biased and limited version *is to be commended*.

The trouble for me is that there are seven plus billion people on this planet, with an equal number of histories behind them. If teaching a severely edited British/white history of Australia was, and is, bad, will our understanding of that history be improved if it is "balanced" by a biased Aboriginal version of Australia's past? The truth is, all histories are severely flawed because all the facts are not known, and if they were, could not be included because of their impossible volume. Histories are biased also by the arbitrary and subjective values used to assess which of the available facts are deemed worthy of inclusion in said histories.

Thus, why is British history, or Aboriginal history, or the history of any nation or tribe or group, more worthy of knowing than any other? How do we decide the veracity and weight to be given to each snippet of the whole picture? What embarrassing bits are glossed over or left out? What are we to *do* with these histories? What can we *learn* from them?

I found it ironic that peppered throughout the magazine's pages were comments lamenting our society's degradation through being "sold a story of competition and separation" that has produced "a crisis of fragmentation", as well as social "atomising" and increasing "tribalism".

And yet these concerns appear unknown to this indigenous lady, who was proud of her work to build "strong indigenous nations", to encourage their "self-determination and sovereignty", to cast off the imposed culture so that Aboriginal kids coming out of school will be "strong in themselves and as sovereign people", who would not have to give up anything or compromise who they are to get through school.

All these sentiments seem to promote separation, which would make interacting successfully with the other ninety-seven per cent of Australians who are not indigenous, harder, not easier. How can these attitudes promote a greater understanding between Aboriginals and non-aboriginals when one side is being taught to be unwilling to give up anything or compromise?

It narks me to think that my criticism of her work will smear me with the racist tag because when I look in the mirror, I see *a human, not* a *white* man. I get the impression that this lady only sees an *Aboriginal* woman. And yet her skin tones, facial features and name, all point to her mixed genetics and cultural histories. By defining herself as Aboriginal, aligning herself with only one "race" of her ancestry, she separates me, and anyone else not of her chosen tribe, from our common bonds, from our shared humanity. It makes me wonder which of the two of us is the racist?

How would she, or the magazine's editor, advise me to consider myself?

Am I to think of myself as African because I was born in Africa, Danish because my father was Danish, English after my mother, or Australian as this is where I was mostly raised? In answering that question, how does the answer promote or lessen the evils of tribalism? How is my new identity going to improve my interactions with the millions of people not of my tribe?

The other question avoided in that interview was what *specifically* do indigenous people want? How would those desires pan out in real life? What rewards come from rewriting history, theirs and ours? Did Aboriginals live in perfect harmony before 1788? Were their spears and clubs used only for hunting, or were they occasionally used as weapons of war? Would she like to live as her ancestors did, in a stone-age hunter-gatherer society where women's freedoms were severely prescribed by the *imposed* dictates of the *Aboriginal patriarchy*?

Non-indigenous culture may be steeped in blood and pain, but how do we benefit by totally denying its many positive endowments?

She is able to spread her message to a vast audience because she has taken on much of the global culture *imposed* upon her (and just about everyone else). In speaking English, she can communicate with at least five hundred million people, not the few thousand speakers of her tribal language. She has access to modern medicine, technologies such as smartphones and air travel, a national judicial system (with all its flaws it still maintains a civil society most others can only envy). She will not go hungry if drought blights her ancestral lands, millions of taxpaying non-indigenous Australians are there to support her, and other Australians, *regardless* of their tribe.

Do indigenous people seek to create an Aboriginal form of Apartheid, with separate laws, and the setting up of a state within a state? That is the impression talk of sovereignty and self-determination suggests.

We also need to admit that *all of us* have *culture imposed upon us*. Our culture is imprinted on us by our parents, our siblings, our schooling and later on by the mass media and our experiences in the workplace. And our schooling, for better or worse, tries to impart knowledge and behaviours that will benefit us in the adult world *of today*. Learning to cope with restrictions, to compromise, to put up with having to be in a certain place at certain times is the price we pay for businesses to be profitable enough to employ people and then pay the taxes that support our social benefits such as hospitals, policing, clean water, telecommunications. Perhaps those restrictions should be less reviled and more understood, if any school kid is to survive in the cities that most of us choose, or are forced by employment pressures, to live in.

My disappointment with many of the magazine's interviews was that they were like a movie star being interviewed by their publicist, or their greatest fan. There was no serious questioning of the meanings of the words used or the opinions expressed.

The Editor didn't ask what Aboriginals *learnt* from the experience of being invaded. He didn't mention that Aboriginals, in having little experience of other societies, were bound to suffer when they finally encountered the first serious incursion by representatives of the rest of the human race.

Both left unquestioned the wisdom of tribal self-determination versus unity, of being split into five hundred (or however many) tribal nations instead of being united. Because of that her ancestors had no central government to raise an army to repel the First Fleet in 1788. And they lacked the interaction with foreigners, and foreign ideas, to enable them to see the huge technological and societal advantages possessed by those British intruders until it was too late.

The Editor's "nonquestions" made me wonder if he'd actually read and considered the other contributors' concerns of the perils of the fragmentation of society. Perhaps he didn't want the aggravation that comes from asking politically incorrect questions, with all their serious social side-effects, such as being labelled a racist, sexist or whatever category seems best to stifle "unnecessary" debate.

Are we to be like the peasants of the Middle Ages in *blindly* accepting the divine right of kings to rule, and a rigid class hierarchy? To accept the way things are. To put up with our earthly miseries because of an *unquestioned* belief that our reward awaits us in heaven. To not debate, to put our critical thinking abilities permanently on hold.

I dream of a better arrangement, of a better relationship with reality.

And if we are to get closer to that better relationship, we need to be aware when we swallow words and ideas without questioning their veracity.

The next interviewee talked about "defeating greed" – a concept as nonsensical as the "war on terror". Greed is an emotion we all possess, as is terror. Both cannot be expunged from our genome, they can only be recognised, understood and *harnessed*. Like the petrol that powers our cars, if its qualities and nature are not understood you can get seriously damaged. But with understanding, and under a constraining regime (controlled burning in the cylinder head of the car's engine) petrol can be used for the benefit of the individual and hopefully society. Likewise with our emotions. We need to better understand where they come from and why. When emotions are too strongly or inappropriately attached to ideas, they prevent those ideas from being modified to better align with reality, which too often leads to unpleasantness later on.

Disappointingly few, ignorant or educated, understand the unconscious mechanisms that attach the emotions of like, or dislike, to facts, and hence fail to understand the importance of that mechanism in controlling our ability to engage effectively and constructively with the world. Too many are blind to how and why we rationalise our viewpoints [1,2].

Because our decision-making is being manipulated by our unconscious, we need to train ourselves to question our own opinions as much as those of others.

Looking back, perhaps my disappointments with the interviews in the magazine actually made it a worthwhile experience because those inadequacies warned me again to be wary of uncritically accepting my own judgements.

The first article, about the *wives* of sex offenders, proved the most illuminating because the counsellor's one success came once the *motivations* behind the wife's denial were altered, via increasing her self-worth and confidence. Similarly, understanding what *emotional needs* Trump gives his supporters is crucial to understanding his power over them, which, once known, can then be satisfied by less destructive ideas and actions.

A good place to start wising up is to read Kahneman [1] and elsewhere [2] in order to learn about the limitations of our brain's decision-making algorithms. So armed, the job we then face is to use that knowledge to understand what is realistically possible given our limitations and those of our fellow humans.

The magazine's presumed goal of giving readers a balanced, truthful exposition of the lives, opinions, and achievements of worthy people would be better served if their editors, contributors and interviewers acknowledged that the truths revealed in one's biography, written by a friend or a fan, are going to be radically different than a biography written by one's enemies. Which one tells "the" truth? And what are the best ways to pitch *nuanced* truth when Joe Public craves certainty, not shades of grey?

If a magazine is to avoid becoming another echo chamber and instead aspires to be a beacon of informed debate, then its staff need to be more critical of their interviewee's words and opinions.

A more considered approach did emerge in the last interview; of a lady who lectures at Oxford University. She commented that though she teaches the brightest minds, too many of her students suffer from being unwilling to admit that they don't know things and have egos so fragile that any challenging of their opinions is found threatening and hence gives offence. With such constraints upon their thinking, they risk being unable to adjust to the novelties and challenges of our evolving world. Their attitudes warn me of what *not* to do!

In her concluding remarks, she offered up ways of uncovering the truths we need to more constructively interact with the world. She encouraged the reader to overcome the follies that ignorance brings by developing and exercising their desire to want to know more of reality, which is easily achievable via the simple act of habitually asking pertinent questions.

She encourages me to continue to be bold, to continue to be curious, to keep asking questions, and to continue to be sensitised to the use of words that deliberately, or unwittingly, restrict my capacity to see and better understand "the" truth.

---

*Copies of this essay were posted to the magazine's editors on 31 May 2021, via email and by "snail mail".

[1] Our cognitive peculiarities are discussed in humbling depth by Daniel Kahneman in *Thinking, Fast and Slow*.
[2] An easy to comprehend summary of our cognitive limitations was discussed in a feature article in *New Scientist* magazine of 23 February 2019 titled: *Why Smart People Do Stupid Things*, (based largely on David Robson's book *The Intelligence Trap*).

51. Like Me!

I may be an opinionated male, but I'm not a control freak.

Okay, so my dear wife would argue the toss on that last bit but I'd have plenty to say in my defence. And she can't talk; she's a woman and hence blind to the many unconscious and unrecognised ways that she, and other women, control the behaviours of us men by simply being female.

So, let's call a truce and admit that, given the chance, *all* humans, male or female, would like to call the shots. Agreed?

As I said, I'm no control freak, but who wouldn't be thrilled to be offered a job that offers so much of what a control freak wants. Such an opportunity arose when a driver assessor job came up: a role tasked with giving directives to candidates, who, if they wanted a driving licence, are highly motivated to do exactly as commanded.

Well; not *exactly*. Once I'd finished my training and began working as an assessor, I quickly found that my commands, no matter how carefully enunciated and phrased, were far too often *not* obeyed as requested.

Australia is a multicultural nation and hence many of my candidates were born overseas and spoke English as a second, third or fourth language. Thus, they often had a very tenuous grasp of English, which caused no end of frustrations for me, and them.

Imagine this scene: we're travelling down a road, conditions are good, and I say: "We'll turn right into the first street on the right", in my most friendly and calming voice and with plenty of time for my driver to get organised.

Nothing happens. No slowing, no head movements to suggest they are looking for any side road, let alone the one I've selected.

I repeat the instruction. Blood pressure goes up a notch, in me, not my driver who is still calmly looking ahead oblivious of the side street rapidly approaching.

We miss the turn.

A plan B is hurriedly cobbled together and at some stage I manage to get my driver to demonstrate their ability to do a right-hand turn, showing the appropriate amounts of looking, slowing, gear changing and giving way to oncoming traffic – that's the clincher. It's then that an assessor's blood pressure peaks, because too many candidates don't understand give way rules, even with an oncoming car, bus or truck about to flatten us!

With time, I dropped the word "street" because too many foreigners hear it as "straight" and do just that, keep going straight ahead. One learns to say: "We shall turn right at the first *road* on the right." in our clearest, calmest diction and, for added clarity, accompanied it with a directional movement of the appropriate hand – you'd be surprised how many people don't know their left from their right.

"Straight", as a word, is further complicated by the fact that some people are literalists. When following a road these secret literalist should never hear it when approaching any four-way intersection, because they'll attempt to go *straight* through that red light or Stop sign!

'But you said, "go straight". I was just following instructions!' would be their explanation should they succeed and survive the experience.

Even "right" can cause trouble if turning right at a

roundabout, because it's an even bet they'll do a U turn and go "*right* around" it!

Yes, I learnt many things in my fourteen years of assessing, the first of which was that any buzz I may have gotten from the idea of being in command soon faded, to be replaced by a more balanced mix of motivations. Constantly living with the underlying fear of knowing that each drive may end in a trip to the hospital, or worse, impelled me to find compensating positives, such as my part in making people better and safer drivers, myself included. Thankfully, for most of the time, the positives outweighed the negatives.

Now, all candidates, irrespective of nationality, were capable of delivering heart-stopping scares, but I found my overseas drivers, if their level of English permitted normal conversation, provided unexpected compensation through exposing me to their novel viewpoints, which were sometimes inexplicable, often refreshing and occasionally; wonderfully life affirming.

That last thought conjures memories of one particular candidate: a young lady from Sudan. She was shorter than most of her countrywomen, comfortably rounded rather than tall and slim; her skin was milk chocolate rather than expresso, but shared that beautiful silky texture common to many African women. She spoke Dinker, Swahili (from her time as a refugee in Kenya) and best of all, had a good grasp of English. A nursing home provided her with employment as a nurse, which was the perfect job for her as she was clearly a people person and very friendly.

Another bonus was that her driving was okay, which made an amicable conversation possible during the quieter sections. In Africa, it seems that families are still important, because she soon plied me with questions about my family background, starting with that one much asked in Australia: "Where are *you* from?"

I confessed that, despite my Danish and English parentage, I had actually been born in Kenya. This unexpected revelation elicited an eye-popping bolt of unconstrained joy followed immediately by this excited proclamation: "You're an African, *like me*!"

Her delight almost undid her driving, requiring me to utter some calming words and a bit more of my family history to get us back on an even keel. When we returned to the Licensing Centre, she suffered further joy by learning that her driving was, "up to the standard", and went home – after paying for her provisional licence – a very satisfied customer.

Her happiness at finding we were "brother and sister" also imparted a lasting happiness in me because she demonstrated that a little generosity, and a single item of commonality, can shrink large cultural barriers enough to see the other as being, just "like me" and hence worthy of understanding and respect.

Hers was a gift indeed!

This anecdote could be deemed an essay on the issue of how to recognise our common humanity. It arose from an exercise set by my writing group as homework for August 2021. We were to write a short piece of no more than one thousand words, then create two shorter versions of it, one half the length, the other a quarter of the full version. It was to test the idea of just right, versus, too much or too little. The above is the long version at nine hundred and ninety-four words and was voted the best of my three permutations.

52. Warrior Culture: Part One

Towards the end of July 2021, for a bit of post-breakfast mental stimulation, I did a random search of an online news commentary site and came across an article written by a white New Zealand academic. It was a declaration of remorse for the actions of one of his ancestors.

The offending ancestor was a policeman who had participated in the forcible eviction of a group of Māori from a patch of their ancestral land. This event occurred in the late nineteenth century – I think – and yet invoked such shame as to motivate an apology to the world a century and over four generations later.

That website is usually a source of informed and balanced debate so this man's ill-considered – though fashionable – apology was an unexpected disappointment because of the deep logical and informational flaws it demonstrated. I shall endeavour to explain.

There is an unpleasant whiff of arrogance wafting from his implication that he is nobler than his ancestor. But can any of us judge ourselves nobler than any other human? To reach such a conclusion requires a lack of knowledge of the human brain's cognitive and operational limitations, as well as a shaky understanding of the nature of the morality that he applied when making his judgement.

To answer whether he is nobler, we need only consider his response if he'd been born into that ancestor's body, experienced that man's life and swam in that man's "cultural soup". My academic would have behaved exactly as his shameful ancestor did, because our thoughts and actions are the inevitable consequence of our evolved genetics, interacting with our specific cultural and physical experiences [1]. If I am wrong, I would be most grateful to learn in what ways I am mistaken.

On a similar vein is his implication that the Māori protesters were nobler than the British. On that occasion, the Māori were staging a peaceful protest and it was the British who applied violence to get what they wanted, which *is* suggestive of the Māori's greater nobility. Again, to resolve the issue we need only consider what would have happened if the roles of the protagonists had been reversed.

Imagine what would have occurred if an island populated by "savage" nineteenth-century Englishmen had been discovered by "civilised" Māori possessing superior weapons, social structure and a considerably larger population. Would those Māori have resisted the urge to use their overwhelming power to leave those English natives in peace, or would they have found cultural justifications to invade, dispossess and subjugate them?

It takes a mountain of denial to *not* conclude that *we are all human*, whatever tribe we align with, be it Māori, Anglo-Saxon or of the educated globe-trotting elite. Being equally human, the odds are vastly in favour of those empowered Māori being quite happy to have annexed that far-off island and enslaved its populace. Recorded history is replete with such episodes, with more ancient and unrecorded conquests stamped in our genome.

His shame also brings into question the usefulness of judging past behaviours from an educated, comfortably well-off, twenty-first-century viewpoint. It is the equivalent of condemning a pair of two-year-olds fighting over a toy for not acting like adults.

In judging his ancestor, he also assumes that the moral dictates of a society are innate and unchanging when the reality is that they are contextual and grudgingly modified when they no longer respond effectively to changed circumstances. He ignores the personal reality that how we see the world as a two-year-old, and our solutions to the problems encountered, will, hopefully, differ from our views and solutions as a twenty-year-old or a sixty-year-old.

The paucity of the thinking behind his apology soured mine because his view again highlighted the near impossibility of having a meaningful conversation, one where both sides accept the sincerity of the other's view, are prepared to *actively* hear what is said, to dispassionately consider it, and then are prepared to modify their own views. Such "true" conversations are unlikely when one, or both, lack sufficient knowledge, generosity and thinking skills. My disappointment arose from assuming that a professor, esteemed enough to be a contributor to the website, apparently lacks such knowledge and skills.

That article highlighted another inadequacy: my inability to articulate a considered response that would not be misunderstood and hence dismissed or reviled.

My main stumbling block was how to explain the notion that seemed to underpin the professor's contrition: his abhorrence of what I call *warrior culture*, which I define as *the excessive glorification of competing and winning*.

Biologically, we are hardwired to *compete* in order *to win*. It stems from our inbuilt urge to develop our capabilities and *use* them to survive and thrive. We want to succeed, but can only do so within society, which is made of like-minded wannabe winners. This forces us to face the brutal reality that we can't always be one of those winners, at all times and in all aspects of life.

Successful societies, and the successful individuals within them, develop optimal attitudes towards the concepts of winning and losing. And to stay successful in a changing world, those attitudes need to adapt, or the individual, and/or society, will fall prey to those groups and individuals better adapted.

My academic's shame, versus his ancestor's presumed comfort with his reference group's justification of his actions, is a demonstration of such a change in societal attitudes, possibly forced upon us by an over-populated world with its hugely increased societal interconnectedness and interdependence.

Throughout recorded history, the warrior ethos of *"might is right"* was cruelly *successful*, if we take a broad meaning of the word. The strong took from the weak, the winners enslaved the losers. It enlarged tribes, city-states, then nations and later empires. It holds true in the corporate world with big firms swallowing the small. It is the credo of the two-year-old who finds itself big enough to wrestle the toy from a weaker rival.

In the modern world and in modern societies, callous and inhuman abuse of power, of winner takes all and the devil take the hindmost, is seen by most as a liability. Thank goodness!

The problem we still face is recognising warrior culture in all its modern guises. It was easy when guns and clubs were used but today's warriors often utilise less obviously repugnant behaviours, and when challenged, are better at justifying them. This makes modern warrior culture more difficult to guard against.

The neoliberal economic dogma that currently rules the minds of most politicians, economists and business owners is one such under-recognised manifestation. The meritocratic idea that social and economic inequalities can be solved by encouraging education is another – convincingly explored in *The Meritocracy Trap* by Daniel Markovits [2].

Both these viewpoints share the warrior's obsession with

competing and winning. They are difficult to argue against because they are built upon seemingly worthy ideas easy to agree with. Businesses should compete to prevent a cosy mediocrity producing substandard products and services. Likewise, access to good education for all, should promote better use of a nation's human "resources" and theoretically raise the living standards of more people.

But a good idea is not necessarily improved by applying more of it.

The excessive, and globalised economic competition that started in the 1970s, changed gears in the eighties and nineties and went into overdrive in the 2000s, resulted in a frenzy of corporate takeovers that massively concentrated power into fewer and fewer organisations, many of whom have become too big to fail and their executives too big to jail. How many economic calamities will it take before governments and their economic advisers admit that free market fundamentalism is a false religion? When will they realise it needs to be replaced with economic policies and institutions that encourage ecologically and socially sustainable behaviours with the aim of a decent life for the majority, not just the elites? Sadly, whilst those elites continue to get richer, and indirectly control public policy, such a change seems a long way off.

The dark side of education as a means to reduce social inequality is harder to see. Markovits does an excellent job of opening our eyes to it.

In encouraging education, governments rarely make it free, which gives the competitive edge to the better off, who then are better able to access the shrinking pool of better-paid jobs that such an education grants access to – a *shrinking* pool of glamour jobs created by globalisation and technological innovations in computing, artificial intelligence and robotics that concurrently expanded the pool of poorly paid dead-end jobs. This process then intensifies educational competition and creates the win-at-any-cost mentality that has the winners motivated to *game the system*. Those at the top have the money to push their progeny into the exclusive schools and universities that are increasingly the gateway to the shrinking number of high-status and highly renumerated positions.

And my New Zealand academic's viewpoint not only lacks accuracy but also consistency.

If his ancestor is to be condemned for carrying out the dictates of the British Empire's unapologetic brand of warrior culture, then he should also show public remorse for all those New Zealanders who shamefully joined the ANZAC forces in 1914 to fight and die in their thousands defending the same brutal "might is right" credo of that odious Empire.

And if the warrior's unrestrained competitive urge that justifies the use of coercion and/or violence is so offensive, then, as a New Zealander, he should also be protesting against the performance of the Haka, a war dance, a ritualistic glorification of *Māori warrior culture*. Admittedly, it is performed before the stylised warfare of a rugby game where few are killed or seriously injured, but surely its prideful display of intimidation demands vigorous opposition from all correct-thinking, educated and civilised persons, irrespective of ethnicity. But I doubt he would be foolish enough to do so because the social backpressure would be too harmful to his social standing and possibly his health.

He also shows a lack of courage because publicly criticising past ideas and behaviours carries little serious risk. It is much more problematic and dangerous when criticising values and beliefs currently in the ascendency.

In an ideal world, we could meet for a face-to-face exchange of views. But what is the likelihood I would more fully appreciate his views and he mine? How would that exchange of views go if the website's review board were there to adjudicate it? Which of us would those "guardians of informed debate" encourage or discourage?

My current jaundiced understanding of human rationality gives little reason to think such an encounter, with or without the audience, would result in a happy conclusion for all involved. I hope I am proved wrong someday.

On the upside, I must thank my academic for pushing me into more fully examining moral viewpoints, which has highlighted their malleable and contextual nature.

He also opened my eyes to the many ways that *warrior culture* pervades and poisons the society I must live in, in particular our societal *obsession* with success and the consequent blindness to *how* such success is achieved, measured and owned.

For these reasons, I am most grateful to him.

---

[1] *How We Became Human* by Tim Dean and *Thinking, Fast and Slow* by Daniel Kahneman are two sources amongst many that provide detailed explanations of the limitations of human cognition and our subsequent attitudes.

[2] *The Meritocracy Trap* shows that seemingly good ideas, when placed in human hands and allowed to run to their ultimate conclusion, produce alarming results: in its case, impoverished wage slavery for the working classes *and* a fabulously remunerated slavery for the ruling elites.

53. Warrior Culture: Part Two

In Part One I defined warrior culture as: *the <u>excessive</u> glorification of competing and winning.* Several weeks after *Warrior Culture Part One* was written, I received, in the mail, the latest issue of the magazine that instigated an earlier essay: *The Truth Issue.* It was accompanied by a brief note tactfully acknowledging my critique of their issue upon the theme of *truth.* The implication of their response was that they had agreed to disagree with my criticisms. Having had little hope of *any* response, it was both unexpected and heartening.

As a music lover, my hopes were raised further when I saw that the magazine's theme was music – a much less troublesome topic than truth.

Sadly, as with the previous issue, those hopes waned by the time I reached the back cover. Had I read it six months earlier I would have said it was a well-balanced, if somewhat a rose-tinted look at music and the people engaged in it. Now, the magazine's stated aim of conversing with extraordinary people seemed another misguided example of our society's *uncritical* glorification of successful people, though it was more graciously done than that found in the pages of gossip magazines.

Their focus on extra-ordinary people had added to society's raucous adulation of the successful that then encourages the extreme rationales of *warrior culture*. And in contributing to the deification of the successful it correspondingly increases the rate at which social value is *removed* from those stuck in the shadows, from the great blurred-out mass of humanity whose unrecognised lives create the conditions that support the noteworthy few.

Don't get me wrong, I, like the majority, am inspired by successful people, *if* their success was morally worthy, and achieved with dignity for them and the people who helped them along the way. Unlike the producers of gossip magazines, I consider the people who kindly sent me that complimentary copy of their magazine to be educated, civilised, and harbouring good intentions. But good intentions are said to pave the road to hell when not enough knowledge and wisdom are employed.

I am also being overly critical because that latest issue was replete with worthwhile interviews and articles. Three that stood out were: learning that *all* the members of the band *Powderfinger* receive equal shares of the profits, that the twenty-eight ordinary blokes of the choir *Dustyesky* were aware of the temporary nature of their current success, and that, after a long career in music, Nicolino DiSipio remained passionate about it and was still motivated by its fun factor. To me, all of the people interviewed were engaged with music for the right reasons, for love, not from an addictive lust for money, fame and power.

They showcased the good side of music. They inspired me.

But I don't only crave inspiration, I also yearn for truthfulness. I need to see the light *and* the dark of reality if I am to recognise whether the road I tread leads to a heaven or a hell.

That dark side of music was hinted at with mention of careers blighted or abandoned because of COVID-19 lockdowns, but more needs to be said about the costs of pursuing music and the realities of musical achievements.

I kept thinking they should have interviewed Kevin Johnson, the Aussie singer-songwriter who, back in 1973, had a paradoxically successful song called: *Rock'n'Roll I Gave You the Best Years of My Life*. It was a catchy ballad of a man's journey into music, from buying his first guitar, joining a band, then years of bands and performances only to belatedly realise that he would never be a star. He sells his guitar and accepts his fate as a rock'n'roll "also-ran".

To have included stories of people who tried and failed, or who succeeded briefly and then faded into obscurity, would have provided a more balanced view of what a life in music entails. Perhaps even interviewed someone who has a dim view of music and is happy to live without it.

As stated earlier, my principal objection to extolling the virtues of extra-ordinary people, is not their striving and their success, if both the methods and goals are morally defensible, but the implied lack of regard for those who don't meet society's restricted and skewed definitions of worthiness. I asked myself: how valid are those definitions of worth?

The more I examined those definitions the more dubious and unhelpful they became. Winners themselves, and the people who write about them, rarely *seriously* question the worthiness of their achievements, whether the conquering of a foreign nation, the swallowing of one's competition to become a corporate juggernaut, or the status given to a rock star.

They almost never acknowledge the multitude of people who directly and indirectly helped them to succeed, restricting any mention to an obvious few. Left out or greatly downplayed is the huge role of good luck, of the received largesse of the goddess Fortuna, because the more her influence is recognised, the more our ownership of achievements is diminished.

The magazine's interviews are like all biographies: misrepresentations of reality. They should be read as largely fictional, not taken as gospel. If we need convincing, try writing our own story, and then give it to our family, friends, colleagues *and* enemies to comment on.

The first thing we will confront is the fact that most of our experiences have been forgotten, with those that remain often drastically reworked – an embarrassing aspect that those who know us will happily bring to our attention.

Most could cope with the comments of an enemy but few would want Lady Luck to critique their biography. Our imaginations are rarely large and brave enough to comprehend her true importance, which encompasses the specifics of existing in our patch of the universe, with our sun and our Goldilocks planet, and then the random course of evolution that led to our creation. Not mentioned will be the luck that gave us the good, and not so good genes we were born with, and the time, place and moment in history that we were born into, as well as all those forgotten people that she forced us to interact with and learn from.

The second embarrassing, or perhaps empowering fact – depending upon our ethics – is the realisation that we can turn ourself into a saint or a sinner simply by careful selection of the parts we reveal and those we choose to forget or reinterpret.

Also unveiled will be the invidious side of silence. The Irish politician Edmund Bourke famously stated that "evil triumphs when good men do nothing". I would add that evil triumphs when good *people do nothing because they are fed a diet of lies, half-truths or silence* in regard to bad ideas.

As an escapee from the world of paid employment, an obvious example was the war on unionism. Decades of media coverage of all the negative sides of union-organised actions, and the misdeeds of some of its members, combined with a complete *silence* on the social benefits, such as safer working conditions and better wages, has resulted in union membership at an all-time low and sinking. The crafting of its "shameful" image then made possible the legislative changes that now severely constrain union capacity to legally exert pressure on employers.

Though in my experience the most beautifully played use of silence [1] was encountered during a TV program about great train journeys. The host was making a train trip through former Yugoslavia and, whilst travelling through Croatia, made the viewer frequently aware of the damage done by Serb forces during the civil war of the 1990s. Eventually, he reached Sarajevo in Bosnia and showed us the city's iconic bridge, destroyed in that war but now rebuilt to make the city whole again. But throughout his explanation of the significance and history of that five-hundred-year-old bridge, he was strangely *silent* on who destroyed it. From all the previous mentions of damage done by Serbian forces, the viewer is left with the assumption it was the Serbs who blew it up. In fact, it was the Croats who were responsible. A prosecuting lawyer or a political spin doctor couldn't have done a slicker job of misleading the viewer via what they *didn't* mention.

When it comes to manipulating attitudes, silence is a powerful tool that we all employ to discourage others, or use to avoid being punished for airing unpopular viewpoints.

But if we are to avoid being duped into accepting ideas that *do* require deeper analysis in order to avoid downstream dramas, for us and broader society, then we need to be more aware of when we are being discouraged from doing so. We need to recognise when we are being manipulated by less obvious forms of the "silent treatment".

Am I equating the work of the good folk at that magazine with those prosecuting the war on unionism, or promoting the absolution of Croatian forces from any destruction of property and lives during the Yugoslav civil war?

No. But I can't help feeling that their magazine's focus on successful people contributes to our society's over-sold concept of success, and its *silent* under-appreciation of the contributions of the "unsuccessful" multitude living the ordinary life.

Reality TV shows, where ordinary folk or minor celebrities *compete*, firstly to get a place in the show, and then against each other in a desperate bid for five minutes of fame, are the latest manifestation of our society's overblown and unexamined cult of success. A brand of success with little dignity or societal benefit.

Again, I am being harsh because the magazine's stories concern morally principled and worthy people, exactly the type whose lives should be more widely recognised. It's a good magazine, but I dream of a better one.

The only one that hints of that dream is *Womankind* [2], published in Hobart. It too has interviews with prominent people, mostly women naturally, but has the added dimension of including stories of more "normal" lives, as well as small doses of philosophy to sharpen the mind's eye.

They also have a challenges section where a small number of women, mostly restricted to young white professionals, are given a relatively simple task to perform over three consecutive days, for instance, finding time to gaze up at the night sky. They then report back their experiences. I find their efforts illuminating in intriguing ways.

The biological world also has the ability to cast light on our topic of discussion. Plants and animals seem to thrive or flounder in accordance with their level of biological *diversity*. Perhaps the same holds true of societies? And do not individuals succeed or fail depending on their *diversity of ideas* and flexibility in using them?

All my knowledge to date has me placing my faith in increasing the breadth and depth of my knowledge to gain the flexibility and humility of thinking to chart the safest way through the reef-strewn waters of life. I need to know of, and understand, the lives of successful *and* ordinary people. And I also need my concept of success and worthiness challenged on occasion to keep it useful and morally defensible.

In our commendable desire to make a success of our lives, it is all too easy to dump ethical considerations, if, or when, our self-focus becomes obsessive and the warrior's lust for achievement regardless of the cost takes over.

It is an outcome more likely to happen if our morality and sense of agency is warped by being shielded from and hence blinded to the innumerable good works of the unheralded majority and the immense but fickle influence of Lady Luck.

To find the middle path between the extremes of mediocrity and megalomania we require the inspiration of true heroes with worthy achievements, on *tiny* pedestals, balanced with acknowledgements of the countless acts of everyday cooperation and kindness done by ordinary folk that make civilised living possible.

It is those unreported achievements and acts of courage and kindness I would like to see and hear more of.

---

[1] A broader discussion of silence can be found in my previous essay on the topic.

[2] *Womankind's* issue twenty-three had England as its focus. The interview with Amy Bradshaw I found particularly interesting. Amy is an ordinary person whose story was both sad and hopeful and somehow extra-ordinarily instructive.

54. Type Two Happiness

In issue thirty of *Womankind* magazine, I came across a new concept in their photo essay section. A full-page photograph, taken by Kate Crittenden, shows a lone woman in a red shirt standing on a boulder on the edge of a precipice. She is looking up at the jagged snowclad peaks of the high Andes. Kate titled the shot, *Type 2 Fun,* which she says is "… any activity that is generally a great idea to start with, but not enjoyable in the doing. Instead, *the real fun is in the reminiscing.*"

After nine years of attending writing courses and groups, producing short stories, essays of varying qualities and finally a novel ready for publication, the idea of two types of fun, of two types of happiness, seemed very true.

Writing a novel is like that young lady's mountain trek, full of arduous struggle and privations, all for a view that gains its true worth mostly upon reflection and less so during the doing.

Whilst writing that novel, as well as many of my essays and short stories, I suffered the frustrations of dead ends, dud words and grammar, and occasional ego bruising negative reviews.

The hours of struggling for the right words, of straightening out plotlines and convoluted thinking interspersed with the shocks of negative feedback seem never quite balanced by those rare and exhilarating moments when everything flows from some magical wellspring onto the page and glowing reviews are unexpectantly received.

That said, I continue writing from a desire for clarification of my thoughts and to have those thoughts presented to others in a way that pleases and possibly promotes new and useful thoughts in my readers.

This writing caper does have enough moments of "regular" happiness in it to keep me going, but its greater reward appears to lie in the delayed production of happiness of the second type. To that end I intend to have a copy of my debut novel placed in my coffin so that my life in eternity will be blessed with some of that precious second variety of happiness.

55. Happily Ever After

On the ninth of June 2020, I gave my dear wife a near final draft of an action-romance I had written. Before turning a page, she shook my expectations by asking: "Can the characters be carried over into another story?"

I'd never considered the idea. I thought the essence of a romance is that two people meet, things get in their way that they eventually overcome, they then get married and are presumed to *live happily ever after*.

My wife's question produced the awful realisation that life *after* wedlock, in the promised land of "happily ever after", to my knowledge is never written of, apparently because it is of no interest to the reading public. It's as though the subject of conjugal bliss and the conditions that sustain it are either a taboo topic, or one too difficult to understand and/or too boring. What is going on?

Was Johann Wolfgang von Goethe correct to sum up our lives as being an endless procession of *wanting and not succeeding, succeeding and then not wanting*? That we enjoy the journey but never the destination?

If the happiness found in long-term and amicable coupledom is what all romantics aspire to, why does it seem to lose its value once we, or the fictional couple, get married? Why can't the romantic glow that attracts and binds people together during the courting continue to outshine the apparent dullness of the everyday activities encountered when running both lives and a shared household? And why is such a shared life not worth reading about?

The physiological foundations of happiness are discussed in depth in *The Science of Happiness* by Stefan Klein but happiness ultimately rests further down, all the way down to our cellular biochemistry. Nick Lane, in *The Vital Question*, quotes fellow biochemist Albert Szent-Györgyi's definition of life as being "nothing but an electron looking for a place to rest".

Such a definition is relevant to our discussion because we can't be happy if we are dead! And when alive, we can only feel happy if all is well in our cells, and they are "happy" only when they are optimally performing their intricate and interdependent biochemical reactions, which, as Albert points out, is no more than a never-ending shifting of electrons from one chemical compound to the next in a sort of microscopic basketball game, where the chemical players must keep the electron "ball" moving in an endless series of passes, with "game over" – death – occurring when the "ball" stops moving.

Thus life, at its core, is an *incomplete* process.

That *incompleteness* also underpins our experience of happiness, which Stefan Klein posits rests mostly in expectation, anticipation, wanting and desiring, all of which are *ongoing* states. They are journeys, not destinations. That is why we feel "alive" only when we are moving/changing/growing, and "dead" when things are static, stagnant and nothing is happening.

And something moving, growing and constantly changing is like trying to hold onto a determined and wriggly baby – we may struggle for a while but eventually we have to put the baby down. Our slippery moment of happiness escapes and again we feel the desire and hope for the next dose.

Whilst happiness ultimately rests upon a cellular biochemistry functioning within an optimal range of parameters, once our body is sufficiently "happy", any consequent happiness increasingly resides in our minds.

It is well to remember that we have a brain, and its attendant mind, primarily to keep our bodies alive long enough to produce the next generation and hence save us from extinction.

We are a social species so our way of working towards that evolutionary imperative is considerably more complex than that of a solitary creature such as an earthworm, or a social but less complex one, such as an ant.

"Happily ever after", that explicit goal of every romance, and the unstated goal of most other individuals, energises our minds to seek happiness in the present *as well as* strategies that will ensure our future happiness, whether as individuals or as members of a couple, both of which require living within a functioning society.

According to Robert Ardrey [1], our quest for both short and long-term happiness is motivated and directed by three broad motivations: security, identity and stimulation.

Security encompasses our requirements for a physical, social and financial situation that is ongoing, relatively predictable and safe.

Two people are unlikely to become a couple if one or both lack some stable health, bodily safety, and a relatively predictable income sufficient to cover the basics of their survival. Two homeless, drug-addicted beggars in a violence-plagued ghetto may find some solace in each other's company but a long-term and happy union is beyond my imagining. In Australia, starvation and violent death are rare but financial insecurities are not and hence are central to the cause of many marital breakdowns here.

Identity covers our innate yearning to develop who we are, what we are good at, and, crucially, to have our personality and achievements then recognised by that section of society we align with.

Once their ongoing security needs are under control, a

couple, to *remain* happy, will need to be able to develop their personalities and skills, at home, and within their communities. On the home front they'll need to develop together, which requires each to commit to each other's developmental aspirations both in quantity and quality. They will have to constantly monitor and negotiate if they are to prevent one being left behind, which subsequently risks their bonds becoming stretched beyond human capacity to maintain. It is a task that requires *time* together *and* a mutual sensitivity of and regard for the other's requirements.

But developing their identities within the marriage is a task involving skills very few of us are *specifically* trained in. They are acquired "on the job", by trial and error, with wildly variable degrees of success. It is a poorly understood art, which produces its best results when both learn to understand and accept their limitations and those of the other, and then endeavour to find flexible responses to any mismatches in aspirations and expectations.

Stimulation appears to be the hardest need to satisfy. I think it was columnist and presenter Philip Adams who said: "we fear boredom more than cancer" and I concur. Our cellular biochemical imperative to *keep things moving* is reflected in our minds having a constant and changing *desire for stimulation* to cure the stagnation and boredom that comes from the satiation of an appetite, or the achievement of a goal.

For the happy couple to stay so, this insatiable desire has to be sufficiently met to prevent them getting bored with each other, which, if left unresolved, will lead to the relationship fading and then ceasing.

A possible strategy for ensuring their relationship is regularly enlivened is for both to actively *rekindle the thirst for knowledge and curiosity* they possessed as toddlers – before such joy was discouraged in school, and then employment, by the need to conform, to fit in, to be a team player. That expanded curiosity, when exercised together, will lead to the couple discovering the extraordinary in the ordinary, as well as new goals worthy of joint pursuit.

In our battle against boredom few ask how much boredom is too much and whether it is realistic to be *never* bored. We would be wise to rethink our attitudes towards the prosaic, the everyday, to those times when not much is happening. If you are running around dodging bullets, scrounging for food and shelter in the middle of a warzone, you can't complain of insufficient stimulation! Boredom seen from that perspective is a *good* outcome and one to be cherished.

According to some, boredom is nature's way of stimulating us to exercise our imaginations and seek something interesting to do because, in our hunter-gatherer past, doing nothing and not learning were often a recipe for a shortened lifespan in their unsecure world of animal predators and murderous rival tribes, not to mention ruthless rivals within their own group. The modern world is considerably less challenging and yet I would suggest we underestimate the long-term risks of not responding to boredom, of not breaking out of a rut that dulls and hence threatens domestic harmony. If it occurs in the workplace, and persists, such stagnation may result in outdated skills that then diminish our future employment prospects.

So, when a lack of stimulation induces boredom, it means we are in the enviable position of having our other needs met! We now have the motivation and the time – that allocated to being bored – to redirect our energies into trying something new. Feeling bored is the body nudging the mind into awakening its imagination and consulting its accumulated wisdom to find useful new activities.

And if life is not exciting at all times, welcome to reality, and be grateful because our bodies and brains are not built to take hyperstimulation for long. Such a condition leads to exhaustion, burnout and pleasures becoming permanently devalued from becoming overly familiar with them. Thankfully, most lives are filled with plenty of the unappreciated neutrality of the routine.

In fact, our appreciation of happiness is to a large extent dependent upon our views on the prosaic.

Happy times are memorable but so are the sad and painful. Unfortunately, bad times are remembered more strongly. That bias and others [2] leave our "remembered self" with a grossly underestimated assessment of our overall happiness.

That happiness rating is further reduced by our underappreciation of the mass of neutral moments that populate our waking hours. Being neutral, those unremembered and hence untallied hours of routine, be it showering, grooming, dressing, preparing meals and innumerable others are missing from our happiness assessment.

Putting those lost hours back in our pie graph of life experiences does two things: it dilutes the percentage of the bad moments, which is uplifting, but also dilutes the number of hours of the happy ones, which is deflating.

Are we then better off ignoring the neutral?

Before we decide, it would be best to consider getting more value from that vast amount of time spent in the neutral zone.

We need to employ our inner spin-doctor and rethink our attitude to the things that must be done. With a bit of imagination, we may come to realise that many of those activities were essential for creating the preconditions that our successes and happiness grew from. We may also recognise that they provided the background against which our stellar moments stand out from.

Putting this rethink on the prosaic into action I now see the unexciting task of washing and drying the dishes, and then tidying up the kitchen after each meal or snack, no longer a grudging must-do activity, but another task that exercises my self-affirming power to create order from chaos through making the kitchen easier on the eye, hygienic, and ready for the next session – a small realignment in thinking that induces tiny increases of happy hormones in my brain, which then promotes a positive mood that makes me a happier and easier person to be with. Perhaps my better mood may even make my dear wife a little happier, and "a happy life is a happy wife"!

That simple reassessment of one ordinary task, when repeated, increases my tally of happy moments which in turn encourages more in a positive feedback loop.

Rethinking the prosaic can also increase happiness by making us realise that some habitual tasks may not be essential, and can either be removed entirely, or drastically reduced, which will leave more time available for happiness-inducing activities.

Reclassifying more of the mundane as 'mildly rewarding and/or happiness enabling' will significantly increase our overall level of happiness. It will also indirectly improve our situation by reducing the relative influence of the bad bits, which now will be seen as not simply opposing the relatively few outstandingly glorious moments but fighting against those wonderful few backed up by a huge army of the mildly happy, happiness-enabling and the neutral.

There is one final aspect of happiness that needs to be considered: its actual nature. What, *specifically*, makes us, singly and/or as one of a couple, happy? What types of "happy" do we make and/or aspire to?

What is oft overlooked is that there are broadly two types: *somatic* happiness as opposed to *philosophic* happiness [3].

By somatic I mean that felt mostly in the body and in the moment. It is the contentment felt after a good meal, the tingling invigoration from finishing a session of laps in the pool, or the invigorating glow after a bout of mutually satisfying lovemaking.

Those moments can be truly memorable but not for long.

Chasing somatic, hedonistic happiness is the least sustainable form of it. That unsustainability was graphically demonstrated in an experiment in which researchers inserted electrodes into the "pleasure centre" of a rat's brain, which were stimulated whenever the rat tapped a bar. The poor thing spent its entire time tapping on the bar *addicted* to pleasure and would have died of hunger and thirst had it not been rescued by the experimenters.

If asked, in our maturity, whether we had a happy life, our conclusion will be based not on faded memories of good meals and lovemaking but on the frequency and quality of events and achievements that gave our lives *philosophic meaning*.

Somatic happiness is mostly inward facing, it is *our* pleasure. *Philosophic happiness* is outward facing, it comes from fulfilling in part, or whole, goals that give meaning and a sense of purpose to our lives from having made an enduring positive impact upon those around us. Philosophic happiness pleases and benefits us *and* society, in the present *and* into the future. As such it is the exception to Goethe's curse. Philosophic happiness gives joy in the process *and* in the possessing, it is never boring; it is a happiness to hold and be proud of.

Surely, the greatest disappointment we could suffer on our deathbed would be to look *honestly* over our life and conclude that it had been a terrible waste of time and energy, that the world would not miss our passing, or worse still, that it would be relieved by our exit from it.

A couple, to enjoy a continuous supply of happy moments, will need shared goals that both feel worthy of expending their lives on, which needn't be grandiose, in fact the more modest they are the easier they will be to achieve. Whatever those goals are they will need to give long-term meaning to their lives such that they give satisfactory answers to the question: what was it all for? If our answers come up short, we will understand unhappiness in its most brutal and inescapable form.

For me, Ralph Waldo Emerson's short exposition on the parameters of a successful life is worth repeating. He defined it as:

> *To laugh often and much;*
> *To win the respect of intelligent people and the affection of children;*
> *To earn the appreciation of honest critics and endure the betrayal of false friends;*
> *To appreciate beauty;*
> *To find the best in others;*
> *To leave the world a bit better, whether by a healthy child, a garden patch or a redeemed social condition;*
> *To know even one life breathed easier because you have lived;*
> *That is to have succeeded.*

For any couple to live happily ever after, contemplating Emerson's view of success should help them define mutual goals that are realistic, achievable and beneficial to them, their family and wider society.

Such goals will transcend boredom, pain and even fleeting moments of physical pleasure. They are the ones that will grant them the sustaining glow of *philosophic happiness.*

This brings us back to the conundrum of why we find a developing romance exciting and worth writing about and reading, but not the living happily ever after.

Again, the answers lie in biology. Our cells must constantly maintain their biochemistry within a restricted range of parameters in a state known as homeostasis. If they don't, they die, and if too many of them die, we sicken and eventually die also.

Our cells want cellular homeostasis *now*, not tomorrow. Again, this imperative is reflected higher up. As social creatures in an uncertain world, we must consider tomorrow if we are to avoid harm biologically and socially, and yet our cells live in the now. This explains why our most powerful and primal inclinations are of *self-interest* and *instant gratification,* aspects that often overrule our intellect's considerations of future consequences. We *feel* the now. The future is a distant and *unfelt* afterthought.

When reading an engaging romance, we experience the thrill of the unfolding story *as we read*. The "ever after" of "happily ever after" is too removed from our senses and visceral stimulation to stir our interest, perhaps because it implies an end state, a boring place where nothing much interesting happens.

But in real life, as distinct from the world of fiction and entertainment, we must think about the unfelt future if we are to have much of one. At some stage, we need to engage the brain and do the seemingly boring work of overruling our myopic cells, do the thinking and then enact the behaviours necessary to bring about a happy and fulfilling future, for both body and soul.

Conscious thinking is laborious but can be made less so if we put the skills developed in reassessing the mundane, and apply them to our moments of forward planning and goal setting.

At this point, I pause. I look around my office, contemplate the many happy photos and inspirational quotes, and then go further afield to contemplate all the good things I have achieved, great and small. Though the small achievements outnumber the great, those few grand moments probably would not have happened without that multitude of lesser ones. When I add in a few of the most memorable moments of somatic happiness, I find that I now, *feel,* pleased! That positive emotion encourages me to keep doing the tasks I have set for myself. Occasionally reminiscing on our past achievements can be a powerful tool for creating a worthy future. Why not use it?

Thus, the oft given advice not to dwell in the past is only

partially wise. The past made us who we are today. If we are not happy, then it is because we didn't learn much from our past experiences, probably because we didn't do enough constructive, honest and *informed* thinking upon those mistakes.

When Isaac Newton was lauded for all his amazing scientific theorems – that still form the bedrock of modern physics – he modestly, and truthfully, responded that his great achievements were made possible by standing upon the shoulders of giants.

Likewise, our future happiness rests upon learning from past mistakes *and* by actively and regularly acknowledging our achievements big and small. Those lessons learned and achievements gained are the giants upon whose shoulders we can create even more achievements of lasting worth.

All forms of happiness are felt in the body and then later interpreted by the mind. Reading a well written romance novel induces the *physically* pleasant sensation of anticipation, which is why we continue reading. But reading about a fictional or real couple buying a house, doing the dishes, driving to and from work is as exciting as reading someone's shopping list. It involves no anticipation and hence induces no positive emotion in the reader. No positive emotion, no reading, which is why the happily ever after is not written about.

That said, we feel our happiness. We wish to *experience it* rather than read about it. To feel it regularly we are wise to consider all the ideas discussed in this essay, especially our reassessing of the prosaic, training our intellect to regularly contemplate our past achievements and then using its glow to energise our thinking and actions towards fulfilling existing goals and/or new ones. In doing so we will feel the joy of anticipating those worthy goals being achieved and enjoyed. It will be a happiness built largely of the philosophic variety, garnished with moments of the somatic.

That promised land of happily ever after is a realm that we

make, experience, and reminisce upon *as we live it*.

---

¹ *The Social Contract* by Robert Ardrey, from 1970, it is dated in some ways, but is still amazingly perceptive in the breadth and depth of its study of our biological and social evolution.

² A pair of easy-to-understand books on the subject of how we think and which kind of thinking is easy (and error prone) versus hard but more rigorous, are: *Thinking, Fast and Slow* by Daniel Kahneman and more recently, *The Intelligence Trap* by David Robson.

³ Type Two happiness described in an earlier essay is an aspect of philosophic happiness.

56. The Law

During a leisurely beachside stroll in the early months of 2022, I was asked by my friend: "Do you believe in the law?" The question was unexpected considering the previous topics we'd touched upon and I'm afraid I didn't really answer it. This is my delayed reply.

The question flummoxed me for a number of reasons not entirely clear to me at the time, that, on reflection, boil down to a) the earnestness of its asking and b) innate recognition of the huge scope of the task hidden within the question.

In the days since its asking, I have concluded the question has two aspects that require untangling: "believe" and "the law".

"The law" in this context is not the laws of physics or chemistry but the rules, formal and informal, by which human society is regulated. This produces the first hurdle: which human society – that pertaining to Australian citizens, permanent residents, and visitors currently living within Australia and its overseas territories, or to humanity as a whole? We shall assume, for now, that we are focusing on Australia and Australian laws passed by our elected parliaments and currently valid.

The second hurdle is laws can only be believed in, or not, if they are known and understood. One amusing formal law that I believe exists in Australia is the quaint notion that: ignorance of the law is no defence from the consequences of breaking the law, or words to that effect. It is a cruelly comical concept because no human alive could possibly remember and fully grasp all the promulgated laws that govern us because there are so many thousands of them and all written in legalese, a language few mortals fully comprehend, including those who draft the legislation.

Living here in Australia, my thoughts and behaviours are constantly being influenced by my understanding of those formal laws known to me. But my attitudes to formal laws are very dependent upon my attitudes to the informal laws that influence me and all societies, those rules of behaviour that allowed our species to stay alive during our evolution on the savannahs of ancient Africa.

To believe in, and presumably obey, a law, one must see its purpose, and, that its benefits outweigh its costs, all of which vary with the individual, and with time and circumstances. How does one decide if a law, formal or informal, should be obeyed, and by how much and in what circumstances?

The answer to when and how much will depend on its why, upon the societal purpose of that law and how much that societal purpose aligns with our unique and malleable moral code.

And where does our morality come from and why do we possess one, no matter how rudimentary?

The most successful animal species on this planet are the social ones [1], because sociability allows such species to transcend the fragility and limitations of the individual and enjoy the power inherent in "economies of scale" to use economic-speak.

We populate the globe in our billions because we mostly know how to work together, whether by consent or coercion. Sociability makes us and breaks us. Few can survive physically or mentally for long in total isolation from our kind.

Knowing and understanding this basic quality of our being is the foundation of our moral code. We feel compelled to firstly stay alive, today and into the future, and secondly to interact with our chosen group, whether as a leader or a follower.

Those two compulsions are not always synchronised, all too often short-term selfishness overrules long-term societal consequences. That imbalance is held in check internally by our moral code and externally by formal and informal laws.

In accepting my dependence upon society, it is easier for me to have faith in the logic of codes of behaviour that benefit me now and into the future and that also help the society I depend on.

But how and when I obey the dictates of the written and unwritten laws of society, as well as my evolved biological desires to function within it, are very much prescribed by circumstances.

Do I believe in the law?

I agree with and understand to a large degree the logic behind formal laws but understand also that those laws are clunky, are open to different interpretations, and often made to best serve a minority. I thus find my obedience to them malleable and situation specific.

On a grander scale, I see much merit in applying the concepts of yin (chaos) and its opposing force, yang (order) to humanity. Societal laws, formal and informal, represent order (yang). Individual freedom to act without heed to our impact upon others, including our future self, invoke chaos (yin).

The happier and better functioning societies will be those with an optimal balance of yang-laws and yin-freedoms, which then evolve as the world changes.

I believe laws, rules, morals are essential for a social species such as ours, but reality is not fixed or totally understandable and hence laws are to be fully obeyed, partially obeyed or ignored depending upon circumstances.

The how, when, and how much credence and obedience to give to human-centric laws, whether formal or informal, is a challenge we are daily forced to consider and resolve. It generates a constant struggle between our responses created by our current level of wisdom interacting with the implacable wisdom built into the formal and informal laws governing our society.

Acquiring sufficient wisdom to choose well is the real challenge that "the law", in all its manifestations, brings to our daily lives.

---

1 *The Social Conquest of Earth* by the biologist Edward O. Wilson.

57. Believe in God

"Do you believe in God?"

I can't remember when I was first asked that fateful question – probably sometime in high school – but I do remember struggling to answer it in an honest and meaningful way. Since that foggy first mention of our supernatural monarch and maker, I have learned much of the world and have done a considerable amount of thinking. This essay is a condensation of my current resolution regarding God, the entity, and the starting point of a response should I again be asked if I am a believer.

The problem with the question is that it is rarely an invitation to discuss aspects of theology. It is almost always a veiled attempt to determine whether I am like them, or not. Though, at a more basic level, it is asked to determine whether I am friend or foe, whether I am with us or against us. It is a question that in times past, and in many countries and circumstances today, could result in social ostracism, persecution, or even death if one answers contrary to what is deemed socially acceptable by the majority.

Five common, but troubling, words, with the trouble held in only two: *believe*, and, *God*.

It is very hard to believe in something difficult to comprehend. In high school, and to the present day, I find magnetism hard to *believe in*, though I can on some level accept it as a concept that explains much, and, that by pretending it is real, we can make predictions that prove true and useful. Unlike heat or light or pressure or sound or taste, we can't directly experience magnetism, so how can we know, in our hearts, that it is real. How can we *truly* believe in magnetism or anything else that we can't directly feel through our senses?

That we humans can believe in things we can't sense directly is one of the wonders of creation. Sadly, for our egos, it is a power not ours alone. Many animals appear to believe in things that don't exist! Let me explain this bold statement, which, if true, would diminish our sense of being unique and *superior* (with attacks upon our precious sense of superiority being considered, by most, to be offensive and threatening).

A lion sizing up a herd of wildebeests is conjuring up and *believing in* the insubstantial, because *it is thinking of a future which does not yet exist*. It is dreaming of how to separate one of the wildebeest from the herd, to be ambushed by other lions, who believe in the same non-existent future, and consequently have gone ahead to lie in wait. A pride of hunting lions is not engaging in random behaviours, they "believe" in the future events they are engineering. It is the same process as our belief that we can create a happier retirement by stashing money into a bank account or a superannuation plan in the belief the funds will be there in a currently non-existent future. To plan ahead, shows belief in that which can't be physically proven, by any means, in the present. That ability to believe in, and act upon *concepts*, is a wonderful power though not without its downsides.

How can I say that lions believe in anything when I can't ask them directly? The same way I determine what another person believes in – through externally observable behaviours, such as body language, what they say, and what they do. God may be able to read minds but I can't, though with advances in neurobiology we are getting closer to that point. Thus, my knowledge of what others actually believe can only be approximate.

Does the Pope believe in the God he claims to represent? He says he does. But why do we believe him when we are quite happy to disbelieve other humans of different rank and occupation.

Thus, if you were to ask if I believed in God and I answered with an emphatic yes, or an equally emphatic no, why would you believe me? And why do I *feel* that my beliefs, whatever they may be, are, firstly, mine, secondly, valid, and thirdly, of relevance to God? Surely God doesn't need my belief in it for it to exist!

The above conundrums were discussed in my essay *Living on Scraps*. In it I conclude that our attitudes to things we cannot directly feel or sense are formed from a subjective assessment of the *probabilities* the event, or concept, are realistic when judged against the current state of our accumulated knowledge.

Since we can't know, or understand everything, our beliefs, no matter how right they *feel*, can never be totally valid. A perusal of findings by scientists [1] on the workings and limitations of our brain will have us taking the opinions and beliefs of others, and ourself, not with a grain of salt, but a handful – assuming we can grant those researchers the same credibility we bestow on persons we currently believe in.

But doubting the source and validity of our own thoughts are very difficult and threatening tasks. Our sanity depends upon having a sense of *agency*, that what we think and do is ours, not the work of outside forces. To be the puppet not the puppet-master is an untenable situation for most, though some would enjoy being relieved of the burden of decision-making and responsibility for the consequences of those decisions, especially if they are harmful to ourselves or others. Many a person has been killed by people claiming to be obeying God's will, but we only have their fallibly human word that God *was* guiding their actions.

Other aspects to be considered regarding belief in God, or

any other concept, are: how strongly is that belief *felt*, how the belief is manifested, and under what circumstances does the strength and shape of the belief change.

As a two-year-old we may truly and strongly believe that Santa Claus gives us presents once a year. Later experiences teach us differently and our convictions regarding Santa Claus's existence and powers fade, to be replaced by more predictable but less magical beliefs.

Fiercely believing in something does *not* make it real. The classic proof of which is the phantom limbs felt by amputees, or the denial of the paralysis of their limbs by stroke victims. Many other neurological conditions [1] affecting the brain's cognitive powers also result in similar strongly held but blatantly incorrect beliefs.

"Do you believe in God?" How can one answer if we don't fully understand how our beliefs arise within us? And why do we accept the changing nature and strength of the other beliefs that we hold, such as the wisdom of saving for a rainy day, and yet when asked about God we are expected to produce a definitive *one-word* answer that is immutable, permanent and entirely ours?

But yes or no are the only answers that will satisfy most people who utter those five fateful words.

Assuming I am prepared to give such a minimalistic response, there remains the problem of whose God I am to believe or disbelieve in?

The question: "Do you believe in God, the one and only" is one that could not have been asked until recently, because, as far as we know, for most of the hundreds of thousands of years our species has existed, gods, plural, ruled. The one God idea is only a little over two thousand years old, and hence for most of our existence people believed in an imaginative team of gods, each with their own responsibilities and powers. The validity of that question and its answers are thus as situation specific as most other question and answer occasions.

The late, great, comedian Dave Allen used to end his show with the line: "Goodnight, and may your god go with you." *Your* god! Said, not entirely as a joke.

If questioned about our belief in God, be wary of remembering Dave Allen and so being tempted to first ask the following clarification: "Describe *your* god to me, so that I can compare it to mine, after which I will know if they are one and the same."

Doing so does several things. First, it will antagonise the other because anything but immediate acceptance implies disbelief. It will then induce further annoyance by placing them in the unenviable position of having to *convincingly* describe their god's nature and powers. Few god descriptions will be such that their god's actions can be ascribed to it in verifiable or predictive ways. They won't be able to give any convincing examples of: if you do this, God is *certain* to do that. Their descriptions of their God's qualities and mode of operation can, with imagination and practice, explain any phenomenon, but objectively predict none. All of which I find unsatisfactory.

The second, is that asking for specific details gives immediate proof that you don't believe in their version of God because, believing their God omnipotent, they assume all *true* believers will share the *same* understanding of it, which negates the need for nit-picking clarification. Asking for such a clarification provides further "proof" that we are not one of them, which risks our being immediately, and negatively, reclassified in regard to how they will treat us and our opinions.

If still reading, by now you will probably have concluded that I am a godless atheist. You would be wrong. I merely can't believe, to any large degree, in the variable and fuzzy visions of God that I have encountered so far in my sixty plus years.

The thing most askers of the God question refuse to accept,

or condone, is the excuse that any belief I can have in a poorly defined and verifiable supernatural entity, who created and then actively manages the lives of its creatures, one who actually listens to and takes heed of prayers and offerings, is, *beyond my imagining*, and hence beyond belief in any depth. Just as I find most mathematics too esoteric for my mental powers – especially that concerning the *meaning* of probabilities and statistics – doesn't preclude me accepting that some people seem to comprehend and make reasonably useable predictions using it. I may not understand higher maths, but I do see its usefulness and *believe* I should be grateful for that usefulness.

Similarly, even though I am sure that concepts like justice, a fair go, and the public good are human inventions which do not exist in the real world – you can't measure their length, breadth and weight – I still *believe* in all three, possibly with as much fervour as many believe in their version of God.

Do I lack a God belief gene? I am not aware such a genetic disposition has been verifiably confirmed and, on the balance of the probabilities that my current knowledge allows me, doubt very much that God belief is genetic and that I missed out on the benefits of such a gene by chance or by divine intervention. Which it is I do not know.

If belief (however strong and situation specific) in God (no matter how subjectively described) is not genetic and instinctual, then such a belief must be a product of a certain set of circumstances operating upon an individual human's mind. This view would explain the evolution and nature of past deities [2] and may help predict the future directions of religious beliefs.

A baby interacting with the physical world learns, by trial and error, that when it does some physical act, such as crying, a response is generated – one of its caregivers comes to feed or comfort it. We learn early about the concept of agency, that things happen for a reason.

But sometimes, the reasons for an action or consequence are not obvious, most probably because they do not follow immediately. "If I didn't make it happen, then who did?" will spontaneously come into our young mind. The who and how are then left to our fertile imaginations or those of our caregivers. A theory is either internally created, or adopted from others, one that we then test as time and experiences allow. If the lack of personal agency lingers then supernatural agents are given the credit.

Such belief in supernatural agents of events in toddlers is evidenced by their comfort in believing in Santa Claus, unicorns, fairies and all manner of other make-believe entities. As we grow up, we learn that some of our supernatural solutions to puzzling events are better and more usefully explained by other theories, generally involving the physical and social sciences.

The same procession in thinking has happened on the society-wide scale. Ignorance of the intimate dealings of the physical world required the invention of numerous and usually capricious deities to explain in some measure the unexplainable, such as the vagaries of the weather, the randomness of diseases, success or failure in warfare or mate selection.

Here in the twenty-first century, science and technology have made most gods redundant. The reduction in the number of gods was also associated with increased urban densities, which put a greater requirement for strangers to work cheek-by-jowl, something that our innate xenophobia makes difficult. Keeping us co-operating, however grudgingly, required stronger forces to counteract that xenophobia. One omnipotent God appears to have been a popular solution [2]. That Christianity came from relative obscurity to prominence in the western world is most likely due to the Roman Emperor Constantine, a man facing internal civil war and external barbarian invaders. He chose Christianity's loving but *all-powerful* God and converted in 312

A.D. This gave Christianity a huge leg up in the contest for religious marketshare [2].

We seem to have invented gods to fill in our ignorance of why and when things happen. Our current God, the one I am usually asked to endorse, has fewer duties than previous ones. It is no longer given direct agency over making clouds rain, the planets move in the night sky, water to spout from our taps, or my laptop to bootup. Most of modern life doesn't require prayers and sacrifices to keep the lights burning or our supermarkets stocked with food. Science, logic, technology and society does most of it for us.

To believe in *today's* all-powerful God, what am I signing up for? And does my belief, or not, in that God have any believable consequences? I haven't been convinced of any so far. To be honest, I find the task of believing in a muscular old guy with a long white beard (as painted by Michelangelo on the Sistine Chapel's ceiling) beyond me. Equally incomprehensible is the idea that by praying we can influence the Almighty into doing us a favour. Surely, we humans are as inconsequential as a grain of sand on an infinite beach. What can we offer God that would be of any worth? Is God so starved of recognition, and/or affection, that our mewlings have meaning enough to be given special treatment and actioned upon?

I am certain true believers would answer yes to God's regard and concern for us. Lucky them for the comfort and certainty it provides. Unlucky me, for apparently lacking that God-given ability.

I am still a God denier, am I? Or, perhaps I am a person of limited ability to comprehend esoteric concepts, be it magnetism or a God that is incorporeal, omnipotent and involved directly with managing the brief lives of its living creations.

If I do have a God recognisable to others, it is definitely the unbribable kind, and one whose only achievement, and desire, was the creation of the universe and the basic rules of physics and chemistry that allows existence to exist. Such a God is hardly one worth boasting of, or promoting, when I know that so many people are nourished and placated by their more grandiose, marketable, and considerably more human versions.

My reduced concept of God may be as ill-defined as the rest, but one clear commonality it shares with other god beliefs is that it manifests itself in all those scraps of subjective experience that can't be proven or disproved.

To me, *God is the magic dust that remains after the torch of fact and logic has been applied to the nth degree*. God resides in the *inaccuracies* of our scientific and subjective predictions, be it formulae to try and predict fluid dynamics, or the timing and precise nature of the weather, the behaviour of stock markets, or even the course of a conversation between a group of friends.

The word "God" attempts to encapsulate the undefinable and is one I cannot use with any confidence. Can we *both* believe, *the same way*, in the *same* God?

I'll let you decide. And, having decided, what then for both of us?

§

Addendum:

I may suffer insufficient God receptors in my brain and hence struggle with the concept, but there are times when I get glimpses of what a loving God may be like. One such glimpse occurred when I watched and listened to the following YouTube video from November 2016:

Amira Willighagen and Patrizio Buanne sing *O Sole Mio* (Amira was less than sixteen at the time)

In that concert hall, on that day, belief in a loving God did not seem impossible.

[1] *Thinking, Fast and Slow* by Daniel Kahneman, *Deceit and Self-deception* by Robert Trivers, and *The Intelligence Trap* by David Robson will illuminate human cognition and belief.
[2] *Sapiens* by Yuval Noah Harari gives some insights into the history and changing nature of religious beliefs.

58. J.P. Uncensored

The other day* I received a link to an interview with Jordan Peterson (J.P.) on a news commentary program called *Fred Blogs – Uncensored*, or some such title, with the invitation to give comment upon it.

That was a week or so back, and having watched it only once, my recollections are undoubtedly highly unreliable and thus exactly what the average person would recall, temporarily, and then, in the fullness of time, forget – though not completely because aspects of it would be squirreled away in the subconscious to bolster one's existing worldview.

My initial reply to the sender was a text to say that I found the interview "interesting but frustrating". If face-to-face, and with sufficient time to discuss it more fully, I would have given it a very different rating, one of an overall disappointment, mostly because of what wasn't said rather than what was.

I am one of the twelve million or so others who bought a copy of J.P.'s bestseller, *12 Rules for Life*. I found it extremely illuminating and worthwhile.

Since then, it appears J.P. has become a celebrity to some – mostly white, male and right-wing apparently – but to many others a pariah prophet. I have only read that book and have not followed his subsequent interviews or online commentaries and so am completely ignorant as to why he now engenders such strong and opposing reactions.

But if he hadn't produced such a polarising effect, it is unlikely that he would have been interviewed because what passes as "news" [1], especially that available online, cannot be viewed – in my estimation – as being concerned with dispersing a breadth and depth of facts designed to enable and promote balanced and rational deliberations.

Most "news" programs, are in fact a thinly disguised piece of entertainment, and, as any budding writer is told, to be entertaining the story must have *conflict* to stir our emotions, and this emotive theme must persist if it is to hold our attention. Attention that will wander or disappear if we only "pander" to our reason. Hence, most electronic "news" is a smorgasbord of titillating factoids and vaguely rational soundbites sufficient to keep the reader or viewer's attention. Attention that keeps them exposed to the advertiser's message, the propaganda of a government agency, or whoever is paying for the show's production.

With that jaded view of what passes for informative articles or programs, my first disquiet was the program's subtitle: "Uncensored".

Disappointingly, J.P. made no comment about that subtitle. But what does "uncensored" mean? And what does its inclusion add to the program and its presenter? It is there for a reason. How would the viewer react if the banner had read "Fred Blogs – Censored"? Would we give the show less, or more, credence?

And why should that single descriptive make such a big, if mostly unconscious, difference to our approach to watching the program?

The only answer I can find is that we don't like to be taken for a ride, or conned into believing falsities only to later suffer the consequences. We want truths, not fictions, especially misinformation and lies that serve another's interests not ours. We yearn to believe that Fred Blogs truly *is* uncensored, and is *truly* seeking to give us the truth, or the best approximation of it.

Sort of.

Actually, most of us, desire truths that are not too far removed from our current opinions because these "truths" avoid the hard mental work of having to rejig, or worst of all, reject, some or all of our hard-won and oft rehearsed opinions [1].

Thus, we are subliminally encouraged by that word "uncensored". But our hopes of receiving worthy information are falsely positive, because, with a little thought we can rightly conclude that, if Fred Blogs were to start asking the wrong questions, resulting in viewers being exposed to viewpoints that are either unpopular or counter to the editorial slant of the owners and/or their advertisers, then he would soon be replaced with a presenter who *self-censors* his questioning and leads the viewer to the "correct" viewpoint.

Fred Blogs is only uncensored in the sense that he was employed, and stays employed, because he has internalised the ethos of his employer. He is like an abused kidnap victim who suffers Stockholm Syndrome, in which long association with their brutish kidnappers, results in them, the persecuted, eventually agreeing with and espousing their persecutor's attitudes.

And, being internalised, the presenter's censored and hence biased attitudes are largely hidden from him, making it easier to speak his self-censored views with conviction, which, to the viewer, is taken as evidence that he knows what he is talking about and hence can be believed unquestioned. This process is discussed at length in *Deceit and Self-deception* by Robert Trivers and probably by other researchers since its publication in 2013.

But none of us have thoughts that are entirely our own. None of us are uncensored. How can we be when from birth we are exposed to other people, who espouse all manner of opinions, whether via words or deeds, opinions and views that we need to understand, and use, if we are to be successfully "socialised" into society.

Biologically, for children to survive the critical early years, the harsh realities enforced by natural selection resulted in children believing as true and worthy everything their adult caregivers say. Becoming an adult, in regard to thinking, happens when we realise that not all that is said is true and we develop some capability for independent and critical thinking. Unfortunately, as adults we can never be totally unbiassed in our thinking because of all the attitudes subconsciously taken onboard as gullible children and adolescents. We can only develop an awareness of those indoctrinated biases but can never fully, or possibly even partially, remove them [1].

"Uncensored" narked me from the beginning. The next disappointment came when the presenter showed a short clip from one of the later "Rocky" movies, in which Rocky Balboa, played by Sylvester Stallone, gives his wayward, teenage/early twenties son a lecture about how tough and cruel the world is, and how to survive he has to toughen up, get real, be a man, not a whining Sissie, or words to that effect.

Again, this is a grossly inaccurate rendition of the interplay between the two characters but it was the sentiment that stayed with me, and also the sentiment that J.P. and the presenter "discussed" – though I would have described their commentary as more a glossing over and denial of the deeper issues presented in that scene than a critical appraisal of them.

Had I miraculously been placed in J.P.'s chair and asked to respond to that film clip, I would have raised the following observations:

The scene is at night, on an inner-city street, presumably in the U.S. There is little activity, suggesting it's very early morning, and it seems cold. Thus, a cold, deserted, unfriendly and, being dark, fearsome backdrop. It is a backdrop designed to unconsciously reinforce Rocky's grim view of the world. An easy view to sell in hyper-capitalist and maniacally individualistic America. But how true is that worldview?

How would that same scene have worked if it was transposed onto a sunny morning, with a backdrop of a wedding in a well-maintained park, with scattered park benches populated by friends swapping sandwiches over a takeaway coffee and an amicable chat, perhaps with an intergenerational family, that includes members of different ethnicities, all having a good time at a picnic nearby?

The influence of the grim background, the "framing" of Rocky's dire assessment, is not questioned. J.P.'s silence can only be read as either a lack of awareness of how context skews our perceptions and attitudes, or, more likely, tacit agreement with Rocky's pessimistic view of society. When he, and we, accept unquestioned that, "that's just the way it is" [2], we consequently put no effort into confirming the *amount* of truth in that summation, or to thinking of ways to construct a better way of being. In our unthinking silence, we act like sheep, doomed to be repeatedly shorn, until eventually led to the slaughterhouse. I exaggerate, but by how much?

Telling a young man that he "has to toughen up" to survive the blows that life dishes out is not without merit, because even the most blessed existence and circumstances produce difficult choices, with the greatest of all being having to deal with our mortality and that of our loved ones.

But "he" has to toughen up, also implies it's a *solo effort*. Again, sort of true. We do ultimately have to make decisions and cope with the consequences, but few of us live alone on a desert island, and hence most of our problems stem from how to handle the impact of other people's behaviours.

Not commented on is that one of the benefits of living in a functioning society is the *option of asking for help*. Rocky didn't get his success as a boxer entirely unaided. I confess to having never seen any of the Rocky movies but his success as a boxer must have involved the support and knowledge received from his trainer, his sparing partners, and even his opponents and enemies, all of whom taught him things he'd not have learnt alone on that desert island.

That unquestioned implication that "he" and "he alone" had to toughen up conjured in my mind thoughts of the young males who commit suicide because they "alone" can see no way out of whatever perceived insurmountable problems beset them.

One such "suicide", though few would see it as such, was encountered in a book I was recently given to read and think upon: *Into the Wild*.

It is the tragic story of a young American man who sees society's ills and is greatly disturbed by them. His solution is to reject society. He then decides to live alone in the wilderness of Alaska. He dies, in an abandoned bus (made by humans), on a dirt road (made by humans for humans) under skies traversed by jet aeroplanes built by and carrying humans. He died from a plant toxin unknown to him but known to others of that "terrible" society of humans he unwisely rejected in *totality*, rather than in part.

We humans are far from perfect, but neither are we totally evil or useless. If we were so we would never have survived and eventually "prospered" to the point of ruling the planet [3]. As a society, and as individuals, we benefit when encouraged to seek *informed* guidance from our fellows, past and present. Those others are often our greatest asset and should not be discounted, actively, or passively as J.P. seemed to do with his silence.

Also not broached is what attitudes and actions a young man must adopt to become sufficiently "toughened up" to become a winner, not a loser. Both these concepts are also left unspoken of and unhelpfully undefined.

Is beefing up in the gym, learning how to box, or do karate

so one can physically overcome obnoxious people the best way to resolve the problems that life produces? Is becoming a "tough guy", or a Trump, or a bullying muscleman of unwavering opinion the message being implied and endorsed by that scene?

Being a doormat is an unappealing lifestyle, but so too is becoming my concept of a "tough guy". It's a pity an alternative approach wasn't discussed. Men in particular would benefit greatly if taught to seek better ways of being assertive, rather than being rewarded for being aggressive, for habitually applying "thump therapy" to resolve issues. We need to encourage men to seek win-win outcomes, not the I win, you lose ethos which is the attitude that underpins today's exploitative, morally and ecologically bankrupt version of Capitalism.

Later on, another film clip was aired for J.P.'s comment. It was of a Senatorial grilling of candidates for a judicial position, with the specific candidate being black and female. She is asked to define "a woman" and gave a limp, evasive response. It was a short, sharp, snippet. Its purpose was to bang the drum of the evils of overblown "political correctness", especially in regard to the heated debate over how to treat people of ambiguous chromosomal sexual designation.

I can't accurately recall J.P.'s response but it wasn't critical or lengthy or apparently much considered. Again, it seemed to be more tacit agreement with the presenter, this time of how ridiculous and "censored" was the woman's refusal to give a definitive answer, which presumably demonstrated the stifling of debate caused by fear of being deemed politically incorrect. It was given as proof of the threats facing the sacred cow of *unrestrained* free speech, with its accompanying demands for *freedom from responsibility* for any of the negative societal outcomes of such unfettered utterances.

Freedom of speech and the treatment of minorities are sensitive issues that need to be considered, coolly and wisely, not with shouted slogans and soundbites. That clip could have led to shedding some humane and fact-based light upon both topics but it was not to be.

The thought that most lingered was: "Did *all* the candidates face that question or only the women, or only black women, and were *all* candidates, male, female or otherwise, asked to define "a man", and if not, why not?" To have seen all the candidates' responses to both questions would have been much more instructive.

That clip seemed to serve no purpose other than to belittle the woman and trivialise the issue of how to treat people who don't conform to the standard biological or behavioural mould. My responses to it would have been to ask: are people of indeterminant gender, human or not? And, what is it that defines a human, and how are we to humanely treat other humans, irrespective of their sexual orientation, and why?

At show's end J.P.'s personal life dramas were alluded to, causing him to shed a tear and struggle for control. It was for me a moving moment that demonstrated that no matter what we think about his books, or subsequent utterances, he is a human like us. He is a person who understands suffering.

Perhaps that was the only useful notion to carry away from that show: "that we are all human, fallible and fragile".

We need to always keep that thought in the forefront of our minds. It will make us more humble and more aware that our opinions are as unconsciously shaped and biased as the next person's. That we need to seek more *facts* before we present our opinions to the world "chiselled in stone".

* This essay was written at the end of September 2022.

¹ *The News* by Alain de Botton and *Manufacturing Consent* by Noam Chomsky explain the outside influences on our opinions, *Thinking, Fast and Slow* by Daniel Kahneman the internal ones.

² This topic I discussed in my essay of the same name.

³ Why we are so "successful" is discussed thoughtfully in *Survival of the Nicest* by Stefan Klein and in *Origins* by Lewis Dartnell, amongst others..

59. Unreasonable People

In *Survival of the Nicest* Stefan Klein posited that humanity's greatest asset is our ability to co-operate. It is indeed a wonderful thing to belong to a group or tribe within which we work for the benefit of our "team", but Stefan also illuminated its dark side. Our "tribal" sense of identity, which inspires us to co-operate, is strengthened by having an opposing group to compare ourselves against, which leads to chauvinism and competition *against* the others. And when the "tribes" or teams are reduced to single individuals, that competition devolves into my interests over yours.

This essay will explore our outward versus inward facing attitudes, especially in regard to their impact upon our ability to be reasonable, co-operative and willing to compromise for mutual benefit, as opposed to our equal capacity to be selfish and parochial and hence unreasonable and uncompromising to the point of hostility against those not deemed to be one of us.

I wish to more fully understand *why* we are all capable of being unreasonable and *how* best to either avoid or cure unreasonableness when it occurs.

The primary causes of unreasonableness are our unique genetics and our unique histories, which then burdens us with unique reasons for thinking the way we do. It is a burden because our unique worldviews regularly produce misunderstandings and associated negativity. Encountering divergent views forces us into negotiations that can be tiring, frustrating and worst of all, may require *us* to change our opinions and behaviours when most of us subscribe, either blatantly or unconsciously, to the maxim: *be reasonable, do it my way*!

And to exacerbate matters, most of our disagreements are also due to the very things we all have in common.

The first commonality is our shared, though uniquely expressed, biological urge to survive and reproduce. But being social creatures, we are compelled to interact with others, initially to survive childhood and then as adults seeking ways to carve out our particular niche within society.

To survive childhood, and beyond, we must often be unreasonable if we are not to be bullied, robbed, marginalised and end up a doormat or worse. We have to stand up for our right to exist, to live, to prosper, even if it diminishes other people's similar rights. Thus, in order to obtain the necessities of life, such as, food, shelter, jobs, friends, spouses, as well as social recognition and status, living within a society compels us to compete as much as co-operate.

And to make the decisions of when and how to either co-operate, or not, we all share a brain with an architecture and operating system that, though brilliant, can easily induce flawed thinking, attitudes and subsequent actions (as discussed in prior essays).

The greatest problem with our thinking is that we each believe our opinions to be true and reasonable and find it inexplicable and annoying that the person, or group, we are interacting with often do not see things our way.

Overcoming our self-blindness towards our unreasonable assumption of the *absolute* validity of our reasoning is the main impediment to overcoming our unreasonableness. It is a blindness shared by the other person, who, like us, also considers *their* logic and viewpoint as the correct one.

Surviving as a social being requires balancing the opposing

forces of self-interest versus consideration of the interests of the society that sustains us. We vacillate between being selfishly unreasonable, or considerate of others and willing to compromise to find mutually beneficial solutions.

This balancing act between levels of selfishness and selflessness is further influenced by the fact that not everyone has the same importance to ourselves or to wider society. It is further complicated by the full effects of our actions, or non-actions, not being immediately evident. The consequences of our behaviours may reveal themselves a short time later, perhaps to our benefit, but one that proves short lived, to be replaced by us suffering later on, or the opposite, short-term pain that leads to long-term gain.

Reasonableness is also influenced by our differing genetics, especially in relation to intelligence, reasoning capacity, and inclinations towards co-operativeness, with that variability then enhanced or diminished by our life experiences.

Some may be predisposed to egocentricity and being uncompromisingly selfish. If so inclined, as a toddler, we may become the playgroup bully from finding that thuggery pays off in the sandpit. Behaviours, which, if left unchecked, can lead us to a successful career in business, politics and elsewhere! But the kindergarten tyrant may also be socially ostracised to the point of them later ending up as social outcasts living in poverty, or finding that persisting with socially repugnant behaviours has them spending much of their adult years in prison.

Those adults who manage to successfully use the bulldozer approach to gain their wealth and status are highly unlikely to see much reason to reject their winning strategy in favour of the "unproven" one of being co-operative and mindful of other people's needs. To them, people are objects, literally human resources to be used up and discarded as they see fit. These persons are the permanently disagreeable. They enjoy getting away with being unreasonable. Dissuading them from *enjoying* themselves is going to be very difficult unless overwhelming coercive force can be applied at length.

Thankfully most people's genetics and histories place them in the *situationally* unreasonable category and as such resolutions to disputes with them are possible (if we understand the key sticking points to such resolutions). It is not generally an easy task and one I am not overly adept at, hence this exploration.

But before we can start to consider ways of changing another's unreasonableness into something both can live with; we must first decide how much effort we are willing to put into the task.

The answer to that question may rest upon who has the power to find and enact a resolution. If we have significantly greater power, we could simply resolve the issue with a "I win, you lose" solution. It is always more difficult for the less powerful to dissuade the powerful because how likely is it that they will *not* use their power advantage to their benefit exclusively?

Another aspect to consider before making a first move is whether we really need to resolve the dispute? What happens if it remains unresolved? Can life go on substantially unaffected if both simply agree to disagree on the issue in question?

If we decide the unreasonableness must be resolved, and that we are not vastly more powerful than our opponent we should then examine the possibility that it may resolve itself simply by delaying any action on it. Sometimes, if we allow sufficient time to elapse, changed circumstances may either solve the problem or make it insignificant compared to the new challenges we both face.

If a win-win solution is important, time is lacking and we do *not* possess an excess of power over the other in regard to the matter in question, then the next step is to clarify exactly what it is that we want, such that if we were to gain it, we would be happy to possess it and its consequences.

I wrote, in an earlier essay, of an area of friction between my dear wife and myself over my monthly motorcycle rides. I knew precisely what I wanted. I wanted to enjoy my day on the bike knowing she too would be happy to let me go and would be happy when I got home. The resolution came from a better understanding of the emotional issues those monthly excursions represented for both of us. I knew what they did for me; finding out what they represented to her was more difficult, but once found, an amicable understanding was gained.

That example highlights the importance of understanding the emotions at play on both sides of a dispute. Why does the issue stir our emotions, which emotions, and what are our justifications for them? Once we have unearthed our emotional imperatives, we then need to discover those at work in the other person. This is the more difficult task because most people will be uncertain of what specific "buttons" the dispute is pressing.

For instance, the intense anger that some felt, and still feel, against governmental regulations designed to lessen the health impacts of COVID-19, to me were, and continue to be, very difficult to comprehend because I do not fully understand the thinking that underpins that anger. I can guess at what that reasoning may be, but if I were to voice my ideas to an anti-vaxxer they would probably reject my explanation as condescending "psychobabble" and then punch me in the nose to end my "offensive lecturing". These people are willing to die for their cause, and equally willing for the rest of us to also die for their "right" to spread the COVID-19 virus, which they deem either innocuous or a conspiracy cooked up to restrict their freedoms. On that issue, they have become permanently unreasonable and hence changing their attitude will be a near impossibility. They can only be tolerated, avoided, or forcibly sanctioned from doing harm to others.

Having examined the reasoning and emotions behind unreasonableness we can now embark upon finding strategies for resolving those issues that invoke low to moderate "heat". In this regard, much can be learned from a reread of *How to Win Friends and Influence People* by Dale Carnegie.

It's been a while since I last read it but several of his strategies still come to mind.

He stated that to catch a fish we should bait our hook with something the fish wants, or likes, not what we want. My prior suggestion to understand what the other wants, to find what specific motivations their contrary views satisfy, is a similar notion to Dale Carnegie's fishing advice. Once we have a better appreciation of the rationale behind the other person's opposing view, we can then fire up our imaginations to see if what they want and what we want can be aligned.

Dale Carnegie also mentions that negotiating with another is much easier if you are both reading from the same page. He suggests finding and stating areas of agreement. Say things that you can both agree on, in broad terms at first, such that they nod in agreement. This puts them in a more positive frame of mind from which novel ideas can slowly be introduced without them being automatically rejected. By getting them to say yes, to have them agree with us, makes us become "one of them" and hence less of a threat to their group identity and self-esteem, after which we can gently introduce grey areas until the possibility of our new idea starts to look less threatening, more plausible, *and* beneficial to them.

Whether fishing or sweet-talking an unreasonable attitude from a person, understanding their *emotional imperatives* are crucial. Forget introducing disputable facts too early because all "facts" are disputable to some degree and the tiniest point of divergence will usually be enough to scuttle any agreement on a sensitive issue.

First, we must slake the emotional needs and only then slowly work on the knowledge base to the point where it can support a resolution.

Again, it is a task I am poorly practised in but one in which one of my previous bosses was quite good at whenever he had to deal with complaining customers. He would nod his head, listen whilst they ranted, and once their emotional need to vent was heard, he would ask what *specifically* they wanted him to do. That question demonstrated his willingness to compromise and his acknowledgement of their wants. Once the emotions are out of the way, their intellect then had a chance to consider new ideas and possibilities.

Another idea to be considered is whether the parties want a short-term or a longer-term solution.

Few, in my experience, give the long-term enough thought, possibly from a disbelief in our ability to usefully predict future events and their consequences, but the future awaits us whether we are semi-prepared or totally unprepared, with the first position being the better one.

Reminding both parties of uncertainty's many manifestations, of the number of narrowly avoided disasters, of the role of unplanned good luck in both lives will reinforce the wisdom of having a more flexible approach to the current dispute, with such a malleable attitude improving the prospects of finding a resolution that works well for the near-term and the foreseeable future.

Thinking long-term also introduces the concept of a use-by date for any solution. Compromises have a time period in which they will operate, and hence any concessions made will not have to be eternal. They can be renegotiated later. Such a notion may make the current solutions more palatable and easier to agree to.

Before we head off imbued with all that we have discussed

above, we need to improve our odds of turning around the unreasonable attitudes of others by an honest look at *our* propensity to be unreasonable.

As stated in earlier essays, none of us are all-knowing and so we are wise to be humbler in stating our opinions. Bringing that humility to the negotiating table will vastly boost the chances of mutually beneficial resolutions to most disputes.

We and our attitudes are part of the context in which any disagreement is played out. Our attitudes and assumptions need to be scrutinised as much as those of the other if mutually agreeable solutions are to be found.

And, lastly, we should be mindful that many of humanity's greatest accomplishments were made by people persevering with ideas that the majority considered unreasonable, that being *too* reasonable can be as debilitating as being too unreasonable.

It appears that unreasonable and reasonable people are another co-dependent yin-yang style duality that needs to be managed like all the other dualities that populate existence, such as love and hate, ignorance and wisdom, growth and decay.

We need verifiable facts and defensible moral codes that are comprehensive enough to recognise the degree of reasonableness in our views and in those of others if the troubles induced by mismatched ideas are to be resolved to the mutual satisfaction of both. We also need to be prepared for the possible consequences of a win-lose outcome.

There is only one certainty when dealing with unreasonableness and that is: we are going to have a lifetime of practice, and we are unlikely to ever become totally unaffected by the unreasonableness of others or that of our own.

60. Philosophising

"Why are you wasting your time with all this philosophising? What good has it ever done you?" is an accusation I have had to respond to on a few occasions, sadly, to date, without any overly convincing answers. In this essay, I hope to remedy that situation.

Why I philosophise is easier to explain than what, exactly, I get out of it.

Firstly, few that I know of, from an early age, aim to become a philosopher. I fell into such a state from my particular mix of genetic predispositions and limitations interacting with my unique history.

Using my experience as a template, I suggest that the process of becoming a philosopher begins with thinking, develops into "thinking too much" and, unless outside help arrives, divine or otherwise, descends into a life of chronic philosophising.

It wasn't until junior high school that I began to realise my physical limitations. I was a skinny gangling youth, who later became a skinny, gangling but balding adult. That youth lacked strength, speed, and hand-eye co-ordination and hence was hopeless at sports – a great disadvantage in sport-mad Australia.

At least I possessed some mental capabilities and did reasonably well in school, enough to get offers to some of the better universities. That said, I scraped through Level Two Maths, and struggled with English, especially when it involved creative writing or the analysing and critiquing of stories and plays – I still struggle in these activities.

Leaving home to move to the big city for university was the start of a decade of highs and lows, filled with a kaleidoscope of new experiences, such as sharing houses, exercising my passion for motorcycling, unsuccessfully chasing women, studying and then losing interest. I dropped out, worked unexciting jobs, eventually found a new area of interest, returned to study and gained a degree to find the economic cycle had turned against me and rendered it and my skills set "surplus to requirements".

By the end of my twenties, I was back in the big city working as a storeman-packer initially, before moving into the office as an accounts clerk. Most disappointing of all was the lack of an intimate relationship with a member of the opposite sex, and seemingly little hope of ever achieving such. The worst part was having no understanding of why I had been shunted off the "normal" life path – education, marriage, children, job in one's field, consolidation of one's career and homelife, to end in a "golden" retirement.

The twenties and early thirties were the years of increasingly "thinking too much" and having little to show for it. That laborious thinking had me trying all manner of solutions, such as buying a car because taking a girl out on the motorbike may have been off-putting – the car had no effect apart from depleting my modest income. I endeavoured to learn about human behaviour and went as far as training in phone counselling but found listening to others troubles just exacerbated mine.

At the end of my era of "too much thinking" I had runout of hope inducing strategies with which to motivate and guide my life towards a happy future. The question then arose of whether or not to continue with my apparently futile, floundering cluelessness.

Thankfully, that turbulent period had produced two useable conclusions: riding my motorbike reliably gave relief from my gloom and that I had no idea how to describe the qualities I was seeking in a future wife, apart from the notion that in her company I would feel relaxed enough to be myself, and be accepted as such.

Not sure if it was before or after I gave notice that I heard about the dolphins at Monkey Mia but at least they gave me a direction: west. So, I headed off on my BMW K100RS with my camping equipment, a few clothes, a couple of thousand in the bank, four thousand owing on the bike and zero thoughts of employment.

By the time I eventually hit Perth I was running low on funds. The motorbike riding had dulled my existential malaise to levels where Monkey Mia had become a lesser priority than that of finding a job.

My luck turned. I took the first job offered (a geological field assistant at a gold mine), which I was pleasantly surprised to learn paid considerably more than I had been making in Sydney, but best of all, it was there that I met my future wife.

The rest of my thirties, forties and early fifties were normality. My thinking rarely got into the "too much" stage and almost no philosophising was required. Married life gave me plenty to keep my mind occupied with things in the here and now, like house payments, home maintenance, travelling, enjoying each other's company and later, after a major health scare, thinking of the future, specifically retirement and beyond, all the way to ill-health and death. That's when philosophising returned to my life.

In my late twenties I had, as a coping strategy, kept a journal in which to temporarily expunge my negative thoughts. Now, having passed life's halfway point, I revived my journalling as a cure to renewed gloomy, circular thinking caused by increasing numbers of unpleasant developments. Later, I decided that writing essays and stories offered another way to untangle the complexities of my "human condition".

Luck again smiled on me, because no sooner had I taken to writing a few short stories followed by a sci-fi novel, than a writing group started up in my neighbourhood. I have been involved with that group for the last nine years and have considerably improved my writing skills (from none to passable) and have learned to use the writing of stories and essays as a way of gaining greater understanding of life's issues. I am now *more*, but not totally, immune to those issues (to be totally unmoved by life's vicissitudes is to be a machine not a human).

All that philosophising, especially in essay form, has helped thicken my skin. But rationality can only go so far. Onlookers may see me as easily upset as I was before. I would disagree with them because, though my emotional responses to life continues to fluctuate, I am more sanguine about my moods. These days I consciously try to maximise my appreciation and memory of my highs, and have made my lows more bearable with the knowledge that they too don't last, especially if I enact all the strategies my philosophising has granted me.

Why do I philosophise still?

It isn't done to artificially dispel boredom with spurious debate on arcane topics, and certainly not from a self-serving and cruel desire to score intellectual points, as seems to be the case with some given the title 'philosopher'. I philosophise because I was born more sensitive than most males, was not over-endowed with attractive physical features, and have faced setbacks in life to which no obvious solutions appeared to me. It is a situation unlikely to change in the foreseeable future.

When circumstances conspire to force one into asking awkward questions and actively pursue answers to them, we soon discover that there is very little that is certain and that those who act with certainty do so from the confidence that limited knowledge gives them. As far as I am concerned, the philosopher, mathematician and writer, René Descartes, only got it partly right when he declared: "I think, therefore I am." He should have thought a bit more. Had he done so he would have concluded: "I think, therefore I am, <u>uncertain</u>!"

So, why do most consider philosophising a wasteful and useless endeavour?

The answer seems to be that they are luckier than me. Their dispositions and personal histories result in their life's problems inducing less psychic pain. Thus, they more easily accept the things they apparently cannot change. They also have greater faith in their opinions than I have in mine, probably because they rarely question the validity of the "facts" underpinning those opinions. And why would they, when our evolved biology selected for, and biochemically rewards quick decision-making because the slow thinkers were either eaten by predators or killed by enemies?

Strong opinions feel good, but just because something feels good doesn't guarantee it will be good in the long-term. Strong feelings are the accelerator, doubts brought on by thinking, questioning or *philosophising* are the brakes. We need both.

Philosophising is generally borne of dissatisfaction. It can lead to either nothing, poor outcomes, or better outcomes, but the same can be said of strongly held "obvious truths".

So, what do we have left?

The following prayer comes to my mind:

God grant me the *serenity* to accept the things I cannot change,
the *courage* to change the things I can,
and the *wisdom* to know the difference.

To which I would add: and the *wisdom* to know what *should* be changed, why, for whose benefits, when, for how long, and what can an individual, or a society, do about it? – all of which requires extensive and reliable facts, thinking, and, philosophising!

If interested in the factual underpinnings of this exploration, please consult the following books:

Thinking, Fast and Slow by Daniel Kahneman, *The Intelligence Trap* by David Robson, *Denial and Self-deception* by Robert Trivers and *The Ethical Brain* by Michael S. Gazzaniga. They will explain our cognitive processes and their limitations.

How We became Human by Tim Dean, *Sapiens* by Yuval Noah Harari and more recently *Origins* by Lewis Darnell examine our evolved nature.

Why We Sleep by Mathew Walker reveals the findings of the latest research into how the quality and quantity of sleep influences our overall health, as well as our memories, cognition and decision-making.

Other books by this author:

Tarkine Mist   - Fiction
> *The thinking person's action novel, spiced with international intrigue and a thread of romance.*

www.ingramcontent.com/pod-product-compliance
Lightning Source LLC
Chambersburg PA
CBHW020137130526
44591CB00030B/66